South On The Sound

"PARTNERS IN PROGRESS" BY RITA HAPPY

Produced in Cooperation
with Historic Tacoma, Inc.

Windsor Publications, Inc.
Woodland Hills, California

*James Everett Stuart, a grandson of
the portraitist Gilbert Stuart, visited
Tacoma in the late 1880s. He
painted this scene of the waterfront
before the tideflats were filled in
and the Puyallup River had been
redirected. Courtesy, Washington
State Historical Society*

South On The Sound

An Illustrated History of Tacoma and Pierce County

Murray and Rosa Morgan

Windsor Publications, Inc.
History Books Division
Publisher: John M. Phillips
Production Supervisor: Katherine Cooper
Senior Picture Editor: Teri Davis Greenberg
Senior Corporate History Editor: Karen Story
Marketing Director: Ellen Kettenbeil
Production Manager: James Burke
Design Director: Alexander D'Anca
Art Production Manager: Dee Cooper
Typesetting Manager: E. Beryl Myers
Proofreading Manager: Doris R. Malkin

Windsor Publications' Staff for
South on the Sound
Editor: Pamela Taylor
Picture Editor: Kevin Cavanaugh
Copy Editor: Taryn Bigelow
Corporate History Editor: Phyllis Gray
Sales Manager: Bart Barica
Sales Representative: Julia Ottolini
Editorial Assistants: Patricia Buzard, Judy Hunter,
    Patricia Pittman
Compositor: Barbara Neiman
Proofreaders: Lynn Johnson, Phyllis Rifkin
Production Artists: Lynn Agosti, Beth Bowman

Layout Artist: Ellen Hazeltine

Library of Congress Cataloging in Publication Data

Morgan, Murray, 1916-
    South on the sound.

    ' "Partners in progress" by Rita Happy
    "Produced in cooperation with Historic Tacoma, Inc."
    Bibliography: p. 195
    Includes index.
    1. Tacoma (Wash.)—History. 2. Pierce County (Wash.)—
History. 3. Tacoma (Wash.)—Description. 4. Pierce
County (Wash.)—Description and travel. 5. Tacoma (Wash.)
—Industries. 6. Pierce County (Wash.)—Industries.
I. Morgan, Rosa, 1918-   . II. Happy, Rita. Partners in
progress. 1984. III. Title.

F899.T2M673 1984   979.7'78   84-5143
ISBN 0-89781-074-0

CONTENTS

Following pages
The Mountain, which gave its
Indian name to Tacoma,
dominates the landscape of the
southern Sound. Max Meyer, an
artist and photographer in Tacoma,
painted this oil in the early 1890s.
The church (to the right) is on the
site of the present Puyallup Indian
Reservation.

ACKNOWLEDGMENTS

One of the pleasures in working on this book has been our collaboration with persons who died before we were born. A few of these helpful spirits were the artists who accompanied exploring expeditions to Puget Sound; most, however, were photographers of the glass-plate era.

The first cameraman on Commencement Bay was Anthony Carr, who in 1866 joined his father on a homestead claim in what is now known as Old Town. Tony Carr photographed the birth of Tacoma, the construction of its first steam sawmill, the loading of the first ship.

In the boom years of the 1880s a score of commercial photographers recorded the trans-formation of the clapboard village into a city. Among these pioneers were F. Jay Haynes, a young Minnesotan commissioned by the Northern Pacific Railroad to photograph the western terminus; the ebullient George Wagness, whose work would be more familiar had he not lost three studios to fires in five years; the energetic Thomas Rutter, who abandoned Tacoma and photography for a career as a veterinarian; the husband-and-wife team of C.E. and Hattie King; the eccentric but gifted Katherine Maynard of Victoria, B.C.; William Holmes Wilcox, a gifted amateur; and the businesslike Arthur French, a journeyman photographer.

Few of these cameramen stayed in town long after the Panic of 1893. They were succeeded by a new generation of photographers, probably equally gifted (surely, A.H. Barnes had no superior) and better equipped, but whose work seems less a revelation, to us, because their later careers overlapped our own lives.

Some pictures in this book are from private collections, but most are drawn from public repositories or the libraries of the Tacoma *News-Tribune*, the Seattle *Post-Intelligencer*, and the *Federal Way News*. We are grateful for the assistance of the custodians of these treasures, who gave so generously of time, knowledge,

MEYER. 1896.

and insight.

Our debt is especially deep to the staff of the Tacoma Public Library. Under the direction of Gary Reese and his assistants, Jean Gillmer and Brian Kamens, what was a grandma's-attic assortment of prints, negatives, and old newspapers dealing with the southern Puget Sound area has been transformed into the Northwest Room collection.

Although the Tacoma Public Library was our primary source of pictures, many other institutions and curators aided us. They include: the Washington State Historical Society (Frank Green and Jeanne Engerman); the University of Washington Libraries (Dennis Andersen); the Washington State Library (Nancy Pryor); Pacific Lutheran University; University of Puget Sound; Tacoma Community College (Morris Skagen, Richard Aiken, and Lorraine Hildebrand); Jefferson County Historical Society; Port of Tacoma (Rod Koon and Gerry Davies); Tacoma Department of Community Development (Patti Sias); Metropolitan Park District, Pierce County Association for Retarded Citizens; Tacoma General Hospital; the Weyerhaeuser Company; Tacoma Humane Society; Tacoma Actors

Guild; North Pacific Bank; Metropolitan Park District; Oregon Historical Society (Susan Seyl); Public Archives of Canada (Gerard R. Huneault); Provincial Archives of British Columbia (Barbara McLennan); Manitoba Provincial Archives; American Antiquarian Society; University of California Berkeley, (Lawrence Dinnean); National Maritime Museum-San Francisco, (Joan Maounis); Todd Shipyards Corporation (Roy T. McMillan); Tacoma Public Schools (Winnie Olsen); McChord Air Force Base; Fort Lewis Military Museum; Tacoma City Light; Steilacoom Historical Society; and the Nisqually Nation.

Individuals who made pictures available from private collections include Douglas and Kathryn McDonnell, Ray Frederick, Jr., Florence Wilson, Katherine Jacroux, Sue Olsen, Mary Randlett, Paul Dorpat, Laughton Gore, Charlotte Brackenridge, Patti Hurlbut, Rowena Alcorn, Frank Sadler, and Lane Morgan.

Our opportunity to write the text and assemble the pictures for this book came when the board of Historic Tacoma, Inc. decided to sponsor a pictorial history in connection with the 100th anniversary of the union in 1884 of

the Tacoma City platted by General M.M. McCarver and the New Tacoma created by the Northern Pacific Railroad. We are grateful for their assignment—and for their total restraint from guidance.

We have aimed not for a formal history studded with dates and names but a reflection of the varying moods of those present during the exploration, settlement, booming, busting, retrenchment, and revival in this land which in spite of all efforts to shape it to older patterns retains a distinctive freshness.

Our interpretations are those of a native son of Tacoma and a third generation daughter of Washington. Our attitudes have been shaped by the Tacoma we inherited and love. We see in the town's slow growth after its mushroom growth not a defeat but an opportunity to avoid the mistakes of those cities that met the immediate hopes of their developers. We hope that in the superb setting there will grow a city whose citizens regard themselves as stewards, not masters, of their environment.

Rosa Morgan and Murray Morgan
Tacoma, Washington

THE INDIAN LAND

From

Wilderness

to White Men

In the spring of 1889, when the great Tacoma boom was at its height, Joaquin Miller checked into the town's finest hostelry, The Tacoma. He was given a room with a view. Although Miller was past the crest of his fame as a poet, he still cut a figure in his sealskin coat, buckskin jacket, red flannel shirt, whipcord pants, cowhide boots, and leather sombrero. He wore his graying hair shoulder length and sported a bowie knife in the sash at his waist.

Tacomans stared with wonder at this apparition of a frontier litterateur, and Miller gazed with appreciation at the scenery, especially at the great mountain that seemed to float on the horizon above the head of Commencement Bay. Even the townsfolk who considered the poet to be a wife-deserter given to committing meretricious verse in erratic meter were delighted with his rhapsody of approval for the setting:

Out of the blackness, above the smoke, above the touch of pollution, above the clouds, companioned forever with the stars, [Mount] Tacoma stands imperious and alone.

You may see a pretty woman pass by as you sit here on the high-built balcony of the new red city on the strong right arm of the sea of seas; but somehow she becomes a part of Tacoma, melts into the mountain of snow, and your face is again heavenward.

You may hear a wise man speak of the actions of great men as you sit here; but somehow his utterances seem far, far away; our heart and your whole soul—they have gone up into the mountains to pray. You can never again come quite down to the touch of that which is unworthy, for you have been companioned with the Eternal.

Come, then, and see the new world, and look up and wonder what fearful convulsions fashioned it. Sit with us in the wilderness and get the balm and balsam of the fir trees in your fibre. It is good for the body as well as the soul to be here in the new red town with its girdle of good green wood.

The slumbering volcano which the Indians called "Tacoma" and the British had named for the Naval officer Peter Rainier, stands to the east of the city. To the north and south are the rivers, Puyallup and Nisqually. The inland sea, which the Indians called Whulge and the British named for Peter Puget, lies to the west. Fire and water have shaped the land that has become Pierce County, and they continue to shape it.

A million years ago volcanoes began to form on the western slope of the Cascades, a range

A.H. Barnes painted this oil of an Indian camp at the head of Commencement Bay in 1911. Courtesy, Historic Photo Collection, University of Washington Libraries

Joseph Drayton accompanied the
Wilkes Expedition to Puget Sound
in 1841. He is credited with this
pastel of Mount Rainier which
could have been made when he
accompanied Lieutenant Wilkes
across the portage to the Cowlitz.
This is the earliest known image of
the mountain by an American.
Courtesy, Oregon Historical Society

The earliest painting of Puget's
Sound is the work of John Sykes, a
master's mate aboard H.M.S.
Discovery. The scene probably
shows their first camp, at Green
Point on Hale Passage west of
Tacoma. Courtesy, The Bancroft
Library

forced up eons earlier as the eastward drifting plate that forms the bottom of the Pacific pushed under the western fringe of Northwest America. Floods of lava filled the valleys carved by mountain streams. The lava cooled into a new landscape which in turn was buried under succeeding flows of molten rock and drifts of ash and pumice. The Mountain grew until its summit rose 15,000 feet above sea level. The highest of the fire-formed peaks between California and Alaska, it made the Cascades its foothills.

Snow fields deepened and hardened into glaciers that flowed rock-solid down the mountain, gouging valleys and adding their runoff to the snowmelt and rainfall that fed the rivers. As the pulse of the glaciers reflect changes in weather, the movement of the continental ice caps reflect changes in climate. During the most recent ice age, which ended some 14,000 years ago, waves of ice a mile deep swirled around the base of the Mountain and scooped new channels for Puget Sound. Melting, the ice left the lowlands covered with a thick layer of sterile dirt and gravel, the scrapings from the mountains of British Columbia.

Then the Mountain was at least a thousand feet higher than it is today. About 5,000 years ago, landslides, starting high on the peak, sent thousands of acres of ice and mud cascading into the valleys. The largest slide carried nearly half a cubic mile down the valley of the White River and left a layer of mud and rock 50 to 70 feet deep on the present sites of Buckley and Enumclaw. Smaller but still enormous mudflows rushed through Paradise Valley and down the Nisqually drainage system, into the Tahoma Creek and South Puyallup valleys.

Henry James Warre, a secret agent for the British government, posed as a young gentleman artist when he visited Puget Sound at the height of the "Fifty-four Forty or Fight" dispute over the Oregon Country boundary. He painted this watercolor near the Hudson's Bay Company fort on the Nisqually prairie on September 21, 1845. Courtesy, Public Archives of Canada

11

The Nisqually (shown here) and the Puyallup rivers flowed from glaciers high on Mount Rainier and shaped the land that became Pierce County. Courtesy, A.H. Barnes Collection, Northwest Room, Tacoma Public Library (TPL)

These cataclysms lowered the rim of the crater. A series of eruptions—the most recent only about 2,000 years ago—imposed Columbia Crest as the high point on the summit that had been left by the collapse. They left, too, nut-sized pieces of brown pumice that climbers bring back, as fresh as when the Mountain coughed them up.

The convulsions of the past 10,000 years were witnessed by the precursors of the Indians. The aborigines left no record of what they saw. Their own existence is known only by the fragmentary evidence of chipped stone—a spearpoint found in the flank of a mammoth dug up from a bog, scattered arrowheads and scraping stones, needles and ornaments of bone found in caves, and petroglyphs etched on cliffs and boulders. Some anthropologists believe there are hints of geologic calamities in the tribal myths of the Puyallup and Nisqually Indians about a being they called Transformer—He Who Changed Things. But all that is known for certain is that not long after the last great ice sheet retreated northward, men were present on Puget Sound.

Their numbers were not great. At peak, in the 1700s, there seem not to have been more than 3,000 or 4,000 Puyallups and Nisquallies, possibly only half that many. But those few lived well. Theirs was an economy of abundance.

The annual runs of salmon, returning to their native streams to spawn, allowed the Indians to harvest in a few days enough protein to last a year. Shellfish, wildfowl, seal, deer, and bear added variety to the diet. The men hunted, the women gathered. Nettles were their spinach, fiddlehead ferns their asparagus, camas their onion, and cattail and skunk cabbage root their potatoes. Nature provided abundant fruit and berries without man's assistance, but the Indians did heel in some roots with digging sticks, and burn the prairies to bring new growth that lured the deer.

In winter the Puyallup and Nisqually lived in family groups in clusters of longhouses of sweet-smelling cedar, set a short distance from salt water out of the path of storms and out of sight of raiding parties from more populous and warlike tribes to the north. In summer they camped in small groups on the saltwater beaches, followed the snowline up the mountainside in search of elk herds and deer, or traversed the Cascade passes to trade with the Klickitats and Yakimas.

Sometime in the 18th century the coastal Indians obtained horses from the tribes to the east, who had obtained them from Indians to the south, who had stolen them from the Spanish invaders. Even after gaining the freedom provided by mounts, the focus of existence for the Puyallup-Nisqually peoples remained the river, the beach, and the pathway of saltwater that led north and west to the restless, far-stretching ocean—beyond which lay mystery.

The earth was their mother; they were kin to all living things. Their fishermen offered prayers of welcome to the returning salmon; their canoe-makers chanted gratitude to the cedar they were about to fell and carve. Myth and ritual reinforced their respect for the creatures that provided food and clothing. Unlucky was the man who profaned his kill.

There was fear and awe in their search for cause, in their attempts to establish connection with the powers in the realm of spirit and dream that controlled the lives of individual and tribe. Their myths peopled the depths of

The omnipresent Mount Rainier lends its majestic power to many views of the Tacoma area.

The Puyallups and the Nisquallies continued in their ways long after the arrival of the white settlers. Asahel Curtis took this photograph in 1905, but the scene is timeless. Courtesy, Asahel Curtis Collection, Washington State Historical Society (WSHS)

The waterpower sawmill built by Nicholas Delin in 1852 at the confluence of creeks running down McKinley Hill and Wakefield Drive was still standing when J.D.S. Conger painted this watercolor in 1878. (WSHS)

Facing page
Henry Holt, who owned an art store in Tacoma, caught the lingering remoteness of the legendary first cabin on Day Island in this painting. (WSHS)

the forest and the far reaches of the sea with beings—some helpful, some malevolent—who were to be courted and propitiated by ritual and tribute.

The peoples of the southern Sound lived in balance with their beautiful land between the rivers and the sea. Their days changed to the rhythm of the seasons. At death their bodies merged into the earth that had nurtured them. Rejoining their ancestors, they became part of the tribal past and future.

On May 20, 1792, when the recorded history of the southern Sound begins, two small boats of strange design brought to the extremity of the inland seamen from beyond the endless oceans. These were the Transformers—The Ones Who Changed Things—

and they were not to be easily propitiated.

At four o'clock on a perfect spring morning, the ships' boats pulled away from His Britannic Majesty's sloop-of-war *Discovery* and headed into the more western of the two passages leading southward from the southern end of what is today the Seattle-Bainbridge area of Puget Sound.

Lieutenant Peter Puget, who was in command of the launch and the cutter, carried a written order from Captain George Vancouver to follow the starboard (western) shore to the extremity of the inlet. This mission was a part of the Vancouver expedition's overall assignment to complete the charting of the Northwest America begun for the British by Captain James Cook in 1776. The Admiralty had also given Vancouver the specific assignment of finding out if the Strait of Juan de Fuca might provide a useful connection to the eastward flowing rivers beyond the continental divide. If so, it would offer a western route of supply for the British fur companies that already were trading for beaver skins on the eastern slopes of the Rockies.

As they rowed south the men of the small boat party saw the sky behind the Cascades lighten with the pastels of dawn, then flare with sunrise oranges and greens, the Mountain still black as the sun rose above the barrier. Seagulls that had been parading the gravelly beach in search of their morning sandflies took off and circled the invading boats, mewing disapproval. An Indian canoe shadowed the little flotilla as it moved along the passage, but the natives shyly refused to be lured alongside by offers of trinkets.

About noon the shore to port curved away and revealed a broad bay leading eastward. As the scientist with the Vancouver expedition, Archibald Menzies, reported:

Up this bay we had a most charming prospect of Mount Rainier, which now appeared close to us though at least 10 or 12 leagues off, for the low land at the head of the Bay swelled out very gradually to form a most beautiful and majestic Mountain of great elevation whose line of ascent appeared equally smooth & gradual on every side with a round obtuse summit covered two thirds of its height down with perpetual Snow as were also the summits of a rugged ridge of Mountains that proceeded from it to the Northward.

Bound by the discipline of British charting procedure, which called for explorers to follow the shore on board and not be lured into interesting detours, the party let the current carry them past Point Defiance and south through the Narrows. When the shore bent west around Point Fosdick the boats turned with it. They even ran the length of a little cove—Wollachet Bay, the "place of squirting clams"—where Lieutenant Puget noted "a quantity of Gooseberry, Raspberry and Cur-

This painting, long considered to be a portrait of George Vancouver, is now thought by Britain's National Portrait Gallery to be "of an unknown person." Still, the officer appears to suffer from an enlarged goiter, as did Vancouver. Courtesy, Provincial Archives of British Columbia

rent Berries now highly in Blossom which intermixed with Roses, exhibited a Strange Varigation of Flowers but by no Means unpleasant to the Eye."

On their way out of the cove, they had their first meeting with the Indians of the southern Sound, a small group of whom were digging clams. As the boats approached the shore, the women and children, according to Menzies, "scudded into the woods loaded with parcels." But when they saw that the British did no harm to one old woman who remained behind they soon returned.

"In their Persons these People are slenderly made. They wear their Hair long, which is quite Black and exceeding Dirty. Both Nose and Ears are perforated, to which were affixed Copper Ornaments & Beads," Puget wrote. Relations were friendly and commerce began. The Indians had only clams to trade—dried clams, smoked clams, and fresh clams—but these they exchanged for buttons, beads, and bits of copper. When the Puget party moved on they were followed by a small fleet of Indian canoes.

The British made camp in a shallow cove at the head of Hale Passage, just east of Green Point. While some seamen raised the tent and marquee, others strolled the beach or lounged under the canvas awning of the cutter. The afternoon was warm, the water calm. John Sykes, a 20-year-old master's mate with a penchant for sketching with pen and crayon, caught the pastel ambience of the moment in the first picture of the southern Sound.

As daylight faded toward dusk, more Indians paddled up to watch the odd things going on ashore. They came by canoe. They did not land but lay a few yards off the beach, their dugouts gently bobbing. Alarmed at the growing number of visitors, Puget rescinded his earlier order to the men not to discharge the muskets they carried primed in the boats. They were customarily discharged at evening so that the powder would not gather additional dampness, but Puget had fretted that the sound of gunfire might unnecessarily alarm the natives. Concerned with the swelling fleet,

however, Puget decided a reminder that the whites were armed would be both cautionary and salutory.

"Bang, bong, bung!" went the soggy powder charges. "Poo, poo, poo!" exclaimed the Indians, who had no way of equating the sound with flying lead. Lieutenant Puget considered their tone mocking, but the night passed without alarm or incident.

The next day brought the first confrontation. About noon the explorers pulled ashore by a small creek for their midday meal. Having a net in the cutter, they decided to try the stream. No sooner did they unfurl the seine than the Indians who had been following them in canoes waded ashore, loud with protest, bows in hand, and arrows in quivers.

For the Indians, to fish uninvited in another man's traditional spot was not merely theft, it was insult most grievous. It implied a master-slave relationship.

The English did not understand how they had given offense. They feared unprovoked attack. Anxious not to demonstrate the killing potential of the sticks that said "poo" and reluctant to appear frightened, Puget told the men ashore to proceed with dinner while those remaining in the boats covered them with their muskets. He also had the men in the launch and gunners fire the one-pound cannons across the open water—"poo" compounded by a big splash.

Thomas Manby, one of the subalterns ashore, later claimed that he saved the day by demonstrating "the external destructive beauties of my double-barrel gun, fitted with a sliding Bayonet." It had been presented to him by the Marquis of Townshend, First Lord of the Admiralty. "Fortunately I got an opportunity of showing its effect in the midst of our parley by bringing down a Crow that was flying over my head. Wonder and silent admiration ensued. I advanced to them with the dead Bird . . . Some shook with fear, terror being on every visage." No other journal mentioned Manby's feat.

By accident or by design, carnage was avoided. The English offered to buy the Indians' bows and arrows. The Indians bargained the price up a bit, then accepted unilateral disarmament in return for fish-hooks, mirrors, and copper.

The incident at Alarm Cove, as Puget called the landing spot, was the only hostility encountered during the explorers' seven days on the southern Sound. Indians brought the English presents of salmon and salad on Anderson Island, traded for clams and fish off Nisqually Beach, and welcomed them ashore with almost total hospitality at a village on Eld Inlet, where Puget noted:

They appear much attached to the Women and hold Chastity as one of the Cardinal Virtues.... Immense Presents would not tempt these Girls, though coaxed with Rage to violate the Marriage Bed and much to their Credit be it Spokan they remained Stedfast in this Refusal.... I may say from these Circumstances that a Contract of that high Importance to Civil Society is among these poor and uncivilized Indians preserved in its greatest Purity.

Six days and 22 hours after setting out, the Puget party was back on the *Discovery* to report that the southwestern branch of the waterway, though verdant and beautiful, led nowhere. Captain Vancouver was off exploring the passage east of Vashon Island. He, too, found the inhabitants to be inoffensive, though there was a misunderstanding on Browns Point where an Indian, after his first taste of British cooking, lectured the white men about the evils of cannibalism.

When he rejoined Puget on the ship, Vancouver added his charts to those of the lieutenant. "By our joint efforts," he wrote, "we had completely explored every turning of this extensive inlet, & to commemorate Mr. Puget's exertions, the south extremity of it I named Puget's Sound."

All officers on charting expeditions were required to write assessments of the lands observed. All praised the scenery, most of them the weather; nobody mentioned rain. Vancouver thought that "the serenity of the

The Puyallups and Nisquallies made excellent and serviceable baskets for many years. The "Z" design represents salmon gills. (WSHS)

climate, the innumerable pleasing landscapes and the abundant fertility that unassisted nature puts forth, require only to be enriched by the industry of men with villages, mansions, cottages and other buildings to be rendered the most lovely country that can be imagined." Puget asserted that "little would the labour be in its cultivation." Most of the officers mentioned the possibility that the forested shore could supply spars and masts for all the navies of the world. All this, plus a native population perceived as civil, helpful, and honest in their dealings, were the advantages of the area as reported by most of the officers.

Two lieutenants sounded a discordant note. Joseph Baker, commenting on the abundant naval products, declared himself "of opinion that their remote situation from the Sea Coast render it most improbable that they will ever be of much use to Navigators." Joseph Whidbey conceded the country to be "equal to any in the world," but thought it so distant from places of importance that the best use for the land at the head of Fuca Straits would be as a depositing area for convicts who had served their time in the newly-established prison colony in Australia, "lest they return to England to become a fresh Prey upon the Public."

Lovely the land might be, but it was half the world away from civilization.

Vancouver's charts and his account of the voyage were published in 1798, the year of his death. They filled in the blank spaces of the Northwest Coast, an area so distant that, earlier in the same century, Jonathan Swift, in *Gulliver's Travels,* populated it with people "as tall as an ordinary spire steeple," the Brobdingnagians.

Puget's Sound was at last on the map, but it was still a six-month sail from England, and a year or more away from the Atlantic seaboard by land. War compounded its remoteness. The French Revolution coincided with the Vancouver voyage, and the Napoleonic wars that grew out of the revolution tied up European shipping and consumed Europe's energies until 1815 when Wellington met Napoleon at Waterloo. With Europe secure, England could again devote attention to the Pacific.

Dozens of American merchant ships visited the Pacific Northwest to trade with the Indians for sea otter skins in the years immediately following the Vancouver voyage. Indeed Yankee captain Robert Gray discovered the Columbia River while Vancouver was exploring the Sound. But as far as is known, no Americans visited the Sound between 1792 and 1824. When white visitors did come, they were again British, and again looking for a way to get somewhere else.

The Hudson's Bay Company absorbed its British rival, the North West Company, in 1821. Three years later the governor of the company visited the Columbia River to see if the former North West posts could be made profitable. One of the ablest of the many able Scots exported from the United Kingdom to America in the 19th century, Governor George Simpson was short, plump, and energetic, a man of strong opinion and quick decision. He and John McLoughlin, a towering Scotch-Irish physician whom Simpson left to run the company's affairs in the Pacific Northwest, made the most crucial decisions concerning Puget Sound.

Simpson declared at once that the old North West headquarters, Fort George (Astoria), was unsuitable. He ordered construction of Fort Vancouver farther up the Columbia as its replacement, a move that increased the importance of the river in relation to the Sound. He decreed that fur posts should grow their own food rather than import it, a move that eventually led to farming on the Sound. And he decided, sight unseen, that the Fraser River would be more suitable than the Columbia as the route to the interior—a misconception that led to the second "discovery" of the southern Sound by the trader James McMillan.

Simpson assigned Chief Trader James McMillan, a dour and durable veteran of the North West Company period, to take a party north in small boats to confirm the navigability of the Fraser. The most convenient route to the Fraser from the Columbia was to ascend the Cowlitz to the Chehalis prairie, portage to the lower Nisqually, follow it to the Sound and row north. The trouble was that the North Westerners had managed to so affront the Cowlitz Indians that they wouldn't allow whites on their river. McMillan was forced to make a wide and awkward detour.

The party of 42 men crossed the Columbia from Fort George to a point near present-day Ilwaco in two large rowboats, which they then carried over to Shoalwater Bay. They rowed north to Tokeland, walked the boats 10 miles north through the Pacific surf, portaged east to Grays Harbor, worked their way up the Chehalis River to the Black, up that twisting, willow-choked tributary to Black Lake, and then widened a five-mile-long Indian trail so the boats could be carried to Eld Inlet on the southern Sound.

Most of McMillan's men were English, Scots, or French Canadians. There was one Hawaiian, an Iroquois, and an American—the first American to be on Puget Sound. He was 69-year-old William Cannon. He had come around the Horn in 1811 on John Jacob Astor's ill-fated *Tonquin.* When the Astor venture collapsed, Cannon remained in the Oregon country, working first for the North West Company, then for Hudson's Bay. He lived for 30 more years, dying at 99, but he left no record of his trip to the Sound. Nor did McMillan. The surviving account was kept by a clerk, John Work.

An Irishman long in the company service, Work was more impressed by the weather than the scenery. His is the first account of winter weather on the Sound. You can almost wring water out of the journal, which is awash with references to "weighty rain," "flowing mud," and a landscape "eternally sodden." There is scant specific detail other than mention of starfish ("a shapeless animal with long toes jointed together in the middle"), a visit to Chelacum ("a village of the Nisqually nation consisting of six houses . . . miserable habitations constructed of poles covered with mats . . .") and a reference to signs that Indians were pasturing horses on Vashon Island. On the return trip from the Fraser three weeks later, Work mentioned only wind and rain in reference to the southern Sound.

From Governor Simpson's point of view, the soggy venture was a complete success. McMillan not only ascended the Fraser some 60 miles without encountering rapids, but he also managed on the return trip to persuade the Cowlitz Indians to allow the Hudson's Bay people to traverse their river. This opened the natural route between Puget Sound and the Columbia—the one that would be used by the first settlers, the first railroad, and later by Interstate 5. Puget Sound became linked with the transcontinental canoe route leading back across Canada to the St. Lawrence River. Never again would a year pass without the Sound being visited by whites.

McMillan's study of the lower Fraser did nothing to disabuse Governor Simpson of the notion that the northern river would better serve the company as a way into the interior. The dangers of the Columbia River entrance, which one captain described as "the seven-fanged horror of the Pacific, the bare bones of the continent, the dread Columbia River bar," augmented his desire for an alternate route. In 1827 Simpson sent word to Chief Factor McLoughlin to construct a post on the Fraser estuary which would eventually become the Company's western headquarters.

The task of construction fell to McMillan, who reported dryly that "this country is very unfavorable for hurry in building forts." Even so he had Fort Langley near completion when Governor Simpson arrived in the fall of 1828 on his second inspection trip to the Pacific Northwest.

Simpson had come by way of the Fraser rather than the Columbia. His intention was to demonstrate that the dangers of the northern river had been greatly exaggerated. Having run the Fraser rapids, he arrived convinced that "the passage down be certain Death in Nine attempts out of Ten." The Fraser wouldn't work as a highway. Fort Langley could not become a major base for the Hudson's Bay Company.

Simpson went by birch bark canoe from the Fraser to the Nisqually. Coursing south on the Sound, he had a new idea. Why not establish the western headquarters on this inland sea? It could serve as a supply base for the Fraser and the Strait of Juan de Fuca, and as a port for Company ships trading along the coast toward Russian America. If necessary, goods for the Columbia could be trekked overland from the Sound to Fort Vancouver.

Developments conspired to reinforce his arguments for a facility on the Sound. The 1828 supply ship, *William and Ann,* was lost on the Columbia River bar with all crew and cargo. The following spring the American vessels *Owyhee* and *Convoy,* owned by Josiah Marshall and Dixey Wildes of Boston, appeared on the Columbia more than ready for a trade war. Not only were they ready to undercut the Company's prices, they offered a greater variety of goods and, not being local residents, they saw no reason not to offer guns and liquor as articles of trade. Their arrival coincided with, and probably precipitated, an outbreak of smallpox that decimated the coastal peoples, reduced the take in furs, and raised prices.

In 1832 the board of directors of the Hudson's Bay Company, meeting in Beaver House under the shadow of St. Paul's in London, authorized the establishment of a Company post on a site yet to be selected between Whidbey Island and the Nisqually prairie. The whites were coming to live alongside the Red Men.

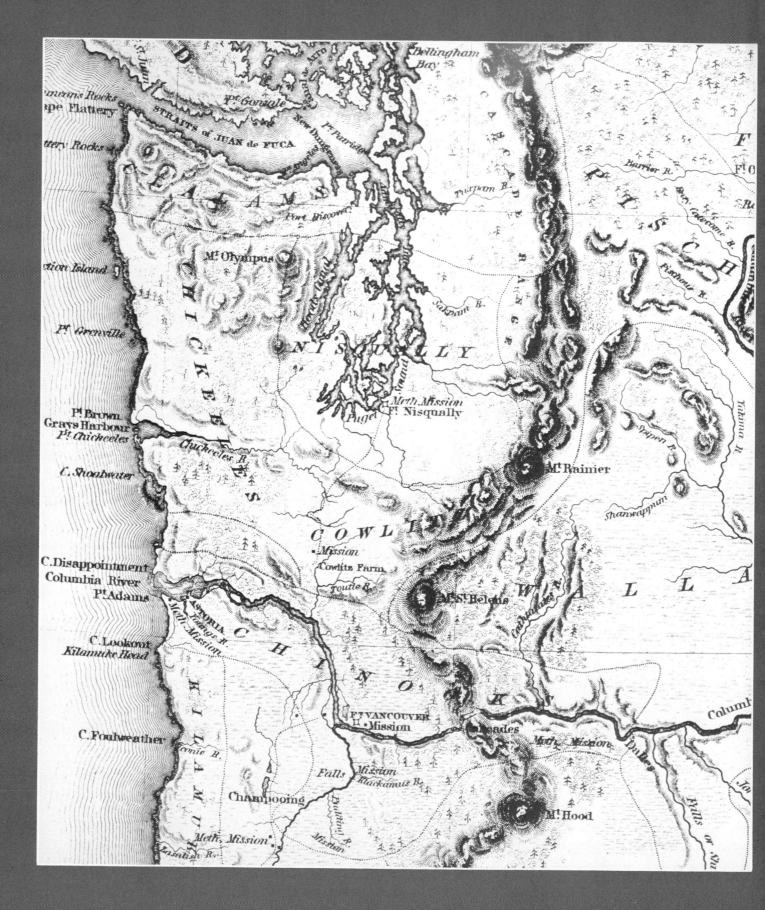

COLONIAL COMPETITION
The Battle
for
Supremacy

Shortly after noon on Thursday May 30, 1833, two Scots on horseback forded the swift-flowing Nisqually River about three miles from saltwater and rode at a brisk canter along the Indian trail north of the stream until they reached the bluff overlooking Puget Sound, calm under a cloudless sky.

On the narrow bench of land below, beside the mouth of little Sequalitchew Creek, were a small shack of cedar boards, an incomplete storehouse being built of logs, and a scattering of Indian mat-and-pole lodges. Some French-Canadians, Hawaiians, and Nisquallies squatted around open fires, roasting mussels and clams wrapped in seaweed, or gambling at the bone game. This was the first white settlement on the sea in the forest, the newest outpost of western civilization: Fort Nisqually.

The riders were Archibald McDonald and William Fraser Tolmie, important figures in the history of the southern Sound. McDonald was in his early forties, an impressive figure well over six feet in height, with red hair, white sideburns, a strong nose, and a notably wide mouth. A man of some formal education, with some training in medicine, McDonald had helped establish Lord Selkirk's colony at what became Winnipeg on the Red River of the North before joining the Hudson's Bay

Company. He held the rank of chief trader and the reputation of being one of the most fascinating yarn-spinners among men whose principal entertainment was campfire storytelling.

"All jaw and no work," was Governor George Simpson's secret estimate of the big Scot, but McDonald was given many important assignments. In November 1832 Dr. John McLoughlin had instructed him to select a site for a Puget Sound post as he traveled between Fort Vancouver and Fort Langley, remembering "your first objective is to observe if the Soil is suitable for cultivation and the raising of cattle; the next, the Convenience the situation affords for Shipping."

McDonald may have been jawing when he should have been listening. On his way to Fort Langley he narrowed the possibilities to Whidbey Island and the Nisqually prairie. Returning in March 1833 he decided on Nisqually. While there he encountered David Douglas who was on a botanizing expedition for the Royal Horticultural Society. The 33-year-old Scottish scientist might well have warned him that the tall grass of the prairie gave a false impression of the fertility of the soil.

McDonald's riding companion on his next

This map, from an unknown cartographer, shows Western Washington when the Oregon Country was in the joint possession of the United States and Great Britain. The notation of the Methodist Mission indicates that the map was made between 1840 and 1842. The dotted lines show trails, though several, like those crossing the Olympic Mountains, existed only in the mapmaker's imagination. Courtesy, Oregon Historical Society

visit in May might also have predicted Nisqually's limitations as a farm area. Only 21 and fresh from Glasgow, Dr. William Fraser Tolmie had studied under the notable botanist William Hooker, who helped him gain an appointment as physician in the Hudson's Bay Company service. A compact young man with a high forehead, sandy hair, and blue eyes, Tolmie looked like what he was, a bookish young scholar anxious to learn about the strange country to which he had been assigned. Experience, not expert advice, demonstrated Fort Nisqually's suitability for raising sheep and cattle rather than grains and vegetables.

Tolmie expected to leave Nisqually within a few days of his arrival, but his stay was unexpectedly extended when Pierre Charles, one of the voyageurs drafted into service as a construction worker, found it more difficult to swing an axe than a paddle. He split his foot, requiring the young doctor's prolonged ministrations. In the seven months before Tolmie moved on, he recorded the transformation of the area from camp to trading post.

The main establishment was built on the high, open ground a mile or so north and east of the mouth of Sequalitchew Creek. With Indian help the log storehouse by the beach was carried to the new site. Quarters were built for the white personnel, along with a company store. A palisade of upright logs, pointed at the top, replaced the flimsy picket fence that blew over in the first gale. Outside the walls the first crop was planted—seed potatoes that were simply scattered on the ground, then turned under by an ox-drawn plow.

Trade began, not only with the resident Nisquallies, but also with visitors who paddled in from the north. One in particular impressed Tolmie, who described him as "a brawny Soquamish with a Roman countenance & black curly hair, the handsomest Indian I have seen." Tolmie wrote his name as "Silah" but the Americans later spelled it "Seattle."

Tolmie's journal is full of exclamations about the Mountain ("stupendous Rainier, enbosomed in cloud.") On the pretext of gathering medicinal herbs, he made the first recorded attempt to climb it, rupturing himself in the process. He also became the first to write down the Indian name for the great presence on the eastern horizon, spelling it "Tuchoma" in his entry for October 29, 1833.

By the time Tolmie boarded the Company schooner *Cadboro* in mid-December, Fort Nisqually, though shy of formidability, had a look of permanence. And, it symbolized the British presence.

The area south of 54 degrees, 40 minutes north latitude (present-day Alaska, then known as Russian America); north of today's California-Oregon border (then Spanish America); west of the winding crest of the Rocky Mountains; and east of the Pacific Ocean was called the Oregon Country. No nation had established ownership, but America and Great Britain shared claims. Under terms of the Treaty of 1818, originally negotiated for 10 years but extended indefinitely in 1827, American citizens and subjects of the British crown shared the right to use any part of the vast area.

British interest was vested in the Hudson's Bay Company, which was licensed by the Crown to conduct all British business in the country. No comparable American monopoly existed; Americans beyond the Rockies found themselves in the position of a mom-'n-pop grocery competing with a supermarket. The Company exploited its advantage by doing all it legally could to keep Americans south of the Columbia, which the British expected to be the eventual dividing line. When Fort Nisqually was created, no Americans lived north of the river.

When, in 1839, Americans ventured to live on Puget Sound, they came not to barter for furs but to save souls. Dr. John McLoughlin at Fort Vancouver had shunted the first missionaries south to the Willamette Valley in 1834, but when two brigs bearing more Methodists arrived in 1837, the Reverend Jason Lee, who was headquartered on the Willamette River in Oregon, decided to expand the Methodist missionary service north of the Columbia. McLoughlin acquiesced to a religious establishment in the shadow of Fort Nisqually.

William Holden Willson was sent by Lee to become the first American to live on the Sound. Faith had brought Willson west but he was at best a marginally zealous preacher. A New Englander of Irish descent, he had sailed as a cooper on New Bedford whalers, fashioning barrels for boiled-out oil, until the spirit of revivalism swept over him and he volunteered to lend his service as carpenter to those ministering to the heathen far north beyond Cape Horn.

So Willson was among the first of the saviours to disembark from the first of two American brigs to reach the Columbia in 1839. He was quick to make himself at home. Tall and garrulous, with a passion for cats, an addiction to tobacco, enough expertise in regard to medicine to style himself a doctor (Jason Lee worried that his advice "might bring some of us . . . to an untimely grave"), and a yearning to be married, Willson was faced with the problem of avoiding bachelorhood in a land where fair-skinned females were few.

There arrived on the second Methodist-laden ship of 1839, Miss Margaret Jewett Smith, a young woman of teacherly inclination who was, let us say, liberated ahead of her time. Willson persuaded her to share his cabin (other arrivals were packed 12 to a two-room house). But when he proposed marriage she refused on the grounds that he had sent with Jason Lee, who was going east in search of recruits, a letter to Chloe Aurelia Clark of Connecticut suggesting marriage. This indeed he had, but the importunate Willson pledged to send a dispatch to Lee requesting that his earlier missive not be delivered.

Double negative. Chloe did not get the word that the wedding was off. With missionary zeal she embarked for Willson, the West, and the heathen. Meanwhile Margaret refused any attachment pending Willson's clearance of previous vows. He not only gave up his courtship but confessed publicly that their cohabitation in the cabin had been in the fullest sense of the word.

Willson's repentance was accepted; in fact, he was even given license to preach and was sent north by Jason Lee to frame up, on the Nisqually prairie, a missionary station. As for Margaret, branded wanton, she was denied the opportunity to instruct the Indian young. Instead she married a drinking doctor from England who had been grievously mutilated by Indians in southern Oregon for atrocities committed by other parties.

Willson arrived at Nisqually on April 10, 1839. He framed up a house and school building before returning to Willamette during the winter. On July 1, 1840, the *Lausanne* reached the Columbia, eight months from New York, bringing what was called the Great Reinforcement, a missionary contingent of 51 persons ready to combat heathenism, Romanism, and the wilderness.

Among the new arrivals were the Reverend Dr. John P. Richmond, a well-educated, near-sighted divine from Maryland; his wife of five years, Amelia (also called America), whom he had married in Mississippi; and their four children, the youngest of whom they had named Oregon. Also on board, bearing Willson's letter of proposal, was Chloe Clark.

Jason Lee assigned the Richmonds and Miss Clark to the Nisqually mission. Willson guided the party down the broad Columbia and up the twisting Cowlitz River to Cowlitz Landing, where they stayed two days at the Hudson's Bay Company farm awaiting the 17 horses needed to carry them and their goods to the Sound. There Chief Trader William Kittson put them up at Nisqually for three weeks while Willson finished the mission buildings. When at last they were ready to take up residence, Dr. Richmond united William and Chloe in what proved to be a long and happy marriage.

The mission was less successful. Dr. Richmond was perhaps the best educated American in the Oregon Country. A graduate of a Philadelphia medical college, he had also studied theology. A big-framed, lantern-jawed man, zealous in his faith, he had brought his family to this remote spot in the belief that Indians by the thousands eagerly awaited conversion. He

Lieutenant Charles Wilkes, commander of the United States Exploring Expedition of 1838-1842, made few friends but excellent charts. From Commemorative Celebration at Sequalitchew Lake

found himself isolated among a people wasted by new diseases introduced by the whites, uncomprehending of sermons delivered in English, and more eager for things spiritous than spiritual.

"Extinction appears to be their inevitable doom," he declared. "No earthly power can rescue them. . . . They will never be reached by the Voice of Gospel." Richmond had promised to stay for 10 years but within nine months, he was ready to resign. Lee expressed consternation. "What will the Catholics who singly are penetrating this whole region to make proselytes to their dogmas think of such Methodists? I am ashamed, I am grieved, I am perplexed. . . ."

Richmond managed to put in two years at Nisqually, long enough for America to give birth to a son, Francis, the first American child born north of the Columbia. The family returned east in July 1842, Richmond forsaking the ministry for the practice of medicine and politics. He lived another 43 years but never again visited Nisqually.

The Richmonds were still in residence at Nisqually Station in the spring of 1841 when American callers came by in abundance: the officers and men of the United States Exploring Expedition of 1838-1842. The Wilkes Expedition, as it is usually called in recognition of its combative commander, arrived on Puget Sound 49 years to the day after England's George Vancouver. His vessels, the sloop-of-war *Vincennes* and the gun-brig *Porpoise*, were the first official representatives of the United States to appear on Puget Sound, and Lieutenant Charles Wilkes was anxious to make up for lost time.

Wilkes' assignment to chart Puget Sound, the Columbia River, and San Francisco Bay and to report on their maritime usefulness stemmed from rising concern in Washington, D.C., about the Oregon Country boundary and the possibility that Alta California might be taken by the British in payment for Mexican debts. Though irascible and vainglorious, disliked by most of his men and officers, Wilkes was an able chart master. His two

months on the Sound resulted in the first detailed outline of the interior waterway, and fixed on the map many now-familiar names.

Commencement Bay was so named because the *Porpoise*, assigned to chart the northern Sound, commenced its survey there. The name of Point Defiance is thought to derive from an entry in Wilkes' journal that says a battery placed on the headland could defy the navies of the world to pass through the Narrows. On May 15 Lieutenant Sinclair, sailing master of the *Porpoise*, took the ship's gig into "an excellent little Bay" which he named Gig Harbor.

Eager to indicate an American presence in an area discovered and developed by the British, Wilkes bestowed the names of his officers and men on many geographic features. Inlets were named for lieutenants Augustus Case, Overton Carr, James Sinclair, George Totten, Thomas A. Budd, and for Passed Midshipmen Henry Eld and George Hammersly. Wilkes, an uncertain speller, spelled it Hammersley Inlet; he didn't even try to spell George Musalas Colvocoresses' surname, settling for Colvos Passage..

Maury Island honors Passed Midshipman William L. Maury; Fox Island, assistant surgeon S.L. Fox; Day Island, hospital steward Stephen W. Days; and Hartstene Island, Lieutenant Henry Hartstene, who had quit the expedition two years earlier after a quarrel with Wilkes.

Quartermasters Dalco, Henderson, Heyer, Neil, Piner, Pully, Robinson, Sanford, Southworth, and Williams had points along the shore named for them individually, and Quartermaster Harbor honors them as a group.

Civilian specialists were also recognized. The artists and draftsmen—Titian Ramsey Peale, John Drayton, and Aldred Agate—had passages named for them, as did linguist Horatio Hale, naturalist Charles Pickering, and geologist Charles Dana.

Since his mission involved strengthening U.S. claims to the most disputed part of the Oregon Country, that lying north of the Columbia River and south of the 49th parallel,

Members of the Wilkes Expedition who fanned out east and south from Puget Sound ended any remaining belief in the accuracy of Ramsay Crooks' report in 1826 that the country north and west of the Columbia River "is extremely worthless . . . with little other timber than pine and hemlock." From Charles Wilkes, U.S. Exploring Expedition of 1838-42, vol. 5

which the Americans proposed as the dividing line, Wilkes had anticipated a cool reception at Fort Nisqually. Dr. McLoughlin, however, had decided it would be good policy to help the Americans see how firmly established the Queen's subjects were north of the Columbia. The U.S. warships were invited to use the landing at Nisqually as their base. Chief Trader A.C. Anderson (for whom Wilkes named Anderson Island) helped find horses for a small land party Wilkes sent through Naches Pass—the first American crossing—to study the Columbia basin. Anderson even furnished the Americans with an ox to roast on Independence Day.

The Fourth of July falling on a Sunday, the celebration took place on the fifth at a natural clearing between Sequalitchew Lake and a larger lake to the north, which in consequence came to be called American Lake. The Reverend D. Richmond (whose "fine fat children, rosy cheeks" were "quite a sight" to Wilkes), committed the obligatory Fourth of July speech, telling the assemblage, which included some of their British hosts, that "We entertain the belief that the whole of this magnificent country, so rich in the bounties of nature, is destined to become a part of the American Republic. . . . The time will come

when these hills and valleys will be peopled by our enterprising countrymen, and when they will contain cities and farms and manufacturing establishments. . . ."

Not all the Americans were as cocksure as the preacher. The British seemed well entrenched. The wooden fort was poorly located and undermined with dry rot but a new one was to be built at a better spot. The fast-draining glacial soil had proved inhospitable to wheat, yielding less than two bushels an acre, and the peltry was in decline, but ranching and fishing were doing splendidly. The company bought salmon taken by the Indians from traps on the Nisqually; Indian women cleaned the catch for brining. The Americans noted "horned cattle in great abundance." More than a thousand sheep grazed on the abundant grass, and the herd was growing in number and quality. The Company had imported fine rams to improve the breed (the first shipment was purchased in California by an officer who knew ships better than sheep and accepted delivery of a flock of geldings), and brought from Scotland experienced shepherds. Nisqually wool commanded premium prices in the auctions in London. Nisqually beef fed the Russians in Alaska.

"I am astonished that our Country should

let them get such a secure footing as they already have got on this land," the purser on the *Vincennes* wrote in his journal. Then, remembering the Indian presence, he emitted some rhyme:

A problem, a problem, oh! hear great and small
The true owners of the country are still on their soil
Whilst Jonathan and John Bull are growing together
For land which by rights belongs not to either.

As for Wilkes, he reported that Puget Sound was not as important as San Francisco Bay but had much to recommend it and should not be yielded to the British.

The advantage obtained by the British in having the Hudson's Bay Company serve as a chosen instrument to manage their affairs in the Oregon Country under joint occupation was that American independent traders found it difficult to survive in competition with the monopoly. The disadvantage was that the Company discouraged the migration of independent Britons as well.

When, in Dr. McLoughlin's phrase, the fur trade became "pretty well knocked in the head," the Company organized a wholly owned subsidiary, the Puget Sound Agricultural Company, to run farm and ranch activities. Retirees from the Company were permitted to establish farms, but independent yeomen were not encouraged to immigrate to the Oregon Country.

In the mid-1830s American fur traders established wagon routes through the Rockies. South Pass opened the way for the migration not of single traders and trappers but of families, on wheels, in groups. A trickle at first, the westward movement across the Mississippi became a flood in 1843 with the ad lib assemblage of a great covered-wagon train. In two years, American population in the Oregon Country equalled British. The Company's subsequent encouragement of migration came too late. When the boundary settlement was negotiated in 1846, only one Englishman not connected with the Company was a resident on Puget Sound.

That loner was Joseph Thomas Heath of Buckinghamshire, a likeable scapegrace. One of five sons of a preposterous but prosperous English gentleman who did not desire his boys to marry, Joseph managed to gamble, drink, and wench away not only his own inheritance but much of that of his mother and favorite sister. An older brother, Will, who took to drink and to sea, chanced to be an officer on Hudson's Bay Company ships. In 1843 Will persuaded the Company to allow Joseph to buy, on time and with a $5,000 surety from other members of the family, an undeveloped estate on what was then called Steilacoom River and is now known as Chambers Creek. It was as far from the gaming halls and watering holes of London as a man could get. There, in splendid isolation and repentant dedication, Joseph Heath spent the few years remaining him planting crops, raising sheep, and hoping (all too often in vain) that the semiannual mail delivery would bring word from home. And he kept a diary.

Heath reached the Sound in the summer of 1844 and, with the help of some Steilacoom Indians, set to work to build a house and till the fairly open land later occupied by the Western State Hospital. He was six miles by wagon road and seven by water from the fort.

Distance was the disease of the pioneer. The sense of isolation in the exile's diary is crushing. Heath spent his first year at Steilacoom without once getting as far as the Puyallup River or Commencement Bay. He measured time by the intervals between the semiannual arrivals of the Company Express, which might bring mail. When it came without letters he was physically ill for weeks.

Tuesday, Dec. 7. Express arrived without letter from home. I shall make no further remark upon it . . .

Sunday, 12. Rode to the Fort and spent a pleasant day when I was not thinking of Home and no letters . . .

Saturday, 18. Fretting every day and almost every hour at not having had any letters from Home . . .

Sunday, 19. Sitting indoors and thinking of all dear to me and making excuses in my mind for their not writing . . .

Monday, 27. Find myself constantly sighing; must be from my not hearing from those dear to me.

Jan. 1. Sat by the fire in the evening and thought of all dear to me; anything but happy; having no letters from them constantly haunts my mind. Rain, gales, frost.

Other problems he met with equanimity. Heath wrote with quiet humor about his dairy and potato house being "in the possession of skunks," with amused resignation about his clothing ("not one of the people about the place is half so ragged as myself"), and with philosophic balance about the loss of a tooth "which does not add to my beauty, but 'twill not bite my tongue again which it had a constant knack of doing." He was calm about a brush with death when he interrupted an outraged Indian's attempt to murder a medicine man who lost too many patients. "I found his gun within a few inches of my breast, which I immediately seized and forced away from him. The next minute he rushed upon me with his knife, when I charged him with the butt end of the gun, beating him off, but not before receiving a smart cut across one of my arms."

There was the pride of accomplishment as the farm took shape. The roof was raised and proved almost rainproof. An old wicker chair was tightened to become "the ornament of the place." The land was ploughed, seeded, and weeded; the crops harvested and stored. Horses strayed and were found. Lambs were born and many lost to wolves. Heath dined on boiled grouse. He marveled at buying from the Indians four magnificent salmon, weighing 16 or 17 pounds each, for a shilling.

Sometimes there were visitors. Heath especially enjoyed Dr. Tolmie, who had returned to the fort as chief trader, and John Edgar, a Company shepherd, and his plump, comely Yakima wife, who sometimes brought presents of bear grease and dried salal berries. On Friday, November 13, 1846, Dr.

Tolmie rode up from the fort with news. Five months earlier the British had signed a treaty yielding the Oregon Country up to the 49th parallel to the Americans. Heath wrote the news "put me out of spirits and out of temper, as I must now look out for a new place of settlement and have to commence *de novo*, which after all the trouble and labour I have had is quite disheartening. . . . Found three fine deer but could not get a shot. An unlucky day with me."

The next Company Express brought letters from home. Heath was cheered too to learn that the Treaty of 1846 recognized the title of the Hudson's Bay Company and the Puget's Sound Agricultural Company to their lands. He would not have to move.

With the boundary settled Americans appeared, looking for land to claim. The first was "Mr. Burkhart, an American . . . Invited him to be my guest until he can build himself a house . . . An unassuming young man, carpenter by trade, much amused me by his total ignorance of other countries. Told me a friend had been to England who thought it was *pretty goodish country but considerably smallish.*"

In November 1848 Heath learned from the officer of a visiting ship that gold had been discovered in California and fast steamer service was planned between San Francisco and Panama. Delivery time of mail from England would be cut to 45 days. "Makes me quite cheerful, distance from Home and all dear to me will be nothing then."

Heath, however, did not live to benefit from the faster mail service. His health was failing, and his efforts to cure himself by starvation, emetics, and laxatives were not beneficial. Within a few weeks he was unable to leave his cabin. Neighbors did what they could. On February 9, 1849, he took the pen he had made from the quill of an eagle he had killed four years earlier and made a final entry. "Dick cut up the pigs and salted them. Unable to do anything myself. Voice gone and myself very weak."

He died on March 7, 1849. The site of his grave is not known.

III

OUTLETS TO THE WORLD
Roads,
Rivalries,
and Rebellion

The American settlement of the Sound moved from the south up. The first pioneer party took up seven claims in the vicinity of the Deschutes River, which flows into the southern extremity of Budd Inlet. Michael T. Simmons, who led the 31 Americans north from the Columbia, chose the area because the swift drop of the river from prairie to saltwater offered waterpower for a mill.

The Simmons group arrived late in the fall of 1845, before the Treaty of 1846 made the area American. They were tolerated by the Hudson's Bay Company, Dr. John McLoughlin having written Dr. William Fraser Tolmie instructing him to let them have credit at the company store at Nisqually. Their presence on the Sound was not known to the British and American diplomats and did not influence the British decision to yield the area. They did, however, serve as magnets for other Americans, especially after they knocked together a gristmill and a sawmill. A community was formed at the mouth of the Deschutes and became the trading center for the new settlers scattering across the prairies. It came to be called Olympia, the name derived from that bestowed on the neighboring mountain range by the British long before.

In 1850 Lafayette Balch, a 25-year-old sea

captain from Maine, sailed the brig *George Emory* around Cape Horn with a load of general merchandise and a precut New England house. Too many merchants had reached San Francisco before him, so he went on to Puget Sound. Olympia looked promising so he began to unload his goods at the head of Budd Inlet. But when he tried to buy a site for a store, Balch found himself at odds with Edmund Sylvester, another down-easter from Maine, who owned most of the townsite. Sylvester was a friend of Mike Simmons, who ran the existing store.

Unable to make a deal, Balch upped anchor and sailed back north in search of a more congenial location. A lovely, low-bank indentation just south of what is now called Chambers Creek appealed to him. Three English sailors who had deserted their ship after it was seized for a technical violation were living nearby; two were cutting pilings for the San Francisco market and the third, William Bolton, was framing up a shipyard with the intention of building sloops. They made Balch welcome. He staked a claim to 316 acres, brought his New England building ashore, assembled it, and opened the first store and hotel in what became Pierce County.

Olympia had a rival. Balch called it Port

The granary at Fort Nisqually, shown here in this 1905 Asahel Curtis photograph, has been placed on the National Register of Historic Places as the oldest building in Washington. The structure was moved in 1934 from its original site to Point Defiance in Tacoma, where a replica of the Puget's Sound Agricultural Company post was built. Courtesy, Curtis Collection, WSHS

Steilacoom.

With the formation of communities, there began the never-ending competition for roads and shipping service. Transportation meant convenience, growth, prosperity, and an end to the loneliness that plagued early settlers like Joseph Heath. It could also mean safety.

The Indians were becoming restive not only at the increasing number of whites in their land but also at the changing character of the whites. The Hudson's Bay Company people had come as employees, under company discipline; the Bostons, as the Americans were called, came seeking personal gain in a land they considered theirs for the taking.

When Balch founded his town, there had already been a serious confrontation at nearby Fort Nisqually. It involved a strapping young Nisqually called Wyamoch by the Indians and

Young Lachalet by the whites (his father was the Lachalet who accompanied Dr. Tolmie on his 1833 visit to Mount Rainier) who was married to the daughter of Patkamin, a small, intelligent, and devious chief, the most prominent of Snoqualmie leaders. Young Lachalet was thought of by the whites as big, handsome, and full of fun, while the Snoqualmies thought of him as a wife-beater. From time to time Patkamin would come down from the north with some warriors to check on the domestic situation in the Lachalet household.

About noon on May 1, 1849, Nisquallies and Steilacooms working in the fields outside the fort rushed in with word that about a hundred Snoqualmies were moving south across the prairie. The party, painted and carrying weapons, assembled outside the water gate. When asked what they wanted the Snoqualmies said they had no quarrel with the whites but wanted to see that Young Lachalet was not inside. Patkamin was invited to enter the fort; his companions were given tobacco and told to wait outside. Two armed French-Canadians were stationed to guard the entrance.

Walter Ross, a company clerk, left the most coherent eyewitness account. After Patkamin was inside, one of the guards fired his gun; "in jest," he explained later. Ross went to investigate. The Indians were angry. There was an exchange of insults, some pushing, and Ross threatened them with his gun. An Indian made two or three threatening gestures at him with a dagger.

Ross and the other whites ducked back into the fort, but after the gate was closed it was discovered that Charles Wren, a cattle hand, had been left outside. The gate was unbolted and Wren ran in but tried to grab an Indian's gun as he came. The gun fell and jammed the gate open. Looking outside, Ross stared into the muzzle of an Indian's gun. Ross fired; almost instantaneously there was a shot from outside. Both missed. The gate was finally closed.

By the time the whites inside had gathered their firearms and reached the blockhouses at the corners of the palisade, the Snoqualmies were in flight. But on the ground below lay an Indian medicine man and a white man, both dead.

The American was Leander C. Wallace, who had a claim on Anderson Island. (Some settlers called it Wallace's Island.) He had come to the company store for supplies. The exact circumstances of his death were never made clear. He may have thought that as an American he was not involved in the dispute at the fort. Some of the Hudson's Bay people said that Wallace was a blusterer who liked to boast that he could drive off a war party with a stick. Perhaps he tried; certainly he died.

During the excitement, Patkamin, who had been in the fort when the shooting started, was helped to escape over the wall by his son-in-law Lachalet. This contributed to a suspicion among the Americans that the wife-beating

In 1850 Captain Lafayette Balch founded Steilacoom, which soon became the first town and the county seat of Pierce County. (TPL)

story had been an Indian ruse to gain entry to the fort with the intention of capturing it, distributing the arms among the Puget Sound tribes, and driving the whites from the country. The British remained convinced that the whole affair was a family quarrel that had gotten out of hand.

It chanced that Joe Lane, the governor of Oregon Territory, who had arrived in Portland (population 20) only two months earlier in March 1849, was paying his first visit to Cowlitz Farms. When he learned of what was described as an attack on the fort, he started for the Sound. With him went Lieutenant George Hawkins and five of the only eight soldiers in all of Oregon. Lane was at Tumwater when a horseman caught up with him to report that Major James Hathaway had just arrived on the Columbia from Boston by way of Cape Horn and the Hawaiian Islands with two companies of U.S. artillerymen.

Governor Lane returned to Fort Vancouver to confer with Major Hathaway. They decided to send Company M under Captain B.H. Hill to Puget Sound with the assignment of apprehending the killers of Wallace. To house the force of 80 officers and men, the government leased from the Hudson's Bay Company the property Heath had been developing.

Captain Lafayette Balch built a store at Steilacoom. From Hunt, History of Tacoma, *volume I*

Fort Steilacoom, a few miles east of the town of Steliacoom, seemed more a parade ground than a defense establishment, as can be seen in this 1866 painting. Courtesy, Western State Hospital

Heath's house became headquarters and lodging for the officers; the outbuildings barracks for the men while other structures were built.

As a defense structure Fort Steilacoom, as it was called, was even less impressive than Fort Nisqually. It had no palisade, but, unlike the trading post, it had soldiers. It marked the first presence of U.S. Army forces on Puget Sound.

Captain Hill sent word to the Snoqualmies to surrender the men who had killed Wallace or face destruction. J. Quinn Thornton, who showed up with a warrant commissioning him to negotiate for the Indian Department, added a promise that if Patkamin turned in the culprits he would be rewarded with 80 blankets. It was a promise, or threat, Patkamin

Edward Huggins was the last chief trader at Fort Nisqually. After the United States bought the land and opened it to settlement, Huggins preempted a claim on land that embraced the best of the buildings, including this bastion. Huggins and his wife, Letitia, are believed to be the couple standing by the fence to the right of the horse. Courtesy, Fort Nisqually, Metropolitan Park District

court officials but also most of the jurors had to be imported from the Columbia area. On Monday, October 1, 1849, the grand jury met and indicted the six, on Tuesday the petit jury found two of the six guilty of murder, and on Wednesday U.S. Marshall Joe Meek supervised the hanging of the pair from a convenient oak in the presence of their fellow tribesmen.

The trial was held at Fort Steilacoom to impress the Indians with white man's justice. It impressed the settlers with its cost—$2,379, which included $480 paid to the Hudson's Bay Company for the 80 blankets—and with its inconvenience, as many of the jurors had to travel 200 miles by canoe and horse to reach the improvised courtroom.

Though there were only 304 non-Indian inhabitants of Oregon Territory living north of the Columbia (an area that included all of Washington, northern Idaho, and part of Montana) and 115 of them were foreigners, an effort began to persuade Congress to designate the northern portion as a separate territory.

On a snowy day in February 1854, in a hall draped with red-white-and-blue bunting and warmed by a pot-bellied stove on the second

couldn't refuse. He sent along six Indians, some of whom may have been present when Wallace was slain.

The Oregon territorial legislature rushed through a special act attaching Puget Sound to the first judicial district so the Indians could be tried at Fort Steilacoom. So sparse was the population around the Sound that not only

General Silas Casey, commander of the regular army troops at Fort Steilacoom during the Indian wars, was one of the many officers who privately sympathized with the Indians. (TPL)

floor of an unpainted frame building on an unpaved street in Olympia, a short, big-headed, frock-coated soldier-turned-politician addressed the first session of the first legislature of the Territory of Washington. Governor Isaac Ingalls Stevens told the 25 newly-elected council members and representatives that they represented not merely the 3,965 non-Indian residents of "our beautiful domain" but "our whole people who have risen in their strength and are now reducing to subjection the vast wilderness between the two Oceans." Statehood lay ahead.

To be sure, there were problems. According to Stevens, the territory needed more and better roads, especially a road through the Cascades that would encourage immigration. It needed improved mail service, a school system and a university, and a trained citizen militia. Most of all, said Stevens, it needed a railroad ("the magnificent and gigantic enterprise of connecting the Mississippi and the Pacific with iron roads"), the purchase by the United States of the lands still held by an alien corporation (the Hudson's Bay Company), and the negotiation of treaties under which the Indians ("for the most part a docile and harmless race") would confine themselves to reservations and relinquish title to the rest of their lands so that settlers could have unclouded deeds to the claims they would develop.

A man of intelligence, eloquence, energy, courage, and ambition, Governor Stevens concentrated all his talents on solving the problems he outlined. But his virtues included neither patience nor the realization he might be fallible. Historians still debate whether he solved more problems than he exacerbated. For a small community gathering on the shore of Commencement Bay, however, there was no doubt. Stevens' policies led to disaster.

In the spring of 1852 Nicholas Delin, a Swedish-born cabinetmaker and carpenter, came to the area by way of Russia, New York, Massachusetts, San Francisco, Portland, and Olympia. At the confluence of two small streams, he built a dam to form an impounding pond, then put up a shed-like building on stilts to house an up-and-down muley saw driven by a water-powered turbine.

Delin's little mill attracted the first commercial ship to call on Commencement Bay, the brig *George W. Emery*, which loaded lumber for San Francisco. The mill attracted, too, a small work force, including an English couple, William Sales, a mill-hand, and his wife, Eliza, a cook. On October 23, 1853, Eliza gave birth to a son, James, the first white child born on the site of what is now Tacoma. The Sales took a claim in the Puyallup Valley, where their neighbors were a Scot who had worked for the Hudson's Bay Company and three German-American veterans of the Mexican War.

Industry diversified. Delin furnished lumber to Chauncey Baird, who began to make barrels in a waterfront shed. Baird's best customers were Peter Reilly and John Swan who, when the salmon were running, made huge hauls with beach seines. They brined the fish for sale in Hawaii and San Francisco.

In the fall of 1853 the Commencement Bay community received reinforcements by an unexpected route. A party of immigrants from the Midwest, seduced by rumor of a shortcut to Puget Sound by way of Naches Pass, set out across the Cascades from the Yakima Valley. Somehow leader James Longmire brought 34 of the 36 wagons and all 171 of the pioneers through to the Nisqually prairie. Most of the newcomers settled in the Steilacoom area or around Yelm. But the Judson family—Peter and Anna; their sons, Steven and Paul; and their orphaned niece, Gertrude Meller—came to Commencement Bay. For $30 they bought a cabin from a discouraged millhand near what became Seventh Street and Pacific Avenue. At once they began to plant wheat and oats in natural clearings on a 321-acre claim that covered most of Tacoma's present-day business district, and they harvested grain on the current sites of the Union Depot and the Post Office. But in October 1855 the seedling community was ripped up by the roots.

Ten months earlier Governor Stevens had summoned the tribes of the southern Sound to a council at Medicine Creek, just south of the

Nisqually. In three days of negotiation with "chiefs" he appointed to represent the Indians, Stevens persuaded the Indian nations to sign a formal treaty under which they'ceded to the United States all of what would form Pierce and Thurston counties, plus parts of King, Mason, and Kitsap counties. In return the Indians retained two reservations of 1,280 acres each, plus a small island known as Squaxin. They were promised instruction in farming and industrial arts, "the right of taking fish at all usual and accustomed grounds and stations, in common with all citizens of the Territory," and payments totalling $32,500 to be spread across 20 years, plus $3,200 in moving expenses.

The Puyallups and Nisquallies soon realized they had been gulled. They could not exist on the space allotted. They asked for renegotiation but Stevens refused; instead he went off to practice more diplomacy with other tribes in western Washington. He proved remarkably successful in getting the saltwater Indians to give up title to their traditional lands. But when in the spring of 1855 he crossed the Cascades to negotiate with the horse-owning tribes of the interior, he found them alert and suspicious. A treaty was signed at Walla Walla; but before it could be ratified, the Yakima—convinced they had been betrayed—took up arms.

To prevent the Indian War from spreading back to the coast, where the white population was concentrated, posses of volunteers patrolled the passes. Eaton's Rangers decided to take into protective custody two dissident Nisquallies, half-brothers Leschi and Quiemuth, lest they stir up trouble. The brothers escaped to the forest and were joined by other rebels. Two volunteer scouts looking for them were ambushed and killed. War had come to the southern Sound. On October 28, a band from the tribes on the White River attacked a scattering of farms between today's Kent and Auburn, burning cabins and killing men, women, and children.

Terror swept the isolated farms and tiny hamlets. The day after the White River massacre, Commencement Bay was deserted. By canoe, by scow, and by wagon the first settlers retreated with their belongings to the town of Steilacoom or to Fort Steilacoom three miles away. Some didn't stop until they got back to where they'd come from.

The Indian War west of the mountains was a siege within a siege. The Indians were kept away from their fishing grounds, the whites from their farms. The Indians found no way to get at the blockhouses, and the whites could not approach the Indians' camps in the deep forest. The Indians, cold and hungry, quarreled among themselves in their hideouts. The white community, though pressed together in the blockhouses, was fragmented. The Americans distrusted the former Hudson's Bay Company people as "Indian lovers." The regular army distrusted the volunteers. The governor arrested the chief justice of the territorial supreme court for defying martial law; the chief justice fined the governor for contempt of court.

As first governor of Washington Territory, Isaac Ingalls Stevens set up the capital at Olympia, organized government, surveyed a route for a railroad from the Great Lakes to Puget Sound, and campaigned for its construction. However, his peremptory dealings with the Indians caused lasting problems. Courtesy, State of Washington Library

Nicholas Delin married Gertrude Meller, one of the young women who came through the Naches Pass in 1853 with the Longmire Party. Their daughter, Grace Alice, was the first white girl born in what is now Tacoma. From Hunt, History of Tacoma, *volume I*

In January 1856 the Indians made a futile attempt to storm Seattle. In March they were driven from an ambush they set near the White River for 50 regular army troops. After these defeats they fled through the mountain passes to Yakima country.

By the fall of 1856 the Indian war was over in the West. Governor Stevens met on Fox Island with the Nisqually and Puyallups who had not joined in the fighting. He acknowledged that the reservations assigned in the Medicine Creek treaty were inadequate to their needs and agreed to recommend new and much larger locations on the Puyallup and Nisqually rivers. In a way, the Indians had won.

The rebel Quiemuth surrendered and was shot, then stabbed to death while being held prisoner in the governor's office. His half-brother, Leschi, was betrayed to the authorities by a nephew who was subsequently murdered by another Indian. Over the protests of the army officers who had fought him, Leschi was tried as a civilian, not a soldier, found guilty of murder, and was hanged.

There was no longer any question of who was in charge on Puget Sound.

With peace restored, the settlers who had fled Commencement Bay could return in safety. They chose not to. Nicholas Delin made a brief attempt to resume sawmilling but there were now several steam mills on the Sound and his water-driven muley saw couldn't cut fast enough to make money. He sold out to a man who worked on the Puyallup Reservation and moved to Seattle, where he put his carpentry skills to work in fashioning the four columns for the portico of the new University of Washington.

Peter Judson abandoned his claim on the Tacoma bluff in favor of land closer to Steilacoom, the metropolis and county seat of Pierce County. Lafayette Balch's town had grown during the war. Many who had come there for refuge, stayed on. By 1858 Steilacoom boasted of being the first incorporated town in Washington, the site of the first Protestant church north of the Columbia as well as the Immaculate Conception Mission,

and the home of the *Puget Sound Herald,* a four-page, six-column weekly put out by Charles Prosch, who had lively things to report.

Steilacoom was a center for culture, high and low. Two dancing academies offered to teach not only standards such as the waltz, schottische, polka, and gallopade quadrille, but also new steps such as the Portland Fancy, the Tempest, and Bash Away Boys.

John McFarland and somebody named Pickering, styling themselves as "Two Gentlemen from the Sandwich Islands," in March 1858 offered the town's first professional entertainment. Their work with violin and piano was well received. An estimated 200 out of a county population of 420 turned out. On April 8 the Sandwich Island duo offered a second concert to be followed by a dance. Tickets: Gent $4; Gent & Lady $4. (Ladies were in short supply.)

Rival entertainment was offered at the Steilacoom jail (another territorial first), where the jailer played fiddle while the prisoners danced with visiting Indian women. Though far from escape-proof, the jail was usually crowded. Steilacoom was a seaport and had a military post nearby. Local authorities tolerated commercial accommodation to the desires of lonely men but excessive boisterousness was penalized, as was being caught red-handed in the act of butchering cattle rustled from the Hudson's Bay Company herd, or for selling liquor to the Indians. Horse racing was tolerated on the Sabbath in spite of the objections of the Methodist minister, but fistfights were considered an improper way of determining the result in a close finish.

The Steilacoom Library Association was granted a special charter by the Territorial legislature. Frank Balch lectured under the association's sponsorship on "The Necessity of a More Elevated Standard of Public Morals Among Us."

Better roads were needed too. Father Louis Rossi, a Belgian priest who came to Steilacoom in 1857, wrote later of his ride north from the Cowlitz:

The ground on which we found ourselves was detestable; we sank up to our knees in the marsh. We tried to keep the horses on the planks. Some fell in the mud; others slipped on the improvised bridge; others tumbled . . . In the midst of all these difficulties no one broke either his legs or his neck . . .

You should have seen me with some big boots which came up to my knees, a waterproof overcoat covering my black habit, and a hat all flattened wtih a very large brim: I had the aspect of a necromancer. A half-pelt of buffalo and a blanket of blue wool rolled behind the saddle in order to serve as a bed in case of need, and double valise which hung on either side of my mount and which contained on one side all that which was necessary to say Holy Mass and administer the sacraments and on the other, some personal articles: that was my baggage.

The young priest soon learned that the best way to get about was by canoe, but only if Indians were paddling. When whites tried the dugouts, he confessed, "My nerves were constantly strained. They do not know the nature of the craft and are complete strangers to the manner of governing it. But with the Indians I found myself perfectly at ease and very tranquil. I sang, I read, I studied, I prayed."

Others prayed when riding the steamers that provided haphazard service around Steilacoom in the 1850s. The sidewheeler *Fairy* was put on the run between Olympia and Steilacoom in 1853 but seems to have disappeared in a cloud of steam. John Scranton and James Hunt brought the *Major Tompkins* up from San Francisco. She lumbered from Olympia to Steilacoom and on to Victoria (round trip six days) for almost a year before impaling herself on a British Columbian rock.

In 1855 J.G. Parker, who was in San Francisco buying liquor for his Olympia business, took a fancy to the *Kangaroo*, a 60-foot iron steamer that had been built in three telescoping sections in Philadelphia for shipment around Cape Horn. Parker changed her name to *Traveller* and put her on the Olympia-Steilacoom-Seattle run. In 1858 her engineer bought her and chartered her to the Indian Department, whereupon the *Traveller* promptly sank at anchor off Foulweather Bluff. The engineer and two Indians swam ashore but the captain, purser, deckhand, fireman, and the only white passenger were lost.

Hunt and Scranton then brought the 185-foot propeller-driven *Constitution* from San Francisco. She cost so much to run that they gutted her of machinery and sailed her as a lumber barkentine. Not until 1859, when the handsome and long-lived sidewheeler *Eliza Anderson* and the larger but lumbering *Wilson G. Hunt* were imported from the Columbia, did steam transportation on the inland sea come to seem as safe as the Indian canoe.

What everyone was waiting for was the arrival of the railroad. There was not a settler on saltwater who could not cite reasons why the western terminus of the first transcontinental to reach the Northwest should not be at his claim. Lafayette Balch was sure his town would be the terminus. Failing that, he proclaimed, the line would have to at least pass through Steilacoom.

Balch did not survive to be disappointed. In 1862 he went to San Francisco to marry his fiance but dropped dead on Market Street before the wedding.

Above
Although no portrait was made of Leschi of the Nisquallies during his lifetime, this representation, painted after his death, is reputedly a good likeness. Courtesy, Historic Photo Collection, University of Washington Libraries

Left
Nathaniel Orr built Steilacoom's first manufacturing establishment, a wagon shop. The sign on the front brought business in the winter, but when the tree leafed out, Orr had to add the sign below the window. (TPL)

THE POWER OF STEAM

Waiting

for

the Train

A reporter for the Portland Oregonian, *visiting Puget Sound in 1871 to study rival sites for the Northern Pacific terminus, wrote: "It is unnecessary to state that Tacoma is also the terminus . . . The founder found it two or three years ago lying around loose, and as it was the only place not then appointed and ordained for terminus purposes, he went for it, bought it, and had it regularly platted and set down as the place where the job of building the world was commenced (hence Commencement Bay) and where the job of building the Northern Pacific Railroad, the next greatest work after creation, is to be finished. . . ." This photo was taken by Thomas Rutter. Courtesy, Ray Frederick, Jr.*

Christmas Day in 1864 dawned clear and cool. The Mountain was out and frost glazed the tips of the evergreens. Three employees at the Puyallup Indian Reservation—the agent, the carpenter, and the farming instructor—thought it a good day to catch salmon. They invited Job Carr to go with them.

The gaunt, framed buildings of the Indian agency offered the only place for travelers to stay between Steilacoom and Seattle. Carr was a guest of A. Williamson Stewart, who taught carpentry and wagon-making. Carr was a wiry little man who had been invalided out of the Union Army at the age of 51 after being twice wounded. He had come west looking for a new life—and more. President Abraham Lincoln on July 2, 1864, had signed legislation that offered up to 40 million acres of public land as reward for completion of a railroad between the Great Lakes and Puget Sound. Carr hoped to claim land where, in the popular phrase, "the iron of rail will greet ocean sail."

The fishing party rowed out along the shore of Browns Point—reservation land, not open to claims—but returned along the south side of the bay. Carr's attention focused on a dip where the bluff lowered to a draw and a fan of dirt spread at tidewater. A shallow bar at the eastern side of the flat screened a brackish pond fed by a small stream. "Eureka, Eureka," cried Carr, standing in the boat. "I have found it."

The spot, today's Old Town, was known to the Indians as Shubahlup, "the sheltered place," because canoes could be left in the pond. There Job built a log cabin (part of which still stands, though it has been moved to Point Defiance) and settled down to wait for the railroad and rising property values. They were slow in coming.

Carr's two sons, Anthony (Tony) and Howard, joined him when the Civil War was over, and later his daughter, Marietta, brought charm and a dulcimer, but Shubahlup, which Carr called Eureka, did not boom. A Quaker by faith, a paper-hanger and grindstone cleaner by trade, Job Carr was no promoter.

On April 1, 1868, a professional developer showed up. Matthew Morton McCarver had been booming townsites for more than half of his 61 years. He had left his imprint on Burlington, Iowa; Linnton and Oregon City, Oregon; Sacramento, California; and Bannock, Idaho, but he still dreamed of founding the great city of the West. With the promise of backing from two Portland bankers, he saddled up his big gray and rode north to Puget Sound to scout out the area the Northern Pacific

Job Carr started the resettlement of Commencement Bay when he built a log cabin near the sheltered lagoon the Indians called Shubahlup. The photograph is almost certainly the work of his son, Anthony, (a Civil War photographer) who, for several years, had the only camera in Tacoma. Courtesy, Rick and Francie Carr

would be most likely to choose as terminus. He got no farther than Commencement Bay.

The map he had picked up in Olympia showed much unclaimed land. The people at the Indian agency told him that people and cattle crossed the Cascades through Naches Pass, which lay almost due east of the bay. Why not a railroad? And Job Carr was willing to sell the low land at Shubahlup—all except five acres around his cabin—to a man so versed in the arts of attracting industry, commerce, and population. McCarver obtained the 163-3/4-acre townsite for $600 cash and land in Oregon that Carr eventually sold for $724. Thus Carr's basic claim brought him $8 an acre.

The boomer's art was uncomplicated. McCarver had the site surveyed by a civil engineer and divided into rectangles. He launched a letters-to-editors campaign that took on momentum after the arrival of his family; for, while McCarver's handwriting was as shaky as his spelling and detracted from the credibility of his claims, words flowed with beauty and precision from the pen of his son-in-law and secretary, C.P. Ferry. Their compositions described turnips of grandeur grown in local gardens, schools of fish so abundant they could be caught bare-handed, and giant clams awaiting easy harvest. They spoke of probable iron in the boglands and coal in the hills. The climate sounded semitropical, the scenery was Switzerland at sea level.

McCarver planned to name the site of all this glory Commencement City but before he got around to filing a plat he was visited by Philip Ritz, a capitalist of prestige from eastern Washington. Ritz was touring western Washington in connection with a proposed Portland-to-Puget Sound shortline railroad. During a day with McCarver, Ritz declined to buy a fourth interest in Commencement City, but he did persuade his host to change the proposed name.

Ritz had just read The Canoe and the Saddle, an account by Theodore Winthrop of a canoe trip on the Sound and a horseback ride through Naches Pass. Winthrop's journey was made in 1853, the book written in 1859, but it was not published until the author distinguished himself by becoming the first Union officer killed in the Civil War. What most impressed Ritz was Winthrop's enthusiasm for the beauty of Mount Rainier and the melodiousness of its Indian name, Tacoma—the only word in the native language he thought worthy of pronouncing.

A month after Ritz's visit, McCarver discussed the question of the name with his Portland backers, then had his son-in-law cross out "Commencement City" on the surveyor's plat and write in "Tacoma." When he got around to taking the plat to the county auditor a few weeks later, McCarver discovered that Job Carr's son, Tony, had already platted his claim under that name. So McCarver changed the formal name on his plat to "Tacoma City."

While waiting for a railroad to materialize, McCarver's Tacoma secured the last major sawmill to be built on Puget Sound for a decade. It took more luck than planning.

Charles Hanson was a young Dane who in the 1850s parlayed ownership of a small freighting vessel into control of the shingle trade in the San Francisco area. The profits from selling other people's shingles he invested in sawmills in Northern California. This venture was so successful that he became known as the Redwood King. He then developed an interest in Douglas fir. A venture in Oregon on the Umpqua having proved more a learning experience than a profit maker, he decided in 1868 to build a big new plant on Puget Sound.

Hanson sent Samuel Hadlock, a millwright, north to pick a site. Hadlock found what he considered a perfect location at Port Orchard, but it turned out to be on school trust land and unavailable. Hanson sent him back accompanied by Hanson's partner, John W. Ackerson, to try again. When they reached Steilacoom, a free-lance logger named Bill Lane suggested they look at the sheltered pond that gave Shubahlup its name. "The best mill site I ever saw," was Hadlock's report on this one.

For $700 Hanson bought 68 acres of Tacoma waterfront from McCarver, Tony Carr, and Territorial Governor Marshall Moore. Work started at once on clearing and grading, which provided the town's first payroll. Tony Carr, a photographer by trade, picked up extra money by working with pick, shovel, and axe on his former land. Fortunately he did not neglect to bring his camera and to record on glass plates the beginning of industry in the hamlet.

Tacoma grew as the mill took shape. Mr. and Mrs. H.N. Steele built a 24-room hotel, which Mrs. Steele ran efficiently while her husband yarned about gold strikes between his fruitless prospecting ventures. John T. Nash started a stage line to Olympia (round trip eight dollars) and bored the folks at the capital with his predictions that within a year Tacoma would have a population of 4,000. (It took 13 years.)

The United States recognized Tacoma with a post office of its own. It was located in Job Carr's cabin. Tony Carr carried the mail by foot, horse, or canoe to and from Steilacoom until the wharf at the mill site was ready to accept steamers.

Pierce County declared Tacoma an election precinct in May of 1869. In their first vote the citizens went Democratic, voting 16 to 13 in favor of Governor Moore for delegate to Congress. The Territory disagreed, however, the majority voting for Selucius Garfielde, who found life in the nation's capital so enjoyable

that when defeated for re-election he stayed on to run a gaming house and brothel.

In September of 1869 the legislature authorized and the county superintendent declared the existence of a Tacoma school district—Pierce County No. 11. J.P. Stewart, a bookkeeper who had come from San Francisco with a consignment of merchandise for the mill store, was hired as teacher. In a dimly-lit, one-room log cabin erected with volunteer labor at the corner of today's Twenty-eighth and Starr streets, the 13 pupils, offspring of only three families, worked their way toward literacy with the aid of *Town's and Wilson's Readers, Clark's Grammar, Town's Spelling, Ray's and Davies' Arithmetics,* and *Cornell's Geography.*

Down by the pond, the 600 pilings that the Lane brothers towed around Point Defiance from Steilacoom by rowboat were tipped into place to support the wharf. While the cookhouse was being erected and the main mill building framed, free-lance loggers delivered some 500,000 board feet of logs to the millpond. The machinery was brought up from San Francisco. Cutting began in November 1869 at a rate of 40,000 board feet a day. The bark *Samoset,* with Captain Martin, docked December 1 and left a week later heavy with a half-million board feet of fresh, steam-cut Douglas fir.

Production increased steadily. First known as Hanson, Ackerson & Company, then as Charles Hanson & Company, and after 1884 as the Tacoma Mill Company, the plant was enlarged in 1874 and again in 1884. It was one of the 10 largest sawmills on the Sound, and the largest in Tacoma, for 20 years.

Opinion varied as to its efficiency. A reporter for the Seattle *Intelligencer* considered it "the best worked" on the Sound. A Pope & Talbot official thought the location so far south a mistake. ("If you should blindfold a man and put him in a boat, wherever he landed would be as well located.") The cost of construction, high even by the standards on Puget Sound where capital investment per mill was the greatest in the nation, rendered the plant "an

Morton Matthew McCarver appears here in this 1870s portrait. A professional town boomer, McCarver led the campaign to interest the Northern Pacific Railroad officials in the town of Commencement Bay. From Hunt, History of Tacoma, *volume I*

The Lane Brothers of Steilacoom first towed in the pilings to support the wharf and mill and then assembled a half-million board feet of fir and cedar for the Hanson mill. The log pond, now filled, is the site of Waterfront Park in Old Tacoma. This photo is attributed to Anthony Carr. Courtesy, Oregon Historical Society

Elephant" in the judgment of an R.G. Dun credit reporter.

Although Hanson-Ackerson was by far the largest enterprise in town it did not own Tacoma as Pope & Talbot owned all of Port Ludlow and Port Gamble, or as William Renton owned Port Blakely. Tacoma never became a town under control of its largest company. But, like all the large mills on the Sound, Hanson-Ackerson was built with capital from outside the Territory. The controlling economic decisions were made in board rooms far from the scene of operations.

After long struggle, the Northern Pacific (NP) in 1870 raised enough money to start laying track westward from a point near Duluth, Minnesota, and northward from the Columbia River toward Puget Sound. The far western section began near the juncture of the Columbia River with its tributary, the Kalama, but where on Puget Sound it would terminate would be decided later in New York.

The economy proved the decisive factor in the selection of a terminus. When work started, times were good, money easy, and cost of little consideration. By 1872 the post-Civil War expansion had all but run its course. The great bond salesman, Jay Cooke, was having trouble moving Northern Pacific paper. Money was pouring out faster than it could be raised. Proceeds from what bonds were sold had to be used to pay interest on bonds previously issued.

With the crisis deepening, NP officials began to share the settlers' dream of sudden wealth through choice of the terminus. If sufficient land could be blocked up near the site chosen, perhaps enough money could be made through selling town lots to allow construction of the railroad to be completed. Eight members of the board of directors were sent to Puget Sound in October to determine the point on the Sound nearest to the Columbia that offered a good harbor, good shore facilities for wharves, and plenty of cheap land that could be acquired for resale.

The ancient side-wheel steamer *Wilson G. Hunt* was chartered to carry the delegation to

Additional purchases to the south in an area of natural parks and beautiful lakes could swell the terminus site to 10,000 acres. Seattle interests offered about 2,500 acres and 450 lots within the city limits, another 6,500 acres near the town, and a cash bonus of $60,000. Only 4,500 feet fronted on navigable water. "As now advised shall unhesitatingly decide in favor of Tacoma."

Tacomans knew the wire had been sent but did not know what it said. Suspense was intense. Job Carr's hamlet had become enough of a community to appear on the map of western Washington published in 1871 by Hazard Stevens. "Tacoma" was listed in the *Pudget Sound Business Directory of 1872* under the heading of "Milling Towns":

A place of about one hundred inhabitants. It is situated on Commencement Bay and is distant from Olympia about thirty-four miles. It was established in 1870. It contains one mill owned by Hanson, Ackerson & Co., one public school, a public hall, a hotel and a store. The country surrounding it is well wooded, but further in the interior it becomes open prairie.
Bowers J., saloon
Byrd W.S., postmaster
Carr, A.P., photographer
Carr, J., painter
Clendenin & Miller, general merchandise
Fuller J.M., general merchandise
Gale J., blacksmith
Hanson, Ackerson & Co., lumber manufacturers,
  shippers, dealers in general merchandise
Lansdale R.A., physician and surgeon
Steel H.N., hotel keeper
Stewart A.W., wagon maker

the sites under consideration. Olympia was crossed off because "the receding tide left its port a wide expanse of mud and mussel shells for half of every twenty-four hours." They felt that Steilacoom stood on a strait rather than a good harbor. The choice narrowed to Mukilteo, Seattle, and Tacoma.

When the visitors returned to the East in December they appointed two well-informed Oregon businessmen, Judge R.D. Rice and Captain J.C. Ainsworth, to negotiate with local interests for property and to make a final recommendation. Rice and Ainsworth quickly dropped Mukileto from consideration because it would require more track mileage to reach. So it was between Tacoma and Seattle with both time and money running out.

On June 30, 1873, the two commissioners wired New York in code, outlining the situation. At Tacoma, promoter Matthew McCarver had blocked up 1,100 acres by purchase and had options on 1,600 more. A terminal site of 2,700 acres with an unbroken two-mile stretch of waterfront was available.

The town's first child, a girl, had been born to Mr. and Mrs. William Baker, who called her Lena Tacoma. Two Methodist ministers, George F. Greer and I.D. Dryer, were the first Protestant preachers to visit the community. On October 26, 1872, Father J.Z.B. Brodel of the Immaculate Conception Mission in Steilacoom noted "saying Mass for the first time in the new borough of Tacoma in the

General John M. Sprague came to Tacoma in 1870 as general superintendent of the Northern Pacific Railroad. He later became the first mayor of the combined towns of New Tacoma and Old Tacoma. (TPL)

home of Mrs. Atkinson at which she alone was present, and that only at the end." All denominations present in 1873—Catholic, Methodist, Presbyterian, Episcopal, and Baptist—held services in the schoolhouse. Everybody prayed for the terminus.

On July 14 Tony Carr, who was working in Steilacoom as telegraph operator, galloped into Tacoma to deliver a wire for McCarver:

We have located the terminus on Commencement Bay.

R.D. Rice
John C. Ainsworth
Commissioners.

The triumph was not total. Tacomans had expected that the rails would stop at the foot of Carr and McCarver streets. Instead, the Northern Pacific chose to create a New Tacoma on property centering on the former Judson and Delin claims three miles toward the head of the bay. The tracks would slant to the water between today's Fifteenth and Seventeenth streets, circle below the Downtown bluff and terminate on a dock below Stadium Way.

There was instant rivalry between Tacoma City and New Tacoma. When the Kalama

Spur was completed, a third community, known as On the Wharf was formed, with aspirations and jealousies of its own. For a time, however, Old Tacoma was able to exploit its advantage as an existing community.

Within a week of the selection of the terminus, the Right Reverend Benjamin Wistar Morris, Bishop of the Protestant Episcopal Missionary Jurisdiction of Oregon and Washington, came up from Portland to preach at the schoolhouse and select a church site. He brought with him Charles Bonnell, a lean, full-bearded Philadelphian, to build the church and serve as its minister.

The Reverend Mr. Bonnell was blessed with a beneficent brother-in-law who forwarded him $500 for church purposes. George Atkinson, the manager of the Hanson-Ackerson mill, was Episcopalian; he furnished the lumber. The minister drew the plans. Townsfolk of assorted faiths made ecumenical contributions of sweat equity. On Sunday, August 10, 1873, only 10 days after work started, the first service was held in St. Peter's on Starr Street. (Fourteen months later a 965-pound bell, purchased with funds raised by

St. Peter's, built in 1874, used an adjoining high stump as its bell tower, which gave Tacoma the opportunity of boasting about "the oldest bell tower in America." This photo was taken by Isaac Grundy Davidson. Courtesy, Oregon Historical Society

children of St. Peter's church of Philadelphia and brought around the Horn in a sailing vessel, was mounted on a 48-foot stump alongside the frame building. Bell and chapel remain in service.) The Reverend George H. Atkinson, a Congregationalist, also arrived from Portland in August 1873, accompanied by a large tent in which he held services until a building known as the Reading Room was completed.

There were other amenities. McCarver and two associates put in a public wharf at the foot of McCarver Street, where the Old Town dock now stands. They also put in a water flume. Up on the hill at the edge of town, on a site later occupied by the Fannie Paddock Memorial Hospital, John W. Pennell, who had pioneered brothel-keeping in Seattle, opened an establishment the pioneers referred to as "the crazy house."

On August 9 young Thomas W. Prosch pulled the first edition of Tacoma's first newspaper off the little press he had brought from Olympia. The *Pacific Tribune*, a four-page, five-column daily and its companion eight-page weekly, ran ads for a half-dozen general stores,

As ivy crept up the bell tower, St. Peter's Church crept deeper into the hearts of Tacomans. The church remains a favorite location for marriage ceremonies. Courtesy, Lane Morgan

and for a tailor, a butcher, a bank, a fish peddler, a cobbler, a physician, a blacksmith, an express agent, and a wood lot. Attorney Hazard Stevens announced himself ready to supply abstracts of title, while J.B. Wren would rent rowboats. Saloons still outnumbered

This photo, attributed to Anthony Carr, shows Old Tacoma in 1871. Forests still pressed in on the rough-hewn village. (TPL)

churches.

Meanwhile, in what the Northern Pacific officially designated as New Tacoma, work crews felled trees, burned slash, and pushed debris over the edge of the bluff, burying in the process a petroglyph etched eons earlier by some precursor of the Puyallups.

Like fireweed after a burn, early entrepreneurs appeared. In September Doc O'Brien, who ran a hotel in Kalama, opened a restaurant in a frame-and-canvas shed, 10-by-30 feet, that he assembled in a swale of skunk cabbage near the northeast corner of today's Seventh and Pacific. Before retreating to the relative civilization of Kalama, O'Brien hired as his entire staff Frank Alling, who had come up from San Francisco on the bark *Dashing Wave.*

Alling later recalled charging his first two customers, Superintendent Wallace of the mill and Mrs. Peter Smith of Lake View, 75 cents each for their meals, a steep price for the time. "Had we given two for ten cents and thrown in a Pacific Avenue lot for a bonus, we would still have had to bank the kitchen fires for want of patronage." He was spared lingering failure when, a month after the restaurant opened, someone stole a leg of mutton hung outside the kitchen door. "That being our last pound of meat and having no coin to buy more, we were obliged to close the doors of the first restaurant New Tacoma ever saw."

Alling next worked as manager of New Tacoma's first hotel, the California House, an eight-room affair to which each guest had to bring his own blankets. When he wished to retire the guest would approach the dry goods box that served as reception desk, give Alling a dime, and receive a tallow candle to light him to bed. Spartan though the California might be, it managed a spread for New Tacoma's first Thanksgiving. The management paid $10 for "two poor small turkeys" but filled out the menu with baked salmon, dried apple sauce, and "plenty of clams."

Gambling was the town's favorite entertainment. The Tacoma Land Company offered a town lot to the first baby born in the community. Two unrelated families claimed the prize, one for a boy, the other for a girl. The company deeded the lot to the daughter of Mr. and Mrs. Anthony Anderson, who lived in a shack down Pacific Avenue from where the Northern Pacific Headquarters Building was later built. For those debarred by sex, age, or lack of spouse from competing in the baby sweepstakes, Alling ran a lottery that paid off in allegedly rare Japanese coins.

Accounts vary as to the first marriage. One version has it that a couple was proclaimed to be in a state of holy wedlock by a town character known as One Armed Chapman, whose claim to being a justice of the peace proved fraudulent. Herbert Hunt in his *History of Tacoma* credits the Reverend Mr. Judy, a Methodist, with performing the first marriage by reuniting a divorced couple named Barr in a ceremony at Twelfth and Pacific.

The first house built in New Tacoma after its designation as terminus was put up where the old Elks Club was later built by a Mr. Angell, the foreman of the site clearing crew. The first meat market, erected by a Puyallup farmer named Vining, in a stretch of wet clay on the water side of Pacific Avenue near Tenth, began dispensing pork, beef, and mutton in November 1873. That same month John Dougherty opened a shoe store. Some say he ran it from the front room of his 10-by-12 foot house; others claim the store was in a three-foot-wide space between two buildings on Pacific Avenue.

The terminus was not booming; indeed it was barely growing. An informal census in November indicated 125 whites in the new town, about 10 percent of them female. There were also about 250 Chinese, most of them laid off railroad workers. (Other estimates set the Oriental presence at an improbable 1,000.)

The Panic of 1873 was the primary cause of slow growth, but its effect was compounded by uncertainty about the design of the town. James Tilton, who had come to Washington Territory as surveyor general 20 years earlier, was at this time in private practice as a civil engineer. Hired to draw up a plan for the town, Tilton was lining out the conventional 19th century grid system, when he found himself replaced by an unconventional genius.

Frederick Law Olmsted was the closest thing America had to a professional city planner. He had designed, among other things, Central Park in New York, the Brooklyn Parkway, and Riverside, Illinois, the first planned commuter suburb. His selection to plan Tacoma was probably dictated by C.B. Wright, a former president of the Northern Pacific and chairman of the three-member board assigned to direct the development of the terminus city and the sale of its real estate. When he was a member of the terminus selection committee, Wright had looked at the southern shore of Commencement Bay and decided "Nature has done everything except build a city." Now he decided that Olmsted should design what Nature had neglected. He may have been influenced less by Olmsted's genius than by his fame. A plan by Olmsted, Wright believed, would attract national attention.

Alas, it was not to be. Olmsted's preliminary plan, which he submitted in 10 weeks without having seen the site, was premature by at least half a century. Olmsted's grand design was to emphasize open space, to create a city with breathing space. The principal avenues were all curvilinear, sweeping gracefully along the contours of the hills, with parks crowning the crests and much of the waterfront reserved as parkway for carriages and a promenade for the citizenry.

Grace and a serene ambience were not attractive to frontier speculators. They coveted corner lots at busy intersections, and Olmsted had done his imaginative best to eliminate the four-way corners of the traditional grid pat-

tern. Six weeks after receiving the Olmsted plan, the Northern Pacific board in New York decided it wouldn't do.

William Isaac Smith, a specialist in designing lighthouses, happened to be on the Sound. He was hired by Theodore Hosmer, the resident manager of the Tacoma Land Company, to come up with something ordinary, and quickly. Smith lined out a variation on the standard grid pattern that made few concessions to the slanted topography but offered no offense to buyers seeking the conventional.

The Kalama Spur—the line between the Columbia River and Puget Sound—was completed in December 1873, two days before the deadline set in the Northern Pacific charter from Congress. Few such projects were finished on schedule, and forfeiture because of tardiness was rare. But the odds against timeliness on this section were astronomical.

The Northern Pacific had gone into bankruptcy late in 1873 and was being reorganized. Work on the main line had halted at Bismarck, North Dakota. J.B. Montgomery, contractor for the final stage of the Kalama Spur, mortgaged his house to meet his own payroll. When mortgage money ran out and workers barricaded the right-of-way at Clover Creek and threatened to take hostages if they were not paid, the Hanson-Ackerson Mill agreed to honor NP pay warrants at the company store. Work went on.

Early in November the first construction train rolled into Tacoma. The locomotive, a small, saddle-tank engine, was in the middle, pushing a kitchen car and hauling a flatcar loaded with two-foot bolts of fir for the firebox and others loaded with equipment. At the foot of the bluff below Eleventh Street, the track gave way and the train rolled over. The conductor, Nickolas Gabriel Lawson, a 24-year-old Swede who looked as if he had been assembled out of cannon balls, managed to pull the cook to safety through the roof of the damaged car.

Lawson conducted the train that brought the first passengers to town a few days after the accident. They were William and Alice Blackwell, who opened a hotel on the NP wharf

The Northern Pacific wharf below today's Stadium Way served as a third world between Old Tacoma and New Tacoma. Its city hall was the Blackwell Hotel, the dark building on the inboard side of the wharf. The Blackwell operated from December 1873 until 1884, when the Tacoma Hotel opened on the bluff. (TPL)

below today's Stadium Way; they became beloved citizens. Lawson was again present on December 15 when, under a clear cold sky in late afternoon, the ceremonial last spike was tapped by such dignitaries as could be found nearby, then settled into place by a mighty blow from John Bolander, who had been head spiker during the three years of track laying.

Tom Prosch's *Pacific Tribune* emitted a celebratory panegyric:

Before the curtain of night was drawn over this day, the long desired connection by rail of the waters of Puget Sound with the Columbia River was completed. The 15th day of December, 1873, will be memorable as marking an important event in the history of our territory and in that of the western terminus of the Northern Pacific railroad. Today, for the first time, the iron horse stood in the presence of the Mediterranean of the Pacific and saluted its placid face with a far-reaching whistle. Make a note of it, readers; for from this day you may date the rise of the second (perhaps the first) city of the Pacific Coast—Tacoma.

The touch of restraint shown by Prosch in conceding leadership to San Francisco may be attributed to his realization that completion of the Kalama Spur meant the end of the construction payroll. Already newcomers were drifting away. On New Year's Day 1874 Frank Alling of the California House estimated New Tacoma's population at 48 whites and 175 Chinese.

For several years the townspeople were absorbed with the competition between the hamlets of New Tacoma, Tacoma City, and On the Wharf, and not with the challenge Commencement Bay might offer to the Golden Gate. New Tacoma and Tacoma City remained separate entities. Though technically part of New Tacoma, the people of the railroad wharf seldom visited the community on the hill. The unpaved, unlit roadway became a creek-bed during the rainy season. There was no road from the New Tacoma wharf to Old Tacoma. When one was proposed, the Northern Pacific managed to block

it. The best way to get between the towns was in J.B. Wren's rowboat which made the trip four times a day (two bits each way), until replaced by a 15-foot, one-lung steam launch.

The towns fought bitterly for prestige and for federal and territorial offices. On July 6, 1874, W.H. Fife, who ran a store at Ninth and Pacific in New Tacoma was surprised to learn that President Ulysses S. Grant had appointed him postmaster for New Tacoma. He had not sought the position. Running a fourth class post office was neither great honor nor a gold mine, but it would bring people to the store and it meant the closing of the station in Old Tacoma. Fife accepted the job and held it for eight years. The first package of mail received in New Tacoma contained only five letters. Fife's son Billy delivered them as a courtesy. (Free delivery of mail in Tacoma was not officially begun for another 13 years.) Receipts for the first three months totalled $21.03. Old Tacoma, outraged at the loss of its post office, complained so much to Congress that its station was reopened and for a time did more business than New Tacoma's. The townspeople of Steilacoom, which handled more mail than both Tacomas together, found the rivalry funny.

Still, the towns grew. A bit. Lots along the streets platted by Surveyor William Smith in the third try at a town plan went on sale in April 1874. Charles B. Wright, president of the Tacoma Land Company, used the occasion to order construction of the town's first masonry building at Ninth and Pacific. By year's end there were 21 buildings along Pacific.

Industry developed. New Tacoma got a small sawmill, Smith & Hatch, which specialized in construction timbers. David Lister, who had lost a factory in the great Peshtigo, Wisconsin, forest fire, built an iron foundry at Seventeenth and Pacific. The Northern Pacific in 1874 ran a branch line across the tide flats, and four years later extended into the hills to reach the Wilkeson coal fields. The NP also installed a turning lathe in its repair shop and described it as "the largest on the coast."

Tom Prosch's *Pacific Tribune* folded and its 40-year-old press was shipped south to San Francisco, but two new papers appeared. Francis Cook built a house for his family at the southwest corner of Eleventh and C (later Broadway), where the Fisher Building later stood, and at Eighth and Broadway he installed a press and type cases in a gaunt frame building supported by stilts. He called his paper *The Herald.* A few months later Mr. and Mrs. M.V. Money, who had been publishing the *Kalama Beacon,* moved their equipment to the NP wharf and began printing the *North Pacific Times.* Mrs. Money sometimes set type with a live parrot perched on her head. Cook was not amused. He looked on the *Times* as a conspiracy on the part of "the interests," and when the *Times* failed in 1878 he saluted its demise with a memorable obituary:

The management of the Oregon Steam Navigation Company, the Northern Pacific Railroad, and Tacoma Land companies—with great promise and bright expectations—infused the first filthy breath of life into the disreputable sheet which has succumbed to its own rottenness.

Culture was honored. A literary society was organized in 1875 and at its first meeting

debated the topic "Resolved: That Chinese Immigration has been an injury to the United States."

The affirmative won. At a reorganization meeting three years later the topic was "Resolved: Women should be granted the vote." Again the affirmative won.

Technology was appreciated. A phonograph, called the "crown jewel of modern invention," was played in 1878, and could be heard for several feet. Particularly admired was the recording of hens cackling. In April 1875 a telephone line was run between the Lister Foundry and the telegraph office on the NP dock. In May the telegraph operators in Tacoma and Olympia tried fastening the phones to their wires. Not only could voices be heard between the cities but also when an Olympian serenaded Tacoma with a clarinet, a Tacoman replied on his accordian.

In June the county assessor estimated the

Above
A clapboard building on the water side of Broadway, halfway between South Seventh and Ninth, housed The Herald, *the first newspaper published in Tacoma. This photograph is from 1882. From Hunt,* History of Tacoma, *volume I*

Left
The first office building in Tacoma stood on stilts to keep it out of the skunk cabbage that sprang up after downtown Tacoma was logged. The building housed the Tacoma Land Company manager who, in the early years, did not do much business. The sketch was made from memory by C.P. Ferry, who was married to McCarver's stepdaughter. From Hunt, History of Tacoma, *volume I*

Far left
Henry Villard, president of the Northern Pacific when the mainline was completed, favored Portland for development. Tacoma regarded him as an enemy and rejoiced when he lost control of the railroad. (TPL)

These illustrations from Harper's
Weekly show the Tacoma waterfront in about 1882. The trestle
leading to the coal bunker in the
engraving at near right identifies the
area as the beach below the present
site of Stadium High. The
engraving at far right shows a
salmon fisherman's beach camp.
Courtesy, Sue Olsen

These illustrations from Harper's
Weekly show the Tacoma waterfront in about 1882. The trestle
leading to the coal bunker in the
engraving at near right identifies the
area as the beach below the present
site of Stadium High. The
engraving at far right shows a
salmon fisherman's beach camp.
Courtesy, Sue Olsen

population of Pierce County communities:
New Tacoma was credited with 614 inhabi-
tants, Steilacoom with 500, and Tacoma
City 350.

Not only did Tacoma spread its industrial
roots in 1878, but the Northern Pacific also
completed reorganization and refinancing.
Construction resumed on the main line. But as
the tracks moved westward, narrowing the gap
in the transcontinental, a new threat appeared
to challenge Tacoma's status as terminal.

Railroad financier Henry Villard, in a
maneuver remembered on Wall Street as "the
blind pool," managed to borrow enough mil-
lions from investors willing to trust him without knowing his intention to buy controlling
interest in the Northern Pacific. What made
Villard's success a threat to Tacoma was that
he already had heavy investments in Portland
real estate and in Northwest transportation
facilities, including a railroad line on the south
side of the Columbia River which he leased to
the NP. Tacomans feared that Villard's self-
interest would cause him to favor the Columbia River over Puget Sound for development.
Tacoma might remain terminus in name while
Portland served that function in fact.

Tacoma's fears deepened when Villard
formed the Oregon Development Company to
direct industrial expansion in the Northwest.
He invested in waterfront property in Seattle
and in the coal fields east of Seattle. Citing
high costs, Villard refused to say when, if ever,
the Northern Pacific would exercise its charter
to build tracks from Tacoma through the
Cascades—a line that would permit traffic to

bypass Portland.

The townsfolk were not mollified in 1881
when the Tacoma Land Company, which was
controlled by the Northern Pacific, broke
ground on the bluff between Ninth and Tenth
streets for The Tacoma, which when completed was the largest hotel north of San
Francisco.

Only three months after work started on
the hotel, Tacoma was struck by a smallpox
epidemic. Its ravages were made worse by a
fruitless attempt to conceal its existence. For
five weeks the town was quarantined. The
steamer Alida was anchored in the bay to serve
as a pest house. A fumigation chamber was set
up on the NP wharf through which passengers
passed to get between steamer and train. All
trains passed through town with windows
closed. Puyallup and Steilacoom stationed
armed men on the roads to prevent anyone
from Tacoma coming to visit. Schools and
stores were closed, even churches suspended
services. The dead, estimated at "from less
than fifteen to more than fifty," were quietly
buried at night. In six weeks the epidemic ran
its course.

Both Tacomas celebrated the end of their
isolation with an almost hysterical welcome for
the ship Dakota, which called to pick up the
first shipment of wheat to be loaded on Puget
Sound for Great Britain. In Portland, which
had monopolized the overseas shipment of
grains, the Oregonian editorialized sniffily that
in five years there might be a second shipload
of sacks ready for export.

As the Northern Pacific approached com-

pletion, growth in the towns speeded. Twenty months after the *Dakota's* visit, a flour mill with a capacity of 100 barrels a day was under construction at the head of the bay, the coal bunkers were being built below Old Woman's Gulch, and, in Old Town, Tacoma's first cannery was buying salmon at four cents each. Tacoma's 11 hotels registered 20,562 guests that year. The two towns had 18 saloons, 15 churches, 12 restaurants, 6 laundries (all Chinese), 5 jewelers, 4 drug stores, 4 bakeries, 4 furniture stores, 4 shoe shops, 4 meat markets, 2 fish markets, 2 printing houses, and one undertaker. There were 19 doctors, 30 lawyers, and an abundance of rooming houses

whose occupants advertised themselves as seamstresses. Tacoma was coming of age.

The last spike was driven on the main line of the Northern Pacific on September 3, 1883, in western Montana. A telegraph key fastened to the spike signaled the final blow of the hammer to St. Paul, Duluth, Portland, and Tacoma. Celebratory cannon boomed and church bells pealed in towns along the transcontinental.

Tacoma joined the cross-country party but joy was restrained. Freight and passenger cars headed Tacoma's way would have to be ferried down the Columbia from Portland to Kalama. Villard held the reins. Portland still reigned.

The Tacoma, a hotel designed by Stanford White, was completed in 1884. Standing on the bluff between Ninth and Tenth streets, the hotel, more than any other structure, symbolized the aspirations of the village to become a metropolis. The stairway on the left leads down to a boathouse at the foot of Eleventh. The water in the foreground is the old mouth of the Puyallup River before it was deepened to become the City Waterway. Isaac Grundy Davidson took this photograph in 1884. Courtesy, Oregon Historical Society

V

A DELIRIOUS DECADE

The

Promise

of Enterprise

Seven ships wait to take on lumber at the Tacoma Mill in this 1888 photo by E.A. Lynn. Tacoma's position on both rail lines and shipping lanes stimulated the city's growth. Courtesy, Dennis Andersen

No month in Tacoma's history presented the townsfolk with so much encouraging news as did January 1884. It was the month when New Tacoma and Old Tacoma united under a single government; when Henry Villard, having overextended himself financially in uniting the Mississippi and Great Lakes with Puget Sound, lost control of his transcontinental railroad; and it was the month when Philadelphia investors allied with Charles B. Wright returned to power on the Northern Pacific board and reactivated plans to lay track directly east from Tacoma through Stampede Pass to Eastern Washington, thus bypassing Portland.

The union of the rival villages of Old Tacoma and New Tacoma was made possible by legislation passed by the territorial legislature in 1883. Even with the legislature's permission, it took a lot of swallowed prejudice for the rivals to accept a common destiny. But in December a committee of leading citizens recommended amalgamation, the townsfolk of each community voted their approval, and an interim body of city officials was elected, with General John Sprague—a handsome, austere Civil War hero and retired superintendent of the Northern Pacific—becoming mayor for a shakedown term of six months.

On January 3, 1884, the last meeting of the old council of Old Tacoma was held preparatory to the swearing in of the new officials on January 7. Finding $250 still left in the town coffers, the lame ducks decided to charter a steamer, go to Seattle for a last supper, and take in a show at Smith's Private Variety Theater. Even the fact that the theater's advertisements defined the program as "unobjectionable to the most fastidious" failed to redeem the junket in the eyes of the citizenry. On second thought the city fathers invested the money in a new fire hose.

Three months later some over-vigorous activity in a Pacific Avenue brothel led to the overturning of a kerosene lamp. The hose proved useless against the resulting fire because of low water pressure. The fire cleaned out much of the block bounded by Pacific Avenue and Railroad Avenue (now Commerce Street) from Eighth to Ninth streets. Another fire in midsummer finished the remaining false-front frame structures that gave upper Pacific Avenue the nickname of Whiskey Row—a traveler's last chance to lift a glass or lay a bet before catching the boat to Seattle. Rebuilding was with brick, stone, and iron—Tacoma's first renaissance.

The combined new and old Tacomas, now called simply Tacoma, claimed a population of

4,000. That total reflected encouraging growth from 1880 when the official census had located 680 persons in New Tacoma, 567 in Old Tacoma, and 5 described only as "living in a gulch."

The boom that had been predicted in 1873 when Tacoma was named terminus was at last underway, with the Northern Pacific back in the hands of the Philadelphia entrepreneurs. These men had chosen the site and personally owned most of the 49 percent of Tacoma Land Company stock not held by the railroad.

The industrial, the commercial, and the aboriginal were cheek by jowl in the developing town. Electric lights were installed in the Hanson mill in Old Town, warehouses and granaries stretched along the docks below the downtown bluff, and shipways cradled schooners and steam vessels in the new yards. Business blocks of brick and limestone studded Pacific Avenue, and a hospital was opened on the site of Tacoma's first bordello. Yet there was not a paved street in town; indeed, few streets were clear of stumps.

Randolph Radebaugh, who published the Tacoma *Ledger,* told of watching from the porch of his house as a bear devoured a fawn bogged down on the muddy shore of Wapato Lake. "Captain" Dave Wallace, who ran a roadhouse across from the Tacoma cemetery in what has become South Tacoma, reported seeing a bear walking south toward Olympia on its hind feet, a yearling lamb cradled in its forepaws. David Lister, Jr., who became manager of his father's iron foundry at Seventeenth and Pacific Avenue, kept a pack of nondescript dogs that he described as "deer hounds" and used to flush game from among the cemetery tombstones. Wolves were deplorably successful in their competition with shepherds for lambs from the flocks that roamed the grasslands south of town.

The wilderness might still be evident, but what the citizenry saw were the manifestations of metropolis. The Tacoma Hotel was the focal point of civic pride. Let a visitor question the likelihood of the city's ascendancy and he was likely to be lectured on the grandeur of the hostelry under construction, at a cost of more than a quarter million dollars, on the edge of the downtown bluff. The rising young architect Stanford White had designed it in 1881 (without visiting Tacoma) on commission from the Northern Pacific and the

Facing page and above
Doug McDonnell, an authority on
early Tacoma, noticed that two
photographs in the Washington
State Historical Society collection
could be combined to form a
panorama of New Tacoma in
1883, just before it merged with
Old Tacoma. The Tacoma Hotel is
under construction on the bluff at
the extreme right. The Central
School is on the bluff to the left.
The large white building in the
central foreground is the Northern
Pacific shop. In the left foreground
is a small sawmill. (WSHS)

Left
After a major fire in 1885,
Tacoma bought new equipment for
the fire department including a
steam pumper drawn by a team of
three. This 1887 photo by Asahel
Curtis shows the men of the "Our
Boys" firehouse in full regalia.
(TPL)

These two pages show the many faces of Pacific Avenue in the late 19th century.

Tacoma grew rapidly with the influx of train-borne Easterners. The photo at upper right shows Pacific Avenue looking north from Twelfth Street in 1884. (From Hunt, History of Tacoma, volume I)

J.T. Pickett, the half-Indian son of Confederate General George Pickett, made the pen-and-ink sketch of the avenue at near right in 1889 as it was rebuilt following the fire. (From The North West, 1889)

Unpaved but cleared of stumps and flanked by board sidewalks (at bottom right), Pacific Avenue is shown from a point near today's exit to Interstate 5. Hannah Maynard, a well-known photographer from Victoria, British Columbia, took this photograph before the completion of the Northern Pacific General Office Building in 1899 and the start of the City Hall tower in 1891. (Courtesy, Provincial Archives of British Columbia)

After the fire the rebuilding was swift and solid. Thomas Rutter took the photograph of Pacific Avenue at left in 1887. (Courtesy, Ray Frederick, Jr.)

When Thomas Rutter photographed Pacific Avenue again in 1890 (below), the street presented an impressive masonry facade. This view looks south from Ninth Street. (Courtesy, Douglas and Kathryn McDonnell)

In 1885 the Reverend Peter Carlson persuaded the Tacoma Land Company to donate two lots between Eleventh and Twelfth streets on Tacoma Avenue for a Lutheran church. A carpenter before he took to the cloth, Carlson helped draw the plans for the church, as well as helping to make the pulpit, pews, altar, and altar railing. Many Swedes arrived in the next three years, and the church sold its two lots for $10,000 and moved to a larger tract at South Eighth and I, near the First Norwegian Evangelical and the German Lutheran Church. Someone suggested that I Street be renamed Lutherstrasse. Arthur French took this photo in 1887. Courtesy, Oregon Historical Society

Indians did much of the hop-picking. The gatherings in the field substituted in a pale way for the potlatch meetings of pre-white times. Here they gamble at the bone game near the foot of Fifteenth Street in Tacoma, the site of a Puyallup village before the coming of the whites. This photo was taken by C.E. and Hattie King in 1888. (TPL)

Tacoma Land Company. The fact that it was Henry Villard who had authorized construction made The Tacoma more cherished by the citizenry; they regarded the hostelry as booty left behind by a besieging army of Oregonians.

The Tacoma was the first of many amenities to be described as "the finest west of the Mississippi and north of San Francisco." Its luxuries included furniture brought by rail from John Wanamaker's in New York, a bathroom at the end of every hall, the largest billiard room in the Far West (84-by-48 feet long, including the bar), a steam-driven potato peeler capable of taking the hides off a ton of spuds each hour, and in the lobby a tame bear named Jack. Jack drank beer from bottles. To reach all this convenience, it was still necessary to wade through streets interminably muddy.

Stanford White's triumph was the pride of Tacoma but other architects had a more lasting impact on the new city, most notably C. August Darmer. He was a Prussian by birth, education, and temperament, who came to America by way of England, Africa, and Australia. After two years in San Francisco he moved up the coast to Portland, then to Tacoma in 1884. Within a year Darmer was chosen to design a building for the newly organized Chamber of Commerce.

The three-story structure at the northwest corner of Twelfth and Pacific featured a cast-iron face topped by a heroic statue of the Goddess of Commerce, modeled (rumor had it) on Darmer's bride, the former Sophie Schultz. The handsome building won Darmer many commissions. During the 68 years he remained in Tacoma, he designed warehouses, breweries, churches, a synagogue, hotels, bars, department stores, schools, mansions for the millionaires, and small, neat cottages for the workingmen.

The possibility of home ownership for blue collar workers became one of Tacoma's most advertised attractions. Lumber was cheap, land was plentiful, and Tacoma soon claimed the highest percentage of residents living in their own houses of any city in the United States.

Growth fed on growth. Not even an act of blatant racial bigotry, one that attracted national opprobrium, stemmed the flow of population and capital toward the booming terminus. By 1885, when Tacoma's population was estimated at 5,000, fewer than half of the residents had been in town three years. In this congregation of strangers, like sought like. Those most unlike were the Chinese. Imported as railroad workers when labor was scarce in the West, many stayed on after the

The grades on portions of the track through the Cascade Mountains demanded the use of engines fore and aft on some trains. The Cascade line allowed goods to be transported in and out of Tacoma without passing through the city's great rival, Portland. From G. Traver, Tacoma and Vicinity

tracks were laid. Rival workingmen, fearful of the ability of the Chinese to survive on minimal pay, regarded their presence as a plot by large employers to hold down the price of labor.

Anti-Chinese agitation, starting in San Francisco, spread along the Pacific Coast and crested in Tacoma in November of 1885, when an organized mob, composed mainly of workingmen but led by city and county officials, drove more than 200 Chinese out of town and put them on trains headed south. Tacoma newspapers claimed the expulsion was conducted without violence and expressed relief at the absence of the Orientals. The national press deplored the mob action, described Tacoma as in the hands of "labor anarchists," and eventually the United States paid China an indemnity for failing to protect its citizens. In the long run the expulsion came to be regretted even by those who had

organized it, but the harm done to Tacoma as a port seeking trade with the Orient was not immediately felt.

As word spread of the new town—and the Northern Pacific publicists made sure it spread—workmen flocked west seeking jobs in the lumber industry, construction, and the railroads, their migration made easier and cheaper by the existence of rails. So many hotels were built to accommodate the newcomers that one booster publication suggested the nickname of "City of Hotels." Even so there were not enough rooms. The Chamber of Commerce sponsored construction of a 250-bed barracks built on the model of an enormous Pullman car. New arrivals could shelter at 25 cents a night while seeking permanent housing.

By 1888, when the Stampede Pass tunnel was completed and the Cascade Division opened to traffic, immigrants were arriving at a rate of a thousand a month. A Northern Pacific brochure, *Tacoma: A City of Cities,* warned newcomers to bring money. "If you are penniless, remember that nothing but hard labor will relieve you, and you had better earn money where you are than come here without it. These busy people have no time to condole with unfortunate people; neither is this or any country especially inviting to penniless people."

Now the town was seeking to lure investors and to alter the image created by the Eastern press at the time of the expulsion of the Chinese: the image of a raw sawmill camp at the mercy of lawless elements. Cultural events would help. In April 1888, Theodore Hosmer of the Tacoma Land Company persuaded 10 community leaders to put up $10,000 each to build a theater which, inevitably, was described as the finest west of the Mississippi and north of San Francisco.

J.M. Wood of Philadelphia was chosen to design the Tacoma Theater, which was erected at the southeastern point of Five Corners, as Tacomans of the day described the intersection of C Street (later Broadway) and St. Helens Avenue with Ninth Street. Thomas Moses, described by an admiring press as "one of the most rapid of American scene painters," decorated the drop curtain with a "Temple of Diana" that he peopled with damsels of heroic proportion.

Not one of the 1,300 seats in the theater was empty on Monday, January 13, 1890, when the curtain rose for J.C. Duff's Comic Opera Company production of "Paola" ("direct from its New York and San Francisco success"), nor at the subsequent offerings of "The Queen's Mate" and "A Trip to Africa." Tacoma's place on the commercial drama circuit was assured. If celebrities got as far as San Francisco, they usually reached Tacoma. Sarah Bernhardt, Mark Twain, John L. Sullivan, William Jennings Bryan, and Susan B. Anthony were among the ornaments on display.

Education, along with culture, was something Westerners feared the folks back East would consider them deprived of. And, indeed, Pierce County's first approaches to schooling had been casual. Melvin Hawk, of Hawks Prairie south of the Nisqually, liked to tell of the time in the 1870s when he rode north to ask Sam McCall for a job on his ranch near Steilacoom. McCall had all the hands he could use. He suggested that Hawk teach school. "I don't believe I know how," the young man replied. "Sure you do," said McCall. "I'm clerk of the school district here and you should see some of our teachers." Hawk maintained discipline in the Steilacoom school for six years.

Standards were raised in 1880 when a college graduate was elected county superintendent of schools. Clara McCarty of Sumner was not only a college woman, she was the first student to receive a degree from the University of Washington. That was in 1876 when, at the age of 16, she earned the degree of Bachelor of Science. Three years later she was certified to teach in Pierce County, and in 1880, at the age of 20, she won election as superintendent of schools. Not only did she become the first woman in Pierce County to hold elective office, she did it three years before women in Washington Territory were first allowed to vote. Miss McCarty did not seek re-election; instead, she married—but she was succeeded as superintendent by another woman, Mrs. Cornelia Greer.

The establishment of Annie Wright Seminary, a private school for girls, was made possible when Episcopal Bishop John Adams Paddock raised building funds and Charles B. Wright gave, in his daughter's name, an endowment of $50,000. The opening of Annie Wright lessened, in the phrase of one Tacoman, "the terror of the thought of being 2,000 miles away from Eastern schools" and incited Tacoma's newly formed labor unions to join women's groups in insisting that tax-supported schools offer quality education to all.

Women took the lead in creating a library. Talk about books during the meeting of a three-woman sewing circle at the home of Mrs. Grace Moore led to a formal gathering at the home of Mrs. Frank Clark in 1886 at which a library association was formed. At first the ladies bought paperbacks, which they bound in hand-lettered cardboard for durability. These were shelved at the Moore residence, where they could be borrowed for 25 cents. By special dispensation, bachelors could for 50 cents indulge themselves in the luxury of using the Moores' living room for a reading room. When traffic became too heavy, the library was transferred to Mr. Moore's law office, where Kate Tiffany, the stenographer, did double duty as librarian.

All this culture may have swayed some Eastern capitalists toward locating plants in Tacoma but the real draw was the existence of raw materials near a point where long-haul railroads connected with saltwater. There was high-grade coal in the hills east of town, lime deposits in the San Juan Islands, and iron, lead, and copper ore in Idaho and Alaska. Rumors set men to probing for oil within the city limits, and a gold strike was expected daily. The bottomlands of the Puyallup Valley yielded hops by the ton, a commodity that sky-

rocketed in price when blight withered most of the European vines. Improvements in the canning process added enormously to the value of the salmon that during the annual spawning run clogged the rivers of the southern Sound. But the most exploitable resource was the forest.

With the completion of the Cascade Division in 1888, the Northern Pacific qualified to purchase nearly two million acres of government land in Washington Territory at 1-1/4 cents an acre. The railroad offered to sell a vast stand of virgin forest in southeastern Pierce County to experienced lumbermen from the Upper Mississippi Valley, where the pine forest was being decimated. The resulting timber rush brought to Tacoma fresh capital, larger and more modern mills, and some talented businessmen.

The most important of the new enterprises was the St. Paul & Tacoma Lumber Company. It was formed by two pairs of immigrants from the Midwest—Chauncey Griggs and Addison Foster of St. Paul, Minnesota; and Henry Hewitt, Jr., and his brother-in-law, Charles

Hebard Jones, of Menasha, Wisconsin. At the urging of the Northern Pacific, the two pairs of entrepreneurs combined to form what became the largest lumber company in existence. St. Paul (as the company was always called) bought 80,000 acres at $5 an acre—the largest purchase of timberland to that time. (It remained a record until 1900 when the Weyerhaeuser Timber Company was formed to buy 900,000 acres from the Northern Pacific.)

C.H. Jones, the most experienced mill builder among the St. Paul & Tacoma founding fathers, insisted that their plant be located not on the south shore of the Bay where the NP land agents suggested but on a tideflat island called the Boot, which lay between the two principal outlets of the Puyallup River.

On April 22, 1889, the mill on the Boot

began cutting lumber. It did not sink into the
bog as many had predicted; nor did it float
away. Production rose until St. Paul & Tacoma
claimed the largest daily production in the
world. The success of Jones' experiment
showed that Tacoma's industrial future lay on
the boggy delta of the Puyallup.

When the federal census takers made their
rounds in 1890 they found that Tacoma's
population had increased 34 times from the
1880 figure. Seattle was still larger, 42,837 to
Tacoma's 36,006, but Tacoma's growth rate in
the closing years of the decade had been
greater. So when it was learned that President
Benjamin Harrison would visit the West in the
spring of 1891 on a non-political tour in prep-
aration for the 1892 campaign, Tacomans
planned a reception they hoped would attract
the attention of the nation to the city's growth
and its destiny.

Early spring had been beautiful, but May
opened rainy and stayed that way. A series of
southeasterly storms swung in from the Pacific.
Tacomans cracked their usual jokes about
"Oregon mist" and "liquid sunshine" as they
sloshed through the mud preparing a welcome
for the 23rd President of the United States.

The little wooden railroad station at Seven-

teenth and Pacific was repainted. The police
were issued new tassels: blue for patrolmen,
white for officers. The fire equipment was
polished until it would reflect any sun that
might chance to shine. Every building in the
downtown area was beflowered and bedraped.
On the evening before the great day, businessmen joined hired laborers in completing a
series of triumphal arches spanning the mud
lagoon that was Pacific Avenue.

Factory whistles alerted the populace at
6 a.m. By 7:30 the parade route was lined with

a gathering that challenged the descriptive powers of the feature writers. "Thousands in gossamer, galosh and umbrella assembled to greet the chief executive," said the *Ledger*. "There were miners of coal and precious metals, sailors from scores of foreign ports, lumbermen from the forests of fir, sealers and fishermen, cowpunchers and ranchmen, squatty Japs and stalwart Scandinavians, jolly Ethiopians and North American Indians galore. . . . Over and above this jam, like black and slippery gas balloons, a choppy sea of umbrellas rolled."

Two minutes before 8 a.m., heralded by a 21-gun salute, Engine 816 pulled the presidential parlor car up to the station. Governor C.P. Ferry and Mayor George Kandle escorted the President and his bodyguard to a carriage drawn by four spanking grays. "It's an ugly day for a drive," said Harrison. But he was game; he ordered the carriage top lowered. His bodyguard held an umbrella over him as the procession started, an honor guard of militiamen in green uniforms with yellow plumes flanking the presidential party.

At Fifteenth Street they came to the first of the temporary arches constructed for the occasion, the Lumbermen's. St. Paul & Tacoma had contributed the pillars, 44 inches square and 15 feet high, which supported a stringer with a clear span of 60 feet that had been cut at the Old Tacoma Mill.

They next passed under the Coal Arch which was crowned by a block of coal 17 feet long, 54 inches wide, and 38 inches thick. It weighed eight tons but fell on no one. Banners assured the President: "We Can Warm the World on Coal."

The Iron Arch, just south of Eleventh Street, was formed with pyramids of hematite from Ellensburg, magnetic ores from Cle Elum, columns of pig iron from the foundry at

The exquisite geometry of rails, wharves, and rigging was caught by Thomas Rutter in this 1890 photograph of the Tacoma waterfront. The tracks horseshoe from the Northern Pacific dock on the right to the coal bunkers on the left. Courtesy, Ray Frederick, Jr.

THE STATE OF WASHINGTON
CAN FEED ALL MANKIND

The Arch of Grain was the fourth of a series of industrial arches spanning Pacific Avenue when President Benjamin Harrison visited Tacoma on May 6, 1891. Designed by Carl August Darmer, the arch was photographed by Thomas Rutter. A banner boasted that "The State of Washington Can Feed All Mankind." Courtesy, Ray Frederick, Jr.

Irondale, and a gas pipe from which was suspended the slogan, "Undeveloped, but Mountains of It."

Last and most elaborate of these monetary monuments was the Grain Arch. It had been designed by the architect C. August Darmer and was constructed with alternating layers of flour sacks and grain sacks. Its banner was unequivocal: "Washington Can Feed All Mankind."

At Ninth Street the militia escort peeled off, while the President's carriage turned left up the hill to C Street where, as the *Ledger* put it, the Gross Brothers store "danced in its flurry [sic] array." As the carriage moved along C to Division, Harrison said, "I wish you would

urge the horses into a trot. This is a rather severe storm." Passing Annie Wright Seminary, where "a troupe of maidens waved flags," he doffed his silk hat. The procession went past the showplace mansions of Chauncey Griggs and Henry Hewitt, then circled by Wright's Park, most of which had been reforested with deciduous trees. When they came to the part that had been left unlogged, the President remarked, "This is an exquisite bit of nature."

The schoolchildren of Tacoma were massed between Ninth and Eleventh on Tacoma Avenue. When the President saw them he muttered, "I wouldn't let a child of mine come out on such a day as this." Mayor Kandle assured him that "Puget Sound children don't mind rain." The superintendent of schools was waiting at Tenth Street, a speech at the ready, but the President said, "We won't stop." Nor did the party pause at Eleventh Street, where 119 students from the Indian school, including a 13-piece band, were prepared to serenade the chief executive. The procession circled back to the Five Corners, where a speaker's stand had been erected. Mrs. Harrison was escorted to dryness in the Tacoma Theater, but the President gamely mounted the uncovered platform.

The rain fell even harder as various dignitaries were introduced. Fights broke out in the crowd as umbrellas blocked a view or threatened eyesight itself. One man bit a hole in another's ear. At last the President arose. Standing under an umbrella held by his bodyguard, he apologized for "prolonging this exposure which you are enduring." He noted that when he visited Tacoma six years earlier, the countryside was enveloped in smoke from a forest fire. Now it was hidden by clouds, "and I still must take existence of those grand mountain tops of which you speak on faith." Still he congratulated his listeners that "this magnificent scenery is frequently hidden from the eye. If everyone saw it, everyone would want to live here and there would be no room."

This led the President into a passage praising "the magnificent, almost magical, transformation that has been wrought in these six years." This is what Tacomans wanted to hear, what they had stood in the rain for hours to hear. And there was more.

A harbor like this, so safe and commodious and deep, should be made to bear a commerce that is but yet in its infancy. I should like to see the prows of some of those great steamship lines entering your port and carrying the American flag at the mast head. . . . We have been content in other years to allow other nations to do the carrying trade of the world. We have been content to see the markets of those American republics lying south of us mastered and controlled by European nations. . . .

The time is propitious for re-establishment upon the sea of the American merchant marine.

The soggy crowd in the triangle at Ninth and Broadway was still cheering long after the President had retreated into the welcome dryness of the Tacoma Theater. Abe Gross of Gross Brothers gave him four grains of quinine to guard against chill. The Women's Club presented the President and Mrs. Harrison with a painting of "The Mountain," and a copy of a poem written by Bernice E. Newell, who had also written a special inscription:

Fair as our Mount Tacoma, in the sunset's glow
Broad as her heights, unsullied as her snow,
Lofty, serene, enduring be your fame.
Your noble acts our nation gain.
And since you to the mountain roam
Why, take from us The Mountain home.

The presidential party was then escorted to the dock, where the steamer *City of Seattle* waited to take them north to a destination the Tacoma papers did not name. A Seattle writer could not resist including in his account a jibe at Tacoma's propensity for overstating its population. "All 36,000 Tacomans turned out to form a crowd of 50,000 to greet the President." But Tacoma was aglow with satisfaction. Surely the nation would realize that a great new city had appeared on the Pacific Coast.

Even the men on telephone poles unfurled umbrellas as they awaited President Harrison's address from the platform in front of the Gross Brothers' store. From Hunt, History of Tacoma, volume I

These are a collection of harbor views from the late 19th century.

(Left) John T. Wagness photographed the crew of the dredge used by the Tacoma Land Company in 1890 to deepen the western channel of the Puyallup River (Courtesy, Sue Olsen); (Above) The western shore had already been bulwarked against erosion when Thomas Rutter photographed these Indian canoes in 1890. (Courtesy, Ray Frederick, Jr.); (Below left) By 1894, when Arthur French took this photograph, the city waterway had reached its present width.

(Facing page top) This 1887 Coast and Geodetic Survey Chart shows the clustering at the head of the bay. (Facing page bottom) In 1888 C.B. Talbot photographed a regatta while high tide covered the mud flats. The area later became industrial land. (Courtesy, Oregon Historical Society)

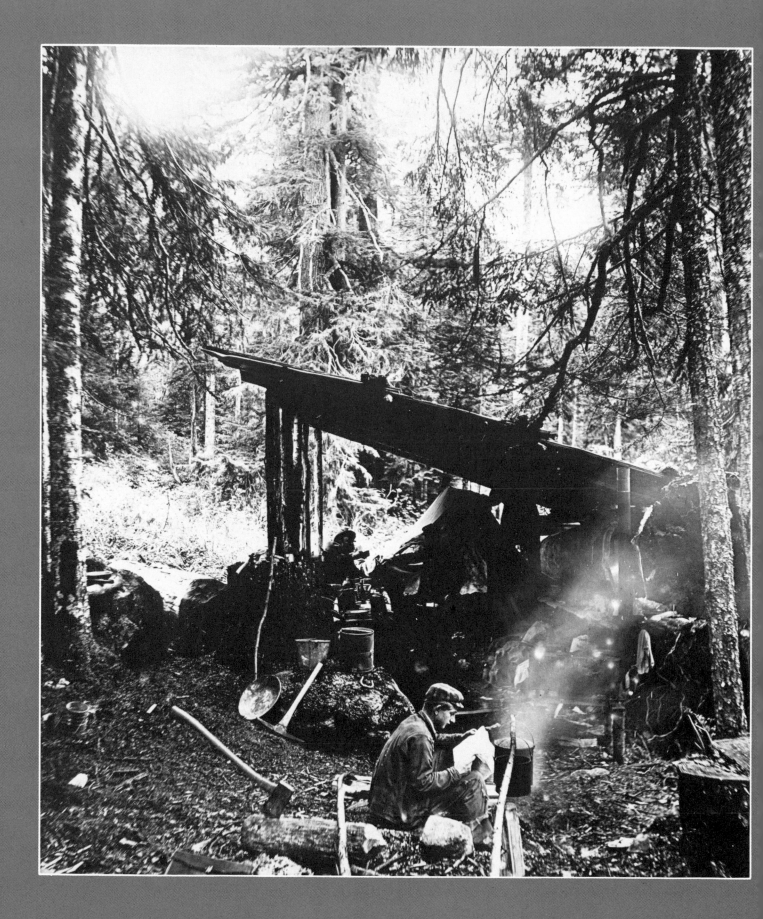

VI

HARD TIMES

Destiny

Turns

Dismal

Facing page
During the Panic of 1893 many of
the unemployed tried their hands at
prospecting. A.H. Barnes recorded
a young gold hunter in camp near
Mount Rainier in about 1895.
Courtesy, Sue Olsen

Right
The Tacoma Opera House at the
Five Corners was designed by the
Philadelphia architect J.M. Wood.
The theater boasted the largest stage
west of the Mississippi—42 by 44
feet and 55 feet to the loft. Ten
prominent Tacomans raised
$100,000 to build it; their aim was
to give the town something more
glamorous than the Frye Opera
House in Seattle. By the time the
Tacoma opened on January 13,
1890, the Frye was no more—a
victim of the great Seattle fire. From
Tacoma Illustrated

The economic slump of the 1890s was worldwide but nowhere did it blight more hopes than in Tacoma. The euphoria stimulated by the completion of the Cascade Division and the metamorphosis of a raw clay bluff and an expanse of mudflat into an almost unbroken line of warehouses, wharves, coal bunkers, shipyards, and sawmills in less than a decade led Tacomans to believe that what they saw happening would keep on happening year after year.

When the eccentric promoter George Francis Train called Tacoma "A City of Destiny," the townsfolk did not remember that he also called himself a "peripatetic humbug." They accepted Train as the voice of prophecy and adopted City of Destiny as a motto. With statistics on lumber, grain, and coal shipments, bank transactions, real estate transfers, and population growth showing an accelerating rate of gain each year for five years after 1886, Tacomans considered their rivals to be not Seattle and Portland but San Francisco and New York.

Some expressed doubts. Chauncey Griggs, president of St. Paul & Tacoma Lumber Company, returned from a business trip to California in 1892 to report the market for lumber "demoralized." He counseled caution and retrenchment. George Francis Train, in the course of an attempt to go around the world—Tacoma to Tacoma—in 80 days, predicted financial collapse within five years. Cyrus Walker, the manager of the Pope & Talbot mills at Port Ludlow and Port Gamble, warned that too many mills were being built and declared, "If they keep on they will burst the business wide open."

More typical was the optimism of Allen C. Mason, a schoolteacher who had made a quick million in Tacoma land development. In an article entitled "Tacoma—Crown City of that Queen of Inland Seas: Puget Sound," which appeared in *The Graphic* in the fall of 1892, Mason praised everything from the climate and geography to the city's financial institutions, singling out for special mention the Merchants National Bank, Pacific National Bank, Wash-

Tacoma's Carnival of Roses was
staged annually in July. The
carnival featured: exhibits of
flowers at the exposition building;
popular concerts at the Tacoma
Theater; excursions to American
Lake, Point Defiance, and
Steilacoom Beach; horse races; a
Rose Ball; and, of course, a
coronation of the Rose Queen in
Wright Park. (TPL)

Bertha Snell was the first woman to
practice law in Washington, but
long before she passed the bar in
1899 she was a famous woman in
Tacoma. She studied business law
in Albany, New York, and she won
appointment as legislative intern
and assistant to Washington's
Governor Elisha Ferry. A woman
of many accomplishments, she
caught the eye of Marshall Snell, a
leading Tacoma lawyer. Snell was
married to someone else but not for
long. Bertha became Snell's wife in
1893 and in 1899 his law partner.
After his death in 1937, she
continued to maintain a law office
in the Puget Sound National Bank
until 1956. (TPL)

This 1893 photo by U.P. Hadley shows a group of musicians whiling away a Sunday afternoon on the outskirts of Tacoma with a fiddler on the porch and a listener on the roof. (TPL)

ington National Bank, and the Traders Bank. In summary he confidently predicted "that in Tacoma's history will be written . . . the marvel of the age in the great modern art of massing men and wealth."

The Panic of 1893 came soon after. Within a year every one of the banks mentioned by Mason had closed its doors. The Northern Pacific Railroad was in the hands of receivers, as was the Tacoma Land Company. Work stopped on the huge Tourist Hotel that the two companies were building at the head of Cliff Avenue. Most of the mills were shut and even St. Paul & Tacoma was running part-time

and selling its lumber at cost. The air went out of inflated land prices. The massing of men and wealth turned to a full retreat as Eastern banks called in their loans and unemployed men went back where they came from, or moved on. Tacoma had claimed an 1893 population of between 52,000 and 54,000. When the census of 1900 was taken, only 37,714 were still there.

The Panic, the lingering depression, and Seattle's emergence as the major city of the state did much to shape Tacoma's personality. In 1890 Tacoma was an assemblage of strangers; three out of four inhabitants had

Only 4 of 21 banks in Tacoma survived the Panic of 1893. Pawnshops did better, with 7 of 12 riding out the economic storm. Ash and Dornberg's, located at the site of the old Alpha Opera House between Tenth and Eleventh on Pacific, was among the survivors. Courtesy, Pierce County Association for Retarded Citizens

The Tacoma Traction Line laid tracks into Puyallup in 1890 but fell into receivership during the panic that followed in 1893. Bicycles were the most popular method of transportation in the lean years, and bike racks were common along Meridian Avenue, Puyallup's main street. Courtesy, Lawton Gowey

lived in town less than five years. With in-migration almost nonexistent between 1893 and 1900, the census of 1900 indicated that four out of five Tacomans had been in town more than 10 years. They knew each other, read the same papers, shared the same hopes and disappointments, and recognized a community of interest that was strengthened by resentment of Seattle's success and by a pervasive feeling that Tacoma had somehow been cheated of a deserved destiny.

Though the 1890s gave Tacomans the sense of a common background, the decade exacerbated economic and political differences. In

the first reaction to the depression, hundreds of the city's unemployed enrolled in Jacob Coxey's "Commonweal Army of Christ" to march on Washington, D.C. in support of a work relief program. The leader of the Tacoma contingent was Frank "Jumbo" Cantwell, a heavyweight prizefighter who had served as bouncer in the town's most notorious saloon. Few of the marchers got as far as Spokane, let alone the nation's capital, but their rhetoric of protest scared the editors of the *Ledger* enough that they suggested deporting the unemployed to Nicaragua and setting them to digging a tunnel between the Atlantic and the Pacific.

Tacoma journalism, even in good times, had lacked decorum. When the *News* in 1886 ran an editorial implying that Samuel W. Wall of the *Telegraph* worked secretly in the interests of Seattle, Wall rushed to the *News* office, braced the offending editorialist, Herbert Sylvester Harcourt, and announced, "I've come to kill you." Harcourt replied genially, "I hardly thought that." Wall thereupon shot him full in the chest, point-blank, only to have Harcourt's tie-pin turn the bullet from what probably would have been a fatal course. A reporter counterattacked the righteous *Telegraph* reporter with a window-shade roller, driving him into the street. Wall was captured, charged with attempted homicide, but never brought to trial, presumably because the prosecutor felt no jury would ever convict a man for defending himself against the charge that he had something good to say about Seat-

When Chief John D. Rainey and George A. Burbank, the secretary of the Tacoma Fire Department, retired from service in 1892, they opened a billiard parlor in the Brunswick at 906 Pacific Avenue. Rainey, in top hat and mustache, stands in the center. Secretary Burbank stands alongside, cue in hand. Bowler-hatted firemen flank them on both sides. According to the Sporting and Club House Directory of Tacoma, Washington, *Rainey and Burbank "spared no expense to make their Parlors what they are."*

Chilberg's Restaurant stood on the water side of Pacific Avenue between Tenth and Eleventh streets. Arthur French, "Crayon Artist and Photographer," recorded this decorous luncheon in the early 1890s, a period when all businessmen brought their hats and most wore facial hair. (TPL)

Child labor laws were obviously not a problem for restaurant owners in the early days. The kitchen crew stands at attention in Chilberg's in this 1893 photo by Arthur French. (TPL)

tle. Harcourt found far-distant employment.

When the *Ledger* went after Harry Morgan, the town's boss gambler, Morgan financed a new paper, the *Globe*, and lured Colonel William Lightfoot Visscher of the Portland *Oregonian* north to turn out a daily dedicated to being nice about vice. Possessed of an orotund prose style and a sneaky right cross, Visscher distinguished himself in duels with the *Ledger* editorialists and in occasional punch-outs with ink-stained wretches of different patronage. His tour with the *Globe* was brief, lasting barely longer than Morgan's ownership, and the colonel moved north to Bellingham to edit the Fairhaven *Herald*.

Soon after the Wall Street Panic of 1893, the *Ledger* dismissed all typographers when they refused to accept a 20 percent cut in pay. The backshop workers immediately created a paper of their own, the *Morning Union*, and called Visscher back to defend the rights of the working man and decry the obtuseness of money barons in general and Nelson Bennett, publisher of the *Ledger*, in particular. Visscher scored a two-punch knockout over one of the *Ledger*'s scab printers when that unworthy said something favorable about Bennett in the Paragon Saloon. Victories were few for labor in

Govnor Teats of Tacoma addresses the Tacoma and Seattle contingents of Jacob Coxey's Commonweal Army of Christ. The 'Wealers, who were marching to Washington, D.C., as a "petition with boots on" in support of work relief programs, had reached Puyallup and were occupying the Park Hotel, which Ezra Meeker was unable to complete because of hard times. From Hunt, History of Tacoma, *volume II*

Harry Morgan's Theatre Comique, on the present site of the Olympus Hotel, attracted more newspaper attention per square foot than any other place in Tacoma. Before Morgan's death in April 1890 you could get a shoeshine at the front door, a drink at the bar, a girl as a companion in a screened-off box seat, and lose money at 21 different games. After his death there was a decade of litigation among his widows, both real and alleged. Courtesy, Historic Photo Collection, University of Washington Libraries

Facing page bottom
William Wilson bought the north half of the Tollantire Donation Claim, 320 acres, in 1872 and built a house at what is today South 123rd and A streets. When Tacoma expanded southward in the 1890s, Wilson hired a mapmaker and platted his farm as a town. Wilson sold part of the land to a developer, Ward T. Smith, who, to promote the proposed town, donated ten acres to the Norwegian Lutheran Synod and commissioned this painting. Courtesy, Pacific Lutheran University

You are respectfully invited to attend, and this card will admit you to the execution of

Salvador Picani,

to occur on Friday July 1, 1892, in the Pierce County jail yard at Tacoma, Wash.

J. H. Price,
Sheriff.

An immigrant Sicilian fruit peddler, Salvatore Conchilla, was found dead in a cottage at South Nineteenth and D in March 1892. His boyhood chum, Salvador Picani, was arrested for the murder, tried, convicted, and sentenced to be hanged. Formal invitations to the execution, in gilt on dark purple, had already been issued when Father Hylebos, his priest and confessor, and four state legislators won a new trial. By then Picani's innocence had been established, and the prosecutor dismissed the charges. From Hunt, History of Tacoma, *volume II*

the 1890s. Visscher drifted off to Chicago. Bennett gave up on the *Ledger,* its new owners made peace with the typographers, and the *Morning Union* ceased publication in 1897.

The Typographers were the first union to form in Tacoma. They were chartered in 1883, the year the new and old cities voted to coalesce. Though they typified the craft union tradition of an organization basing its power on the right of skilled workers to withhold their services, the Typographers participated actively in politics. They sent official delegates to the Anti-Chinese meetings of 1885, endorsed the successful campaigns for women's suffrage, and joined the politically oriented Tacoma Trades Council after its formation in 1890.

The Trades Council, which grew to be the Tacoma Central Labor Council, was formed after some union men meeting informally at the Knights of Labor hall on Pacific Avenue discussed the swap of property worked out between the Chamber of Commerce and the

The First Battalion of the Washington Regiment of the National Guard marched down Pacific Avenue on its way to embark on the S.S. Senator, *en route to the Philippines during the Spanish-American War. They lost 43 men before their return: 23 in battle, one by drowning, one in an accidental shooting, two of unknown causes, and the rest by disease. Courtesy, Paul Dorpat*

City of Tacoma that made possible construction of the campanile-towered city hall. The working men felt that the business organization, which obtained the corner where the Winthrop Hotel was later built, was the clear winner in the trade. If the city council wanted to bargain away valuable property to the bosses, the workers felt they ought to get some too. But if their request for an old fire station, which they wanted to use as a union hall, were to be granted, they would have to have an organization comparable to the Chamber to receive ownership.

On April 3, 1890, delegates from the Bricklayers, Carpenters, Cigar Makers, Cornice Makers, Stonecutters, Longshoremen, Stevedores, and Riggers met to create the Council. It did not get the fire station but the Council organized Tacoma's first Labor Day parade later that year and not only served as the dominant voice for organized labor but played an active role in reformist politics throughout the 1890s.

The Tacoma Trades Council sent delegates to the Confederation of Industrial Organizations meeting in North Yakima on July 18, 1891, which drew plans for the People's Party of Washington. The Populists in 1892 elected nine representatives to the state legislature, including three from Tacoma, on a platform calling for curtailment of strikebreaking by private detectives, an end to inflationary economic measures, the nationalization of railroads and lowering of rates and fares, and the establishment of free employment agencies. Two years later, following the Panic, the Populists elected 23 legislators, including John Rankin Rogers of Puyallup, an eccentric but effective reformer who looked on cities as "sink holes of civilization" but won favor with labor by working for mine safety legislation and state support of public school financing. In 1896, at the bottom of the depression, a Populist-Democratic fusion ticket captured both houses of the state legislature and elected Rogers as governor, although the Republicans won nationally.

New to responsibility and torn between the conflicting demands of special interests, the "Pops" immediately went bang. Their performance alienated the electorate and drove

many working men toward the position held by the American Federation of Labor, that a union's mission was organizing for effective bargaining, not running candidates for office. Economic recovery, spurred by the Spanish-American War and the discovery of gold in the Alaskan Klondike, ended the Populists' effectiveness as a party.

Another answer to bad times was the utopian colony, three of which were started in the Tacoma area during the 1890s. The first was the Glennis Cooperative Industrial Company which in 1894 manifested itself on 160 acres of homestead land belonging to Oliver A. Verity, a part-time carpenter. The colony was based on Edward Bellamy's *Looking Backward: 2000-1887*, but Bellamy's directions for creating the utopia he described in detail were vague. The Glennis group was split asunder, Verity averred, by "the desire of the many at Glennis to make by-laws restricting others from doing things that in reality were private matters, causing . . . many meetings which were noisy and bred inharmony from the diversified views of what should be done."

In reaction, Verity joined George Allen, a discursive, college-educated dreamer of mechanical bent who was also disillusioned by Glennis, and B.F. Odell in founding an alternative to their first alternative society. Located at Von Geldern Cove on Carr Inlet, southwest of Tacoma, it was formally called The Home Mutual Association and informally, Home Colony, or just plain Home.

The founding fathers hoped for a place where, in Verity's words, residents would have "the personal liberty to follow their own line of action no matter how much it may differ from the custom of the past or present, without censure or ostracism from their neighbor." Allen explained that "We had heard and read of many isms, and had tried some with varying success. We wished to give each ism a chance to prove its usefulness to humanity."

The Mutual Home Association's stated purpose was to assist "members in obtaining and building homes for themselves and to aid in establishing better social and moral conditions." Membership cost a dollar. Having joined, a member could use from one to two acres of

Washington College, which had opened its doors in 1885, graduated its last class in 1892. These young graduates posed in mock celebration. The institution thereafter changed its name to DeKoven School and moved to the suburbs, first locating at the former Ainsworth Farm on Clover Creek, then at the old Davisson farm on Steilacoom Lake. Courtesy, Historic Photo Collection, University of Washington Libraries

Utopian colonies flourished near Tacoma in the late
19th century. (Near right top) In 1898 an agent for
the Co-operative Brotherhood agreed to pay $5,917
for 260 acres of bottomland on the Burley Lagoon
at the head of Henderson Bay. Sixteen people moved
to Washington State to "secure control of the politics
and start the co-operative commonwealth." Utopia,
in winter, looked like this, circa 1900. (Courtesy,
Washington State Library); (Near right bottom)
The colonists at Burley built their own schoolhouse,
rented it to the school district, and used the rent to
help pay the teacher's salary. The building doubled
as a community center where the co-operators held
meetings they hoped would "make Burley the social
and intellectual center of a considerable district."
(Courtesy, Mary Randlett); (Far right top) Jay Fox,
a tall, lean intellectual who came to Puget Sound
bearing a bullet in his shoulder from the McCormick
Harvester Machine strike in Illinois, published a
paper called The Agitator at Home Colony of Joe's
Bay. He was convicted of criminal libel for advocating that colonists shun their neighbors who had
complained to the sheriff about nude bathing.
Governor Ernst Lister (of Tacoma) granted him full
pardon. (Far right bottom) The Burley Co-
operators built a hotel, published a newspaper, made
broom-handles, sold jam, rolled cigars, and failed to
raise tobacco. Their major product was lumber, cut
in a mill rafted down from Bellingham. Here a
bargeload of cedar shingles starts for Tacoma in
1909. (Courtesy, State Capitol Museum)

Tacoma interests, headed by the elder William Fife, outbid Seattle and Port Townsend for a floating drydock built in 1891 at Port Hadlock on Port Townsend Bay. They had the dock towed to Quartermaster Harbor, where the town of Dockton grew up on Maury Island and helped to attract shipping to Tacoma. Here the S.S. Victoria, a ship famous in the Nome gold rush and also (as the Parthia) for an attempt to carry supplies to Chinese Gordon in Khartoum, rests in the cradle while her bottom is scraped. (WSHS)

land. The Association retained title to the land; the purchaser was a steward of the property and could bequeath or sell improvements he put upon it. He was subject to taxation by the Association but the taxes could be spent only upon the purchase of more property which would be available at cost to new members.

Though threatened with attack by self-appointed guardians of the status quo, riven by dissent over such ponderous issues as nude bathing, and picked on by the authorities who jailed the editor of a Home based paper, *Discontent—Mother of Progress,* for disrespect to George Washington, Home survived as a corporate entity until 1919 and lives on in growing myth.

The neighboring Burley Co-operative Colony, though more political, attracted less hostility. It was the outgrowth of a suggestion by the socialist leader Eugene V. Debs—after the strong showing of the Populists in Washington in the 1896 election—that socialists migrate there "to secure control of the politics of the State and start the co-operative commonwealth."

A splinter faction of Social Democracy of America—to whose convention Debs put forth the idea of a cooperative—obtained acreage on the Burley Lagoon at the head of Carr Inlet in 1898. In spite of issuing publications such as *Soundview,* "a Magazinelet

Washington Automobile Company displayed a line of horseless, roofless carriages for Tacomans at 708-710 Pacific Avenue. Established in 1904, the company claimed to be the first automobile dealership in the state. (TPL)

Devoted to the Obstetrics of Thought and the Philosophy of Existence," Burley survived as a legal entity until 1924. But for Burley as well as Home the Princess Utopia had gone back to sleep long before, when the return of prosperity brought with it goddesses more graspable than the perfect society for dreamers to pursue.

Seattle survived the 1890s in much better shape than did Tacoma. The great fire of 1889 had allowed rebuilding of the waterfront and the downtown area, the arrival of the Great Northern railroad in 1893 cushioned the shock of the Panic, and an alert business community enabled Seattle to exploit the gold rush to the Klondike and Nome and expand not

only its waterborne trade but its shipbuilding industry. By 1900 Seattle's population was more than twice that of its younger rival, and Tacoma was referring to itself as "The Manufacturing City of the Northwest."

Years after the Panic touched off an exodus, Tacoma again claimed 50,000 inhabitants and was growing fast. A Chamber of Commerce publication cited more than 300 separate mills and factories with an annual production of $23 million on invested capital of $14 million. The 8,000 industrial workers received an estimated $500,000 a month, and the city averaged 25 new factories, with 1,000 employees, a year.

Most of the expansion centered on lumber. The Weyerhaeuser Timber Company in 1900 had made the largest purchase of timberland in history from the Northern Pacific land grant, and chose Tacoma as headquarters. Weyerhaeuser would not start cutting its holdings for another decade, but St. Paul & Tacoma, which had doubled the size of its plant in 1901, was turning out 150 million board feet of lumber and 75 million shingles a year—world records. Thirty-eight other sawmills, shingle mills, and woodworking plants in or close to Tacoma were in operation. Wood products ranged

(Top) Dennis Ryan of St. Paul built a smelter in Tacoma in 1888. William Rust and Associates bought it a year later and rebuilt the plant. (From Ye Official Souvenir: Western Washington Industrial Exposition, 1891); (Middle) Hanson's mill by 1888 was known as the Tacoma Mill. Until St. Paul and Tacoma Lumber Company opened its plant the following year, the Tacoma Mill was largest. (Courtesy, Historic Photo Collection, University of Washington Libraries); (Below) This Thomas Rutter photograph shows the Tacoma Smelter in 1891. (Courtesy, Ray Frederick, Jr.); (Bottom right) The coal bunkers lay just below Old Woman's Gulch, where the Stadium was later built. (From C. Clark, Tacoma: The Water Terminus)

from water mains to broom handles, from cradles to caskets, and from pulley blocks to the knees for wooden ships—indeed, to wooden steamships.

The Tacoma Smelter was the largest on the coast, capable of processing 700 tons of ore

daily. The Northern Pacific shops were the largest foundry for car wheels and for repairing cars in the West. The Northern Pacific had deepened the city waterway and built more wheat warehouses, totalling 2,300 feet in length and 148 feet in width. The Puget Sound Flouring Mill, largest in the state, had a capacity of 2,000 barrels a day, and three smaller plants raised daily production to 3,800 barrels.

Tacoma's shipments of wheat and flour were now fourth in the nation, rivaling Portland's, and Tacoma boosters loved to quote the comment of the *Portland Oregonian* when the first sacks of wheat were carried aboard the *Dakota*: "They have shipped a cargo of wheat at Tacoma and have had a banquet; perhaps at the end of five years they may ship another cargo, then they will have a clam bake."

Above
The officers and men of the Buckingham posed in 1895 for William Hester, a noted photographer of maritime activities, while the ship was loading in Tacoma. (TPL)

Left
Sperry grain warehouses lay below Buckley Hill, as the area north of Old Woman's Gulch and south of Old Tacoma was then called. Second-growth Douglas fir sprouted among the notched stumps left by loggers who had worked from springboards when they harvested the virgin forest. (TPL)

(Facing page) (Upper left) The tentacles of transportation reached out from Tacoma into the suburbs in the 1890s. This map was drawn by Frederick Shaw. The steamships of the mosquito fleet connected Puget Sound ports, but land travellers faced problems with the rivers. (Top) Sam Pehyo provided dugout service across the Nisqually. (Middle) Another solution was the swing ferry, which was propelled by the pressure of the current against hull and rudder. (Courtesy, Historic Photo Collection, University of Washington Libraries); (Bottom) The Tacoma and Steilacoom Railway Company began operations in 1890, connecting the Court House to Steilacoom. In good weather the cars were open, but sidewalls were bolted into place during the rain. The line was abandoned in 1916 having averaged a loss of $17 a day. (Courtesy, Lawton Gowey)

(This page) (Above) The Point Defiance Railroad Company was franchised in 1889 to run a line to the Smelter. The line connected Division and Broadway with the Smelter but soon merged with a line to Edison (South Tacoma). (Courtesy, Lawton Gowey); (Right) Tacoma used cable cars to climb its hills. This 1893 view looks up Eleventh from Pacific Avenue. The E.N. Ouimette Building housing Washington National Bank is where the Rust Building now stands. (Courtesy, Oregon Historical Society)

VII

THE CHALLENGE OF ADVERSITY

A

Modern City

Emerges

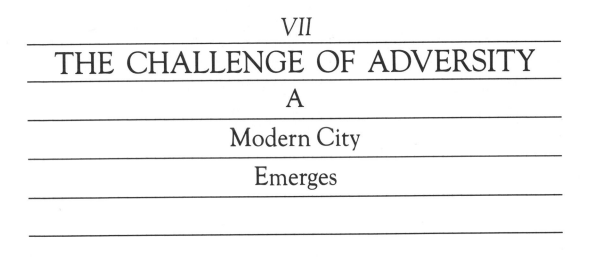

Students parade in the new Stadium Bowl in the annual May exercise in this 1912 photo by Chapin Bowen. Tacoma High School and the stadium symbolized Tacoma's growth in the early years of the 20th century. (TPL)

Seen from the Bay, the pile of masonry looked romantic to imaginative tourists—a ruined castle from a fantasy past. To Tacomans the abandoned hulk of the Tourist Hotel—roofless, windowless, and smudged with smoke from the 1896 fire that gutted its unfinished interior—stood as a symbol of the unfulfilled promise of civic destiny: a blight, a police problem, civic scar tissue. But when the Northern Pacific let a contract for the building's demolition and the shipment of its bricks to Idaho and Montana, there were stirrings of rebellion.

While walking downtown to work one morning in 1902, Conrad Hoska, a popular mortician, and Eric Rosling, an attorney, paused by the gutted building and deplored the demolition in progress. Hoska, who had served on the school board, mentioned that Tacoma High needed new quarters. Before reaching the foot of Cliff Avenue the two men had convinced themselves.

Tacoma was small enough so that nearly everybody knew everybody. Hoska and Rosling went directly to William Coffee, who ran a plumbing business across from the Tacoma Hotel. Coffee, who was president of the Board of Education, liked their idea and called Frederick Heath, the school board's architect.

Heath visited the site and shortly after noon called on Coffee to say that the hulk could be transformed into a school. Coffee summoned the board to a special meeting at 1:30. After Heath outlined the possibilities, Coffee telephoned George H. Plummer, the Northern Pacific's land agent. Plummer said the railroad would sell the ruins and the six-acre site for what they had paid to acquire it: $34,500. The board said, "Sold." When Hoska and Rosling walked home together that afternoon they noted that the demolition crew had been called off the job.

Between the purchase of the ruin and the opening of the high school lay the usual delays of community enterprise: a lawsuit over the legality of the deal, an election to approve financing, arguments over the safety of foundation stones that had been exposed to great heat, and debates over design, but in September 1906 teenagers and faculty moved into the new Tacoma High School. The city celebrated the creation of a unique facility for only $6,000 above estimated cost. Those who had doubted joined those who had promoted in bragging about the edifice that some called the Chateau, and others, the Brown Castle: "Why, mister, they are even printing postcards of it in Germany!"

Above
The school system prided itself on providing state-of-the-art equipment for its classes in business skills. This 1908 photo shows a class at Tacoma High School. Courtesy, Tacoma Public Schools

Above right
The intramural basketball champions of 1902 pose amid the statuary stored in the basement of the old Central School. Courtesy, Tacoma Public Schools

The new school stood at the edge of Old Woman's Gulch—a ravine carved by a small stream that, originating near South K Street, wound through Wright Park (picking up water from the spring-fed swan pond), then cut across G Street, Tacoma Avenue, and E Street and descended to the Bay. A trestle, 240 feet above sea level, carried E Street across the head of the gulch toward Buckley Hill, the site of many fashionable Victorian homes. The gulch itself was an unsightly tangle of alder, second-growth fir, and salal. Near the Bay were a few shacks occupied by widows of fishermen and longshoremen. According to architect Heath it was "the utter incongruity of the extremes, palace and jungle," that suggested to him the idea of turning the gulch into an athletic field.

Two years earlier, Harvard had dedicated the nation's first large-scale sports stadium. Greece, in 1906, was restructuring an amphitheater in Athens as a site for Olympic-style competitions. Heath argued that what was good enough for the Ivy League and Athenians was none too good for Tacoma's athletes. The

Left
Miss Emily Caskey holds the attention of the listeners in the front seats at the Saturday story hour in the Carnegie Library, but the boys in the back row seem to find the camera more interesting. (TPL)

Below left
A heavy cruiser anchored off of the Stadium Bowl to add emphasis to a May Day parade in this photo by Chapin Bowen. (TPL)

city's young agreed. The Tacoma High literary magazine announced that "progressive boy students" were organizing to transform Heath's dream into concrete. The student body president of the last class to graduate from the old high school urged students "to leave no stone unturned until you have secured a stadium of the first order only."

The cost-conscious Board of Education agreed only to log the gulch slopes and sluice some dirt from the banks to create a level area. But concrete grandstands? The old women were evicted from their shacks (there is no record of where they went) and the gulch was made tidy. It looked so promising as open space that a group of businessmen offered to build a stadium for the school district if they could lease it for 10 years. The board agreed, then reversed itself and decided to finance construction from public funds.

The field area was increased to two-and-a-half acres by sluicing 185,000 yards of dirt from the banks. Concrete pillars were sunk to hardpan, reinforced beams placed across them, and a latticework of steel girders raised to support a terraced fabric of heavy wire. Concrete was poured to form 31 tiers of seats. Heath de-

Passenger vessels from the mosquito fleet swarmed into City Waterway in this Wesley Andrews photograph for the dedication of the new Eleventh Street Bridge on February 15, 1913. The 112-foot Verona *(left) and the 140-foot* Nisqually *had been launched not long before from the Dockton yards in Quartermaster Harbor. The beloved* Flyer *was about to be taken off the Tacoma-Seattle run after 21 years of service, during which she made four round trips a day at an average speed of 18 miles an hour. Courtesy, Oregon Historical Society.*

scribed the monolithic concrete horseshoe as "a poem in masonry . . . a great athletic field set in the midst of superb natural scenery. In the symmetry of its terraced seats, in the enthusiasm that built the structure is the grandeur of the poetic spirit."

Twenty-five thousand spectators assembled for the dedication on June 10, 1910, to watch 4,000 schoolchildren form a living American flag and 7,000 perform a dance routine. The next day there was a track meet with Tacoma High competing against Queen Anne, Lincoln, and Broadway of Seattle. You could see almost anything in the Stadium—football, baseball, balloon ascensions, fireworks displays, Wild West shows complete with "a real stage coach robber and Indians burning settlers' cabins," opera stars from New York, military demonstrations, and politicians. Tacomans agreed with former President Theodore Roosevelt when he said, "The building of this stadium will influence your city for decades and will influence every city in the nation. During my travels I had heard of this extraordinary feature

of your municipal life. . . . I know of nothing like it on this side of the water or abroad."

The high school and stadium were but part of a surge of public projects in the early years of the century. They were championed by Republicans of the Theodore Roosevelt stripe, reformers left without a party with the collapse of the Populists, and hometown boosters who just wanted something done. The railroad and the land company didn't come through. "We'll have to do it ourselves," they said.

Tacoma had owned its water and light utilities since 1893 when Charles Wright unloaded them on the city for a price the courts later determined to be exorbitant. The municipal activities of the early 1900s revitalized both systems. Tacoma acquired water rights on the Cedar River, guaranteeing a supply adequate not only to the needs of its growing population but also those of the electrochemical industries that would arrive in the 1930s and 1940s.

City Attorney Theodore L. Stiles, who had helped draft the state constitution, persuaded

Women who campaigned for the right to vote in the election of 1910 were counseled by their leader, Emma Smith Devoe of Tacoma, to be well groomed no matter what their activity. This group, photographed by Asahel Curtis on September 16, 1910, took her seriously. Courtesy, Curtis Collection, WSHS

the state supreme court to interpret it in a way that gave Tacoma the right to condemn land beyond the city limits for public purposes. Not only did this court victory allow Tacoma City Light to build a hydroelectric dam in the 700-foot deep LaGrande Canyon on the Nisqually, but it also cleared the path for the public power movement throughout the state. For the next half century City Light supplied residential customers with electricity at less than a penny a kilowatt hour, the lowest rate in the nation.

The reformers restructured city government. Freeholders wrote a charter putting legislative and administrative power in the hands of a city council consisting of a mayor, trea-surer, public safety commissioner, utilities commissioner, and public works commissioner. The mayor was assigned only the garbage department to administer but as titular head of city government could take the lead in campaigns for civic improvements.

Such leadership was the specialty of Angelo Fawcett, the first mayor elected under the Commission Charter of 1910. A Populist turned Republican turning Independent, Fawcett campaigned successfully for a farmer's market at Eleventh and D streets, which was so successful that D became Market Street; for a new lift bridge across City Waterway at Eleventh Street, which in turn led to a municipal trolley line on the tideflats to carry workers to

Ida M. Tanner and her husband, Prince A. Tanner, both seated on the ground, hosted the Calenthe Association at their home at 6119 South I Street on September 3, 1915. Prince was an elevator operator, his son Ernest was a prominent figure among Tacoma longshoremen (and one of the best high school athletes ever to compete in Tacoma), and Ernest's son, Jack Tanner, a third generation Tacoman, is the first black federal district court judge in Washington. Courtesy, Charlotte Breckenridge

Facing page bottom
The 1906 San Francisco earthquake created a demand for lumber that had all the mills on Puget Sound running overtime. A railcar shortage brought scores of old sailing vessels out of retirement. Old Tacoma came alive with industrial activity for the last time. (TPL)

the expanding industries; and for a municipal dock to bring maritime traffic to the foot of the downtown bluff.

The new dock serviced the vessels of the mosquito fleet—the passenger steamers and cargo boats that plied between the cities of the Sound. Though trains and electric interurbans connected Tacoma with the other waterfront communities, most cargo traveled by water, as did many people. Oil was replacing coal and wood as the energy source for ships; diesel in the oceangoing craft, the gasoline engine in small boats. The Slavs and Scandinavians who had created a fishing community at Gig Harbor no longer rowed to the San Juan Islands to intercept the sockeye salmon runs; internal combustion saved time and spared muscles. The advent of the privately owned powerboat also stimulated the growth of beach communities. Like the Indians before them, Tacomans were beginning to migrate between solid houses built to withstand the winds and rains of winter, and beach cabins—often referred to as "camps"—for the summer.

The waterfront was in its busiest and most varied period. The great square-riggers of the age of canvas, exiled from runs demanding speed and punctuality, called at Commencement Bay for cargoes that did not deteriorate in passage: lumber, wheat, and coal. Steamers hauled passengers and mail around the Sound on schedule; launches delivered commuters to Salmon Beach, Spring Beach, Manzanita, Day Island, and way points. Visiting journalists called Commencement Bay "a hive of activity." A tourist wrote home that "you can rent a rowboat and row to snow." The Chamber of Commerce hyperbolized Puget Sound as "the American Mediterranean. . . . rainless from June to September."

The Mountain loomed over the Inland Sea, adding to Tacoma's attraction. Mount Rainier had been made a national park in 1899. In 1903 a government road was authorized; construction started from Ashford, where both the Tacoma and Eastern Railroad and the Pierce County road ended. In 1905 the road reached the snout of the Nisqually glacier; by 1910 it was graded to Paradise Valley, but not passable. The following year, though, one automobile, aided by a team of mules, made it through the mud to paradise, carrying all 280 pounds of President William Howard Taft. Tacoma papers hailed the achievement: "From sea to snow-line by automobile in one day."

When the Commercial Club and the Chamber of Commerce commissioned the veteran engineer Virgil Bogue to draw up a comprehensive proposal for development of the Commencement Bay waterfront, his 1911 plan made provisions for tourism as well as industry and commerce. It called for small boat moorages between the Stadium and Old Town; a ferry slip between Old Town and the Smelter for commuters to Browns Point, Dash Point, and Redondo; and a terminal at Point Defiance for ferries to Vashon Island and Gig Harbor, along with moorages for pleasure craft. Bogue's top priority, however, was improving tideflats for industrial use.

When he delivered his recommendations Bogue declared:

Tacoma has the advantage of cheap coal and coke

of good quality and cheap electric power, and with her enormous area of tideflats, which reach all the way up to Puyallup and beyond, opportunity for industrial enterprises practically unexcelled. . . . With the courage and help of her people, Tacoma will become one of the great ports. . . . Without that courage and help, development will at best be slow and uncertain.

Although lumber and other freight was hauled on the Seattle-Tacoma Interurban line, passengers provided 80 percent of the revenue. Parlor cars had open observation platforms, velvet curtains, and spittoons. As many as 1,600 passengers made the trip each day. Courtesy, Lawton Gowey

The slopes of Mount Rainier became Tacoma's playground. (Right) A hiker paused on the trail from James Longmire's resort to the alpine meadows of Paradise Valley. (A.H. Barnes Collection, TPL); (Middle) While guiding a party of climbers on the lower slopes of Rainier in 1882, James Longmire released his horse to graze. The horse, named Old Spot (shown here), ran off, and Longmire found it in a valley of hot springs. In 1883 Longmire built a ranch there and promoted the curative qualities of the water. (A.H. Barnes Collection, TPL); (Bottom) By 1913 it was possible to reach Paradise by carriage. Dr. Park Weed Willis of Seattle, complete with cap and moustache, sat beside the driver. (Courtesy, Mary Randlett)

(Above left) By 1920 it was possible to reach Paradise in convertible comfort. (TPL); (Above) Pierce County built a road from Tacoma through Ashford to the new Mount Rainier National Park. (TPL); (Left) This photo from the 1920s shows the neat tents at Paradise nestled in the pine and fir forest. (TPL); (Lower left) Asahel Curtis photographed these intrepid mountaineers on the slopes of Rainier, the "Switzerland of America." (Courtesy, Sue Olsen)

Three of Tacoma's four newspapers chanted hosannas, fortissimo. The *Ledger* called the plan "a clear guide in the right direction." The *Tribune* gave "hearty endorsement." The *News*, after warning that "certain old mossbacks will raise their roaring voices against anything that will take a few dollars out of their fat and padlocked purses," urged that the citizenry "stint, if required, and sacrifice without a whimper." Only the *Times* demurred, giving heavy coverage to those who feared "municipal socialism" and the possibility that a

The Smelter was rebuilt in 1906 after the plant was acquired by American Smelting and Refining Company. The Smelter then specialized in copper—the great metal of the age of electricity. (TPL)

port commission might be duped into "buying mud at high prices."

Bogue's plan subsided into a swamp of citizens' committee studies, never to reappear in its original form. In 1914, however, the county commissioners put before the voters a proposal to create a countywide port district and commission. A ticket of three commissioners committed to developing the first phase of the Bogue plan appeared uncontested on the ballot. In spite of wide publicity for the special election, only 14 percent of the electorate voted. Those within the Tacoma city limits favored creation of the public port by a modest margin but the county precincts were overwhelmingly opposed. The commissioners were elected, but the port district was not created.

The proposition was resubmitted in the general election in November of 1914 and again was defeated. It looked as if the Tacoma-Pierce County lust for economic self-improvement had abated. But in 1916 a new opportunity was presented. The federal government was seeking a site for an army camp. That would mean a federal payroll.

Little in Tacoma's early association with the military indicated development of a cordial, lasting, and profitable relationship. Army regulars had been sent to Tacoma in 1885 to arrest the mayor and other city officials after the expulsion of the Chinese. The first encampment of the National Guard at American Lake in July 1886 was officially described as a "failure," partly because promised accommodations in town were not forthcoming, but

Tacomans had always been aware of the beauties of their surroundings, but during the new century they exploited tourism as a major resource. Puget Sound became "a place where no rain falls from June to September," and Tacoma was "The Pearl of the American Mediterranean." Courtesy, Paul Dorpat

Tea, crockery, liquor, and textiles from the Tacoma Maru *were the first cargo to be handled at the Oriental Dock on the tideflats. Critics said the warehouse would be carried away by the first high tide. (TPL)*

also because the guardsmen assigned to prepare the camp area were "incapacitated due to premature celebration of the Fourth of July." The second encampment had such a cost overrun that the training exercises were suspended for eight years. The guard was sent to the Philippines during the Spanish-American War, but the court martial and conviction of its ranking officer, Colonel William J. Fife, for telling dirty stories in the presence of impressionable enlisted men, provoked more mirth than respect.

Nevertheless, when Tacomans learned that newly enacted legislation permitted the Secretary of War to accept, as donations, sites adapted to military purposes, they set out to acquire by purchase and condemnation a tract of 140 square miles east of American Lake, of which more than two-thirds was private property. A committee composed of Steven Appleby, a bank cashier; Elbert Baker, publisher of the Cleveland *Plain Dealer*; and his son, Frank Baker, publisher of the Tacoma *News-Tribune*, persuaded Secretary of War Newton D. Baker (no relation) to agree to accept the property if it were acquired. Immediately after his re-election in 1916, President Woodrow Wilson endorsed the project.

The Pierce County commissioners submitted to the voters a proposal to issue $2 million in bonds to pay for acquisition of the land. The campaign, carried on during the surge of indignation over the German resumption of unrestricted submarine warfare, was no contest. To oppose the bond issue was un-American. The vote was 25,049 to 4,150.

"It is impossible at this time to grasp the full significance of this magnificent gift to the Government," wrote Belmore Browne, a Tacoma artist and explorer:

A new spirit is making itself manifest, a spirit that is based on the realization that we are no longer an isolated nation, but a vital part of the life of the great globe on which we live. With our new position has come a flood of grave responsibilities. Already the principle of Democracy on which we stand has been assailed by the forces of Militarism. Every resource of our great land must be used to guarantee the spiritual freedom of mankind.

The courts responded with the same emotion. Few property owners resisted condemnation of their farms and homes, and those who did go to court fared poorly. Within two months all but a few parcels of the land were possessed by the county and deeded to the United States for use as a permanent military station.

Three days before the United States declared war on Germany, a party of army engineers began a survey of the military reservation to select the best site for the central buildings. They chose the plain directly east of American Lake. Captain David L. Stone, the constructing quartermaster, quickly drew plans

The big snow of 1916 was Tacoma's worst until the blizzard of 1950. Some streetcars stood abandoned on the tracks for more than a week. A.H. Barnes braved the February cold to take this picture. Courtesy, Dennis Andersen

for the cantonment, a horseshoe sweep of buildings on a 2,500-acre area with Mount Rainier looming behind the central parade ground.

Construction of the quartermaster's office and two warehouses began on Monday, June 25, 1917. Within the week the warehouses were in place and the headquarters was occupied. The following Monday, workmen started to assemble 36 barracks; within 10 days 1,080 of the workers were housed in them. By then orders had been placed with Tacoma mills for the greatest single purchase of lumber in history. Seventy carloads of raw boards were arriving at Camp Lewis by rail each day. Two sawmills were built on site to recut wet planks to blueprint specifications. Each plank was stamped with a symbol so that inexperienced workmen could knock it properly into place. Every eight hours the rough carpenters slapped together 11 barracks and 6 stables. (Some still were in service when the Second World War rolled around.) Ninety days after building began all of the officers and 90 percent of the

enlisted men for the 91st Division were answering reveille at Camp Lewis.

While barracks materialized on the Nisqually prairie, new shipyards rose on the Commencement Bay tideflats. The Todd yards were the largest. When the Todd Shipyards Corporation was created on June 29, 1916, bringing under one management shipyards in Brooklyn, Hoboken, and Seattle, William H. Todd, the 52-year-old founder, doubted that much money could be made building ships, especially on the West Coast where wages were high. His plan was to repair vessels. Germany's success with its U-boat campaign changed his priorities. Orders poured in from abroad for dry cargo carriers, submarines, and cruisers. Todd's Seattle yard (formerly the Moran Brothers Company) had more orders than it could fill but no room to expand. Todd found needed space on the Tacoma waterfront at the head of Commencement Bay, between Hylebos Creek and the northeast Tacoma hill.

A subsidiary corporation, known as Todd Dry Dock and Construction Company, was

Black troops were given special segregated assignments in the war "to make the world safe for democracy." The Forage Detachment was assigned to gather materials needed in construction. (TPL)

formed with Todd putting up half a million dollars and Tacoma interests investing a like amount. The original plan was for a 12,000-ton floating dry dock to be built in the Seattle yards and towed to Tacoma, where Todd's West Coast repair work would be centered. When the United States entered the war, the Emergency Fleet Corporation, which was established as the acquisition and construction arm of the United States Shipping Board, decreed that Todd's Tacoma yard should concentrate on building Cascade-type freighters.

The Cascades were 380-foot, 7,500-deadweight ton ships of a type originally designed by Todd for Danish and Norwegian shipping companies. The Tacoma investors in the Todd subsidiary asked to withdraw from the operation so they could concentrate on building wooden ships, while Todd turned out the steel Cascades.

Never before had government played such an active role in industrial development. The United States helped pay for construction of the new shipyards, granted cost-plus contracts

under which the builder could not lose, and then allowed employers to grant a wage scale and working conditions that would keep labor content. The government financed the expansion of the Todd yards to provide ways for 12 ships at a time, financed the building of barracks to house a thousand workers, and advanced the money the city needed to extend the Tacoma Municipal Railway (renamed Tacoma Municipal Belt Line), along Eleventh Street so it could serve the Todd yards.

Though conscious of patriotic duty, workers in the mills and shipyards were also aware that labor was in short supply and profits guaranteed. When the Tacoma Railway & Power Company discharged 10 men for union activity, the workers struck, demanding better working conditions, better pay, and union recognition. They brought in a brass band and—reinforced by Seattle streetcar workers who arrived on a chartered steamer—paraded on Pacific and Broadway distributing pamphlets detailing their complaints. Workers were asked to report at 4 a.m., drive a trolley

until 9 a.m., take two hours off without pay, work two more hours, rest again, work from 4 p.m. until 7 p.m., and hold themselves available for the graveyard shift from 11 p.m. to 1 a.m. For this they were paid $3 a day. It took federal intervention for the trolleymen to win better hours.

Inspired by the success of the shipyard workers, the lunch-bucket patrons of the Belt Line rioted on the tideflats and won better waiting conditions. Longshoremen, on threat of a strike that would tie up shipping, won a National Adjustment Commission ruling that gave them, at least temporarily, control of the hiring halls. The government imposed an eight-hour day on the sawmill operators, then extended it to the camps in the woods. Most Tacoma department stores voluntarily adopted the eight-hour day. Telephone operators had to strike for five weeks to win shorter hours and union recognition.

Amid such alarms and diversions, production surged. Trees were felled, lumber was sawed, and the great frames of shipways rose around the rim of the bay. The Todd yards stood on the north side of Hylebos Creek, the

Foundation yards on the south bank. The Wright yard turned out steel freighters while Tacoma Shipyards, partially owned by St. Paul & Tacoma Lumber Company, specialized in wooden vessels.

The first Todd hull, the Cascade-type freighter *Chebaulip,* hit the water only eight months after work started on the shipyard itself. The Foundation yard launched and commissioned the first of 20 wooden schooners ordered by the French government only six months after acquiring the site for the yards, a feat made more remarkable by the fact that the yard was built on land that had been eight feet under water at high tide. (The William D. Tripple Foundation Company, which owned the shipbuilding facility, had an international reputation for laying foundations for skyscrapers.) By November 1918 Tacoma's shipyards employed 14,500 workers, and Tacoma estimated its population at 135,000. But on November 11, Germany surrendered.

Many of the ships on order were completed. The Foundation yard made its last delivery—the *Egalite* to the French government on the first anniversary of the armistice, then towed a

dozen unfinished hulls, for which orders were cancelled, to Minter Creek and burned them. The Todd yards remained active for four years after the war. But peace on the international front marked the end of harmony in the yards.

During the war, with ships urgently needed and labor in short supply, the Federal Fleet Corporation agreed to high wages in return for a pledge of no work stoppages. Employers, their burdens lightened by contracts guaranteeing profits, raised little objection. But with soldiers coming home and ship bottoms in oversupply, labor was abundant and employers were anxious to retrench. The shipyard unions insisted there be no cut in wages. The government had reluctantly allowed West Coast yards to pay above the national average when ships were needed. But in January 1919 when Charles Pietz of the Federal Emergency Trades Council wired the Seattle Metal Trades Association, an employer organization, to warn that if they agreed to union demands their allocation of steel would be cut off, the wire was some-

how delivered to the Metal Trade Union council. Labor was outraged.

The Metal Trades Workers struck the Seattle and Tacoma yards. In Seattle their walkout led to the first general strike in America. It faded away after three days in which all but essential community services were suspended. In Tacoma, as in Seattle, the Central Labor Council called for a general work stoppage, but several key unions refused. The shipyards were shut but the tie-up did not become general. In both cities the result was the same. The workers lost. Wages were cut but the yards could not compete successfully with those in the East, much less those abroad. By 1920 only the Todd yard was still in operation and it was abandoned in 1924.

When the federal census takers made their rounds in 1920 they found 97,432 inhabitants. This was a gain of 60,000 in 20 years, but still disappointingly below boosters' estimates. The city's period of greatest growth was over.

The bucolic Camp Stand By was set up by civilian agencies to provide rest and rehabilitation for doughboys returning from overseas. Marvin D. Boland recorded this tranquil scene on June 20, 1919. (TPL)

109

The forests have long supported Tacoma's existence. (Above) In 1907 lumberjacks still notched a tree with axes to guide the direction of its fall; then, standing on springboards to be clear of undergrowth and be free of the pitch-filled swell of the butt, they teamed to saw through the trunk. (Courtesy, Paul Dorpat); (Top) Before World War I, the work day in the woods was "bird-song to owl hoot," and most meals were gulped in the cookhouse by lamplight. Few camps served meals in the picnic atmosphere recorded by Arthur French in this 1902 photo. (Middle) Conditions in the lumber camps improved dramatically during World War I when the government intervened to enforce an eight-hour day and sanitation. (Courtesy, The Weyerhaeuser Company); (Bottom) When the tree was down, a bucker with an 11-foot saw cut it into sections for easier movement. It took two hours to cut through a tree that had taken nine centuries to mature.

(Top) In the early days, the logs were dragged to water along skid roads by teams of oxen. This photo was taken by U.P. Hadley. (Courtesy, State Capitol Museum); (Middle) By 1890 the steam-powered donkey engine, which didn't have to be fed when it wasn't working, supplied the energy for yarding the logs to salt water or to a logging railroad. Thomas Rutter took this photo. (Courtesy, Ray Frederick, Jr.); (Bottom) By 1922 there were 37 sawmills in Tacoma cutting an average of 4,036,000 feet of lumber every day. Seven local shingle mills had a combined daily capacity of a million shingles. Mills and woodworking plants employed 10,222 men. Thomas Boland took this photograph of the St. Paul and Tacoma Mill pond. (TPL)

VIII

THE BITTER YEARS

Doldrums,

Depression,

Disasters

The 1920s found Tacoma still seeking a suitable nickname. The promoter George Francis Train had popularized "City of Destiny" in 1885. But after 1893 its ringing promise clanked like a lead bell.

During Tacoma's resurgence after the turn of the century, suggested sobriquets included references to industry ("Harbor of Smokestacks"), expansion ("Watch Tacoma Grow"), felicities ("You'll Like Tacoma"), and comparisons ("Philadelphia of the West," "Chicago of the West," "The New New York," and "The Venice of the American Mediterranean"). Real estate developer Allen C. Mason, whose instinct for public relations was not usually so askew, came up with "The American Liverpool." An official of the Wheeler-Osgood door manufacturing plant argued that because of Tacoma's role as gateway to the Mountain it should call itself "The Doorway City." Instead Tacoma decided it was either "The Lumber Capital of the World" or "The Lumber Capital of America."

The claim had merit. St. Paul & Tacoma had rebuilt its mills B and C in 1920 and added Mill D in 1928. Its annual cut remained among the largest in the industry. The Weyerhaeuser Timber Company, which owned more standing timber than any company anywhere, sawed no boards in Tacoma but its vast holdings were administered from the Tacoma building.

The great Japanese earthquake of 1923 stimulated the export of lumber. By 1926 mills on Puget Sound produced almost 58 million board feet of lumber. But the industry was subject to quick fluctuations of production and price. A small operator could still set up a secondhand saw under a leaky roof and turn a short-term profit. High prices led quickly to overproduction and a glut on the market. Even before the Wall Street crash of 1929, the industry was in deep trouble. Too many people were cutting too much lumber without much thought of the future. "To look at the waste around the logger," the veteran Cyrus Walker of Pope and Talbot wrote to a friend, "gives you a weird and dreary feeling."

Shaky though the industry might be, Tacoma was lumber's leading producer. The curve of Commencement Bay was rimmed with a dozen mills; at night the waters reflected the orange glow of the cones of refuse burners that rained ash as well as dollars on the community. An occasional sailing vessel called for lumber but most shipments left aboard diesel-powered freighters. Sometimes half a dozen lumber ships swung at anchor in the

bay, awaiting dock space.

On March 25, 1921, the Pacific Coast Steamship Company's *Edmore* tied up at Pier 1 of the Port of Tacoma, where lumber for Los Angeles was swung aboard by cranes from a line of waiting flatcars. Tacoma at last had a public port facility to compete for cargoes with the Port of Seattle. The proposal to create a countywide port district with an automatic two-mill tax base and the right to issue bonds, which had been defeated twice in 1914, appeared on the ballot again in November 1918. With the help of the longshoremen's union and the *Ledger*, it passed. The voters then approved a $2.5 million bond issue to buy and improve 340 acres lying between the Todd yards and the Puyallup. A year to the day after the first piling was driven, the *Edmore* was loading at Pier 1.

The urge for civic improvements that might broaden Tacoma's economic base remained strong. The Municipal Street Railway, which had been established as a public utility to carry workers to plants on the tideflats, was in 1924 transformed into the Tacoma Municipal Belt Line. Its passenger service was subordinated to that of shunting freight cars to manufacturing plants from the lines of privately owned railroads. The Belt Line claimed title to being "America's shortest railroad, and busiest."

Tacoma City Light, already successful at bringing cheap electricity to the citizenry, expanded so it could offer bargain rates to industry as well. The city bonded itself to develop a hydroelectric plant fed by water from Lake Cushman in Mason County, and strung the world's longest single span of wire— 6,244 feet—across the Narrows as part of the power line to Tacoma.

The Water Division replaced with concrete and steel tubes the 43 miles of wooden-stave pipe that carried water from the Green River; it also sank wells to the aquifer in South Tacoma. Tacoma was able to offer industry electricity at less than a penny a kilowatt hour and water at 2 cents per 100 cubic feet when two million gallons were used daily, 1 1/3 cents when three million or more were used.

Such attractions persuaded the Union Bag and Paper Corporation of New York to buy 26 acres at the tip of the tideflats Boot. There they erected a kraft pulp mill, which eventually was taken over by St. Regis. This was the first of Tacoma's timber-based industries that was devoted not to dividing logs into geometric boards but to breaking them down with chemicals and transforming them into new materials. Tacoma gained a new payroll, an entry to the electrochemical age, and a distinctive aroma.

Always image conscious, the lumber capital launched a new fight to get Congress to decree that the Mountain be called by its Indian name rather than that of Admiral Peter Rainier, whose favor Captain Vancouver had curried in 1792. A bill declaring that it was Mount Tacoma passed the Senate but failed to get out of committee in the House. Rainier it stayed.

Seeking to attract international attention to his home town, John Buffelen, one of the lesser lumber barons, posted a prize of $25,000 for the first aviator to fly nonstop between Tacoma and Tokyo. A barnstorming stunt pilot named Harold Bromley doggedly tried to become the Lindbergh of the Pacific. On his first attempt his monoplane, *City of Tacoma*, crashed on take-off from a ramp at the abandoned race track south of Tacoma. On his last try he got airborne from Tokyo only to turn back after reaching mid-Pacific. Tokyo to Tokyo did not put Tacoma on the map.

The Thirties brought more disappointments and even worse publicity. The beloved

Nine-year-old George Weyer-haeuser, now president of the Weyerhaeuser Company, was abducted while walking home from Lowell School in May 1935. He was released unharmed after a ransom of $200,000 was paid. His kidnappers were later captured. When one of them finished his sentence at McNeil Federal Penitentiary, George found him a job with the company. Courtesy, Tacoma News Tribune

Above left
A few weeks after the stock market crash, winter winds blew in from the north. The cold weather froze streams, reduced the reservoirs, and kilowatt-happy Tacoma faced an unexpected power shortage. The aircraft carrier Lexington *came to the rescue, tying up at the Baker Dock on December 15. The ship cut into City Light's power system and for a critical four weeks helped Tacoma glow. (TPL)*

Tacoma Hotel was destroyed by fire. A slide washed out the open end of the Stadium bowl. Half of the mills closed, never to reopen. Two kidnappings attracted national attention. George Weyerhaeuser, later president of the Weyerhaeuser Company, was abducted as he walked home from Lowell grade school but was released unharmed. Charles Matson, son of a prominent physician, was snatched from the family home and murdered. A crescendo of strikes brought major gains to Tacoma workers but left an impression of an industrial city in travail.

A gleam of promise shone at the end of the dreary decade with the July 1, 1940, dedication of the Tacoma Narrows Bridge. The day was clear and the bridge beautiful—a thin band of concrete more than a mile long, the third longest suspended roadway in the world. Arching across the narrowest part of Puget Sound, it linked Tacoma with the Kitsap Peninsula and opened the city to shoppers previously dependent on Bremerton. Few Tacomans among the dignitaries who spoke at the dedication could resist the phrase, "a dream come true."

In 1932 Elbert Chandler, a civil engineer who operated a toll bridge at White Salmon on the Columbia, organized a Tacoma Narrows Bridge Company which, with the blessing of the county commissioners and the Chamber of Commerce, sought to raise over $3 1/2 mil-

lion, the estimated cost of construction. For openers he asked the Reconstruction Finance Corporation (RFC), an agency created during the Hoover administration, for $3 million. For closers, the RFC said no.

The 1934 state legislature passed a bill permitting counties to build and operate toll bridges. Pierce County at once declared itself

willing. Governor Clarence D. Martin set aside $700,000 in state funds to meet the requirements of the Public Works Administration (PWA), an agency created by the Roosevelt administration, for local participation in projects of public benefit. PWA Administrator Harold Ickes, citing high costs and low potential traffic volume, refused the grant.

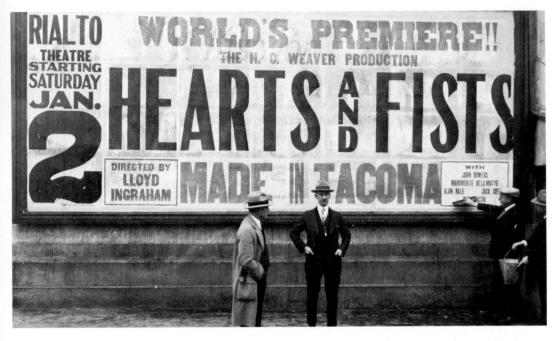

RIALTO THEATRE STARTING SATURDAY JAN. 2 — WORLD'S PREMIERE!! — THE H. C. WEAVER PRODUCTION — HEARTS AND FISTS — MADE IN TACOMA — DIRECTED BY LLOYD INGRAHAM — WITH JOHN BOWERS, MARGUERITE DE LA MOTTE, ALAN HALE, JACK CHES...

In 1925 H.C. Weaver, a Hollywood producer, decided that artificial lighting would make it possible for the movie industry to move out of Hollywood. With several wealthy Tacomans, he acquired a lot at Titlow Beach where he built a 180-by-105-foot barn, "the largest floor space without supporting pillars in the Northwest." His first movie, Hearts and Fists, "a tale of tall trees and big men," was written by Clarence Buddington Kelland, directed by W.S. Van Dyke, and starred the husband and wife team of John Bowers and Marguerite de la Motte. It was shot in 34 days. Weaver Productions went broke in 1929. Photo by Marvin Boland (TPL)

The dream of the few had become the wish of a multitude. Tacoma wanted that bridge. Senator Homer T. Bone of Tacoma endlessly lobbied the PWA in Washington; the Pierce County legislators in Olympia joined their peers from King County, who wanted a bridge over Lake Washington, in successful championship of a bill to create a Washington State Toll Bridge Authority. The state, rather than Pierce County, became the applicant for federal funds. In 1937 the feds gave in. The Public Works Administration granted half of the money needed to build the bridge (by then estimated at over $6 million), and the Reconstruction Finance Agency loaned the rest.

Tacomans watched with delight as concrete was poured on the bluff for cable anchors and into the tiderips of the Narrows to form the piers on which the 502-foot towers were placed. Townsfolk gloried in statistics: 8,702 strands of wire with a total length of 19,823 miles were woven into the pair of cables that looped over the towers and stretched 5,450 feet from anchorage to anchorage. They cheered as sections of roadbed were hoisted up to the bridge deck from barges fighting the tides more than 200 feet below. Because traffic was expected to be light and building costs

were known to be heavy, the roadbed was only two lanes wide. Everyone marveled at the gossamer grace of a structure so long.

When the roadbed was in place and the finishing touches were being put on the bridge, workers remarked that it "acted funny." Sometimes the roadbed seemed to ripple as though someone were pulling on the loose end of a clothesline. F. Bert Farquarson, a professor of civil engineering at the University of Washington, was commissioned to test a model of the bridge in a wind tunnel used for studying airplane structure. He suggested some minor ways to reduce wind resistance but urged a more comprehensive study. Engineers in charge of construction denied there was a problem. Chicken Littles were in short supply. A savings institution put up a billboard on the Tacoma side of the Narrows proclaiming itself as safe as the bridge. An insurance agent had so much confidence that he pocketed the premium on bridge insurance and neglected to forward the policy to headquarters. After the bridge opened many motorists waited for the wind to be "right" before taking a joyride across the oscillating span. It was amusing to watch the car ahead dip from sight, then reappear. Tacomans called their bridge Galloping Gertie.

On the morning of November 7, 1940, Gertie took the venturesome on one last wild ride. The wind was blowing from the southwest, steady at 42 miles an hour. Shortly after nine o'clock Gertie's up-and-down ripple changed to a twisting, corkscrew motion with the north railing rising above the south in some sections while the south was above the north in others. The engineers closed the bridge to traffic.

Leonard Coatsworth, a *News Tribune* editor, was between the towers at the time. He abandoned his car and his cocker spaniel, Tubby (she bit him when he tried to get her out), and crawled to safety on the Tacoma side. Winfield Brown, a student at the College of Puget Sound, risked a walk across the bridge. His worst moment came when the roadbed twisted to such an angle that he seemed to be looking straight down at the white-capped water. Professor Farquarson, who had raced down old Highway 99 from Seattle to film Gertie's death dance, was thrown to the deck when he tried to rescue Tubby but managed to reach safety by keeping to the center strip, where his engineering training told him the torque was least.

Lampposts waved, then snapped off. Chunks of concrete rolled back and forth across the roadbed until they smashed through the guard rails. About 11 o'clock a hundred-foot section of the roadbed plunged into the Narrows, and within minutes two-thirds of the road between the towers had disappeared. Freed of its weight, the towers leaned back toward the nearest shore, their tops bending 12 feet before being arrested by the cables that stretched taut, humming like giant harpstrings.

On the bank, Tacomans wept.

The 1940s were a remake of Tacoma's experience in the First World War, but on a larger scale. Again civic concerns were set aside. Everything focused on the production of lumber, ships, and soldiers.

As with the earlier conflict, the buildup began well before the United States was formally at war. In 1938 the War Department created, out of Fort Lewis property and adjacent land, the first of eight military airfields Congress had authorized three years earlier. The area included a dirt strip and wooden hangar, grandly called Tacoma Field, which served as a hangout for civilian pilots who flew by the seat of their pants. WPA workers, on an appropriation of $61,000, cleared and graded the landing strip to a level suitable for anything the Army Air Corps was flying. The B-17 and B-24 bombers of the 17th Bombardment Group were the first planes to use the field, which was named for William A. McChord, a colonel who died in a 1937 crash. But Mitchell medium bombers, B-25s, became the predominant craft using it during the war. Some of the aircrews that made the first strike on Tokyo— the Doolittle raid from the carrier *Hornet* in April 1942—trained there. By 1943 McChord was the largest bomber training base in America.

After the First World War, Camp Lewis faded away like a proper old soldier. By 1925, when the government auctioned off half the remaining buildings, the camp was accommodating fewer than a thousand officers and men. Tacoma had expected more. The Pierce County commissioners and the *News Tribune* joined in chorus: "Love it or leave it. Give us a payroll or give the land back to the county."

The War Department did not choose to surrender a site it had described as the best training area in the United States. Camp Lewis was bucked up in status to Fort, and a 10-year development program was carried out. In 1937 Fort Lewis hosted the nation's largest military exercise, a maneuver involving 7,500 soldiers of the Third Division. Brigadier General George Catlett Marshall, of later fame, commanded. Also present was Major Mark Clark, newly arrived at the Fort. Major Dwight D. Eisenhower arrived later.

After Hitler invaded Poland in 1939, troop strength at Fort Lewis and McChord jumped in four months from 7,000 to 26,000. With the passage of the draft act in September 1941, a $14 million construction project began at North Fort Lewis. After Pearl Harbor the post found itself handling more than 50,000 trainees at a time. Expansion continued as the Axis powers collapsed; there were German POWs to be housed, and American GIs to be discharged.

The war years witnessed the transformation of the Fort Lewis hospital into a major general hospital, renamed for Colonel Patrick S. Madigan, the "father of Army neuropsychiatry." Madigan specialized in treating the gravely wounded and those whom war had damaged in non-physical ways. By the end of the war, Madigan, McChord, and Fort Lewis had a population half as big as Tacoma.

A month before the war began in Europe, the Todd Shipyard interests joined West Coast companies to incorporate a new entity known as the Seattle-Tacoma Shipbuilding Corporation. Workmen immediately began reconstructing the Todd yard on the tideflats on the same plan as the original but with cranes carrying the loads that in the earlier war were moved along two miles of overhead cable. Within weeks of incorporation Sea-Tac had a contract to build five 6,750-ton diesel motorships. The keel of the *Cape Alava* was laid March 5; on August 3 she was delivered. The other four were commissioned in September.

Sea-Tac's next contract was for six larger cargo ships but while they were on the way, Japan attacked Pearl Harbor. The government ordered that two of the freighters be converted to combat troop carriers (*Frederick Funsten* and *James O'Hara*) and the other four into escort aircraft carriers. The navy called them CVEs, the public knew them as "baby flat-tops," and German Admiral Karl Doenitz was later to credit them with being a primary, perhaps decisive, factor in neutralizing the U-boat threat.

One of the Tacoma-built freighters with built-on flight decks, the *Bogue*, was credited with the first CVE submarine kill. In time the baby flat-tops became more purposefully designed, but of the 56 launched at Sea-Tac, 37 were civilian cargo carriers drafted for combat. Besides the CVEs, the Tacoma yard fabricated five tankers, five seaplane tenders, four destroyer tenders, and three barges.

The rat-tat-tat of riveting ended in July of 1946 when the tender *Isle Royale*, the destroyer *Eversole*, and the baby flat-top *Tinian* were delivered. The Todd interests, having decided to consolidate their Puget Sound shipbuilding, traded their tideflat area to the United States in exchange for government-held land adjoining the Todd repair yard in Seattle. Activity slowed on the waterfront and in the woods as the nation began to demobilize. Yet when the 1950 census was taken, Tacoma's population had grown to 143,673, a gain of over 30 percent, during a single decade.

Inspectors walked the cables to determine the amount of damage three days after the Narrows Bridge collapse, as fog hid the western shore and the waters below. Courtesy, Historic Photograph Collection, University of Washington Libraries

IX

THE OLD AND THE NEW

A

Time Again

to Dream

Traditionally, Tacomans had been inclined to think of their town as a quiet place, unafflicted with the disorders of big cities. Even after the Second World War, it was an article of faith that in Tacoma there were few traffic jams, little racial tension, scant corruption in local government, and no organized crime. True, prostitution was tolerated as bootlegging had been during Prohibition, but Tacoma was a seaport, a lumber town, still almost on the frontier—and, after all, somebody had to accommodate the soldier boys after dark or they'd go to Seattle.

But in the last week of November 1951, Tacoma caught a view of itself from a different perspective. A committee of state legislators under the chairmanship of Senator Albert D. Rosellini (a Seattle attorney who had been born in Tacoma) held public hearings in the Tacoma armory as part of a statewide investigation of organized crime and vice. The sessions were carried live, gavel to gavel, on the only Puget Sound television station. For five days the audience for the cinema verité soap opera grew.

The cast subpoenaed to discuss law non-enforcement included cops of easy virtue and unusual affluence; a city official who accounted for several thousand dollars in currency traced to his safety deposit vault by explaining that he must have won it gambling in Alaska; and the commissioner of public safety, who described himself under oath as a practicing alcoholic and testified to a long evening spent on "an inspection trip" to a three-story brothel operated by a lady known variously as Amanda Truelove and Lil Buckley. Miss Truelove-Buckley, duly sworn, could not describe the man she paid protection dues to because the transaction took place under a red light.

Such revelations hardly qualified Tacoma as a Mafia satrapy, but they were grubby enough to persuade many citizens that the tolerance policy had become intolerable. Blame fell on the commission form of government. Effective in its early years, city government had hardened into an alliance of small fiefdoms with each commissioner seemingly more attentive to guarding his own turf than looking after the community interest. The commissioners were forced by public opinion to authorize the election of freeholders to review the city charter and make recommendations. The recommendation was for total change: adoption of a council-manager charter under which nine part-time council members elected at large would establish policy to be administered by a

George Kahin, counsel for the state Legislative Committee on Vice and Crime in Washington, questions Public Safety Commissioner James T. Kerr about brothels in Tacoma at a hearing in November 1951. Courtesy, Tacoma News Tribune

professional city manager.

The new charter was adopted in November 1952, just a year after the crime hearings. In the ensuing election of the new city council, a professional wrestler, cast as the good-guy type, received the most votes. The entire council, however, laid claim to being the best educated in the nation, averaging six years of college per member. They chose as the first city manager a veteran of the political wars against the Boss Tom Pendergast machine in Kansas City. He in turn chose as chief of police an old-shoe policeman of impeccable rectitude. The days of fun and games were over. The brothels closed and, although streetwalking persisted, Tacoma was dropped from the American Social Hygiene Association's list of venereally dangerous playgrounds. There were no more national magazine exposes of "Seattle's Dirty Back Yard." Instead Tacoma was declared All-America City by the National Municipal League.

The decorum did not extend beyond the city limits. Tacoma's bordellos retreated into the county, sometimes under the guise of massage parlors or topless taverns. With the benign neglect of the sheriff they prospered. One major operator was accused of arranging for fires in his competitors' establishments. Eventually a grand jury returned indictments, a series of petit juries returned guilty verdicts, and a county freeholders' group proposed a restructured county government. The voters endorsed reform. The fires died down, and the

Far left
Two Tacoma-born governors are
shown together in 1968. Albert D.
Rosellini, an old pro who held the
governorship for eight years, shares
a luncheon joke with Dixy Lee Ray,
who won the office in her first
political campaign. She was
defeated in the Democratic primary
four years later. Courtesy,
Tacoma News Tribune

Left
Jack Tanner, a native of Tacoma,
became the first black appointed to
a federal judgeship in Washington
when President Jimmy Carter
named him to succeed U.S. District
Court Judge George Boldt in
January 1978. Courtesy, Tacoma
News Tribune

county, like the city, was ready to concentrate on more orthodox enterprise.

The Port of Tacoma, meanwhile, responded to the economic sag after World War II with the introduction of new personnel rather than a change in the form of government. With the election of Maurice Raymond to the port commission in 1953, the Port moved toward programs of modernizing and expanding facilities, competing aggressively with Seattle for cargo and industry, and cooperating with rather than confronting the longshoremen.

Tibbetts-Abbett-McCarthy-Stratten, an engineering firm, drew up a program for the Port. It centered on extending the Hylebos and Industrial waterways deeper onto the tideflats, thus creating new areas for industrial and distributing enterprises. When the Navy declared its property on the Industrial Waterway to be

surplus, the Port—with a major assist from Senators Warren Magnuson and Henry Jackson—acquired it for the bargain-basement price of $2,100,000. Within six months the Port Industrial Yard, as it was renamed, operated in the black.

Roy L. Perry was brought in to serve as the Port's first executive director. A retired colonel from the Army Corps of Engineers, small, soft-spoken, and elaborately polite, Perry proved to be an innovative administrator, an effective salesman, and a disarming diplomat. He steered the Port through the difficult period of

Sugar Ray Seales of Tacoma, the
only American boxer to win a
medal at the XXth Olympiad in
1972, was honored with a special
day when he returned to town.
Seales turned professional and won
the North American middleweight
championship but was blinded by
ring injuries. Courtesy, Tacoma
News Tribune

adjustment that followed ratification of the coastwide Mechanization and Modernization Contract between the International Longshore Workers Union and the Pacific Maritime Association.

Labor peace prevailed while the massive equipment of the bulk-cargo and container-ship commerce sprouted at the head of the Bay. Giant cranes were imported from Germany to swing containers into and from the vast interiors of the new vessels; equipment was installed that could pick up a boxcar full of wheat and pour its contents, to the last grain, into the elevator; two huge domes mushroomed on the tideflats to hold alumina powder imported from Australia and store it for shipment to the pot-lines of the aluminum plants; and buildings 10 stories high were fabricated and loaded on barges to be towed north through the Bering Sea and the Arctic Ocean to the Prudhoe Bay oil fields.

Cooperation between the Port officials and the work force remained so good during the 1970s that Perry's successor, Richard Dale

Smith, found it appropriate to involve officers of the longshore Local 23 in negotiations with prospective tenants. Most notable was the successful attempt to persuade Totem Ocean Trailer Express (TOTE) to transfer its roll on/roll off container terminal for Alaska shipments from Seattle to Tacoma—a victory especially cherished by old-timers who still fretted about the loss of Alaskan trade to Seat-

tle during the Gold Rush.

While the Port was adding space for industrial development, City Light increased the available power supply. First, the Nisqually was dammed, creating Alder Lake as its reservoir. Then, after protracted battles with sportsmen and conservationists in the legislature and in state and federal courts, Tacoma won the right to build the Mayfield and Mossyrock

dams on the Cowlitz.

Tacoma's position as a distribution center was strengthened by the completion of Interstate 5, which shortened distances north and south, and by the Echo Lake cutoff to Interstate 90, which brought eastern Washington closer. The State Toll Bridge Authority rebuilt the Narrows Bridge, four lanes wide this time, and designed to offer less resistance to the wind. Galloping Gertie's successor has earned the nickname Sturdy Gertie.

For all this firming up of the city's industrial-commercial base, a considerable agenda of problems remained. Access to downtown Tacoma from Interstate 5 was inconvenient and ugly. The air often smelled of pulp mill sulphur and carried smelter arsenic. The bay was freighted with years of industrial waste, and the aquifer was tainted with chemicals of uncertain origin. Indian treaty rights complicated plans for further development of Port industrial land. City Light, made overconfident by many successes, had enmeshed itself in the Washington Public Power Supply

Completed on schedule and within budget, the Tacoma Dome stands beneath crossed searchlights in this photograph taken on April 25, 1983. Even Seattle had to admit the dome surpassed its own. Courtesy, Tacoma News Tribune

125

Right
Ramona Bennett wrested the leadership of the Puyallup Tribal Council from Satiacum, who was later convicted in federal court of racketeering. He was also found guilty of hiring an assassin who shot at Bennett but missed. Satiacum fled to Canada but was captured in 1983. Under Bennett's leadership, the Puyallups focused on educational programs. Courtesy, Tacoma News Tribune

Below
Bob Satiacum, Puyallup Indian (shown with his sons setting nets in the Puyallup), was repeatedly arrested during the 1950s and 1960s for disobeying fishing regulations. He claimed that the State of Washington was misinterpreting the provisions of the 1854 Treaty of Medicine Creek. The United States Supreme Court agreed. A ruling by U.S. District Court Judge George Boldt guaranteed that the Indians could catch up to 50 percent of the salmon and steelhead that passed through their traditional fishing grounds. Courtesy, Tacoma News Tribune.

System's nuclear building program, a fiasco that threatened to erase the long enjoyed advantage of low-cost electric power. Wood stoves became popular as electric heating systems were turned off, and industries threatened to leave with their payrolls.

Perhaps the biggest problem of all was the old-timers' pervasive "Can't Do" attitude. After the economic collapse of 1893, skepticism concerning development proposals was ingrained; sometimes it bordered on paranoia. "In Tacoma," a city official once mourned, "you could be arrested for optimism."

Early in the 1980s the miasma of civic self-doubt began to fade. Fairchild Camera and Instrument announced that a high-tech industrial campus would be located in neighboring Puyallup. The Port—which already claimed to be the 12th largest in the world—lured Sea-Land, the world's largest containerized shipping operation, away from Seattle. The University of Puget Sound moved its law school into the former Rhodes Department Store, bringing new life to downtown. The Old City Hall, after a handsome but unprofitable renovation as a vertical shopping mall, was again transformed into elegant office space. The move was so successful that work began on a similar restoration of the former Northern Pacific Headquarters building across the street.

Tacomans, who had mourned the loss of the Tacoma Hotel to fire and the transformation of the Winthrop Hotel to a retirement home, were cheered as the Sheraton-Tacoma, with its cascade of glass-roofed terraces, rose across from the new Bicentennial Pavilion. A hotel and marina was announced for Old Tacoma, and the Dome Hotel took shape below McKinley Hill. There were new restaurants everywhere and the food was as good as the view.

A group of local investors bought most of the block between Thirteenth and Fifteenth, Pacific to Commerce. It had once been the pride of the city; its buildings from the 1880s caught the attention of engravers. But time had darkened it. In the years after the Second World War, tarted up with false fronts and neon, the vintage structures served as porno parlors and pickup bars. In 1983 a restoration program began to make it worthy of its official status: the Pacific Avenue Historic District.

The urge to preserve, rather than tear down, was strong. The Pantages Theater, built in 1916 as one of the showplaces of Alexander Pantages' vaudeville circuit—but more recent-

ly a dusty echo chamber for movies—was turned into a gleaming recital center for the performing arts.

Four blocks south of the Pantages on Broadway the Cornerstone Development Company, a subsidiary of the Weyerhaeuser Company, was unmodernizing three old buildings in what a University of Washington architecture professor hailed as "a textbook example of adept architectural coordination." With the Pantages, the Sheraton-Tacoma, and Cornerstone renovations as anchors, and the University of Puget Sound Law School building at Eleventh Street, the 20-year-old Broadway Mall gave hope of fulfilling the promise of the early architectural sketches. That promise had faded as a decade of squabbles led to budget cuts and compromises that subordinated grace to concrete.

In the residential districts, where restorations depended more on individual initiative

Above
A man and a woman pause to talk on the ramp that led from Stadium Way to Pacific Avenue. A favorite track for jaywalkers, the shortcut became a part of vanished Tacoma in the 1970s when it was sacrificed to improve access to Schuster Way and the waterfront. Courtesy, Paul Dorpat

Left
The Tacoma Actors Guild has brought professional theater back to Tacoma after an absence of more than half a century. Actress Cheri Sorenson, a graduate of Pacific Lutheran University, is seen here as Blanche DuBois in Tennessee Williams' A Streetcar Named Desire. *Courtesy, Tacoma Actors Guild*

(and a friendly banker), the change was even more impressive. Those ornate wooden mansions that Rudyard Kipling derided in 1889 as "the castlemented, battlemented bosh of the wooden Gothic school" were returned to their Victorian glory. Like the trees their early owners had planted, they looked better in their maturity.

Of all the manifestations of regained confidence, the most conspicuous was the Tacoma Dome. When it was proposed, there were the questions characteristic of any civic project in America: Is it needed? Where should it be built? Who should build it? How should it be decorated? There were also the congenital doubts of those who remembered past disappointments. But this time the project was neither stopped nor stultified by doubt.

When the dome began to rise beside the freeway below McKinley Hill, within a stone's throw of the spot where, 130 years earlier, Nicholas Delin put together his little sawmill, the arched framework looked beautiful. A wooden building seemed right for Tacoma. It remained handsome when coated with plastic and painted. Its charm was not lessened by the fact that it was completed on time and within budget. The dome became a symbol of the city's renewed belief in its future.

A hundred years after the merger of Old Tacoma and New Tacoma, something surprising, and promising, took place. A reporter was sent down from a neighboring city to the north; his city editor had sent him to discover how Tacomans were managing their city's renaissance. Now that's progress.

Cleveland Rockwell of the Coast
and Geodetic Survey painted this
timeless watercolor of Mount
Rainier as seen from Nisqually
Reach in the autumn of 1891, but
the scene is little different from the
one that Peter Puget's party
observed a century and a half
earlier. Courtesy, Collection of
Mrs. Robert Jacroux, Oregon
Historical Society

129

After the construction of the "Mile of Grain Warehouses" in the early 1890s, Tacoma could challenge Portland for supremacy in the export of wheat from the Inland Empire. Courtesy, Lane Morgan

Top
A few of the old buildings from the Hudson's Bay Company era remained standing at Fort Nisqually into the 20th century. (TPL)

Above
The stump of a giant cedar was converted into a bandstand near the ponds in Wright Park. The stump supported concerts and speeches until it was destroyed by fire in the 1930s. (TPL)

The roadway from the Northern Pacific dock to Pacific Avenue was still considered "The Gateway to Tacoma" in the early years of the 1900s. Half Moon Bay had been filled in, and the "Mile of Grain Warehouses" stood between the city and salt water.

Below
During the heyday of public transportation at the turn of the century, streetcars ran to Point Defiance every 15 minutes, and boats left the point on the hour for the small towns on the southern sound.

Streetcars and horse-drawn floats move north along Pacific Avenue toward Ninth Street in this 1905 postcard.

Right
The Old City Hall and the Northern Pacific headquarters building loom over Firemen's Park. The viaduct that connects with the waterfront Schuster Parkway can be seen at bottom right. Courtesy, Tacoma Chamber of Commerce

Facing page near left
The campanile tower, a separate building that was integrated into the Old City Hall, remains a Tacoma landmark, although skyscrapers now overshadow it. Courtesy, City of Tacoma Community Development

Facing page top right
The Washington State Historical Society Museum was built on a bluff overlooking Commencement Bay in 1911 and enlarged during the 1970s. The museum contains a wide range of local history, from Indian artifacts to recent industry. (WSHS)

Facing page bottom right
The only known collection of Salish Indian prayer boards is on exhibit in the Washington State Historical Society Museum. (WSHS)

Right
The Seymour Conservatory, built in 1907 as a donation from a former mayor and recently restored to its original elegance, has been placed on the National Register of Historic Places. Courtesy, City of Tacoma Community Development

133

Above
The Northwest Trek on the road to
Mount Rainier preserves native
animals in their natural habitat
without cages. Courtesy, Tacoma
Chamber of Commerce

Above right
The bucolic beauty of the Puyallup
Valley sets off the rustic charm of
these old wooden barns.
Photograph by Mary Randlett

Facing page bottom
Red tulips—with a few brave
yellow renegades—cast their glory
across the floor of the Puyallup
Valley, Photograph by Mary
Randlett

The Tacoma Land Company
donated the 27 acres of Wright
Park to the city. The park is named
after Charles B. Wright, a former
president of the company. The
park's pond, fed by a natural
stream, has long been a favorite of
ducks, swans, and midnight skinny-
dippers. Courtesy, Tacoma
Chamber of Commerce

The University of Puget Sound
moved to its present campus in the
north end of Tacoma in 1923.
Jones Hall was the first structure to
rise on the new site. Courtesy,
Tacoma Chamber of Commerce

Park Place, a part of the old
Fireman's Park, provides a spot of
green in downtown Tacoma. The
tower of the Northern Pacific headquarters building, now remodeled
into offices, can be seen to the left.
Courtesy, Tacoma Chamber of
Commerce

Yellow daffodils surround this quaint old house in the Puyallup Valley. Photograph by Mary Randlett

The reconstruction of the downtown area has been aided by renovation in residential districts. These restored row houses are on south J Street near Seventh. Courtesy, City of Tacoma Community Development

Tugboats ply Tacoma's harbor in their dual role of draft horse and sheep dog. Photograph by Gerry Davies, Port of Tacoma

Near right
Although a bit cool for swimming, the Sound invites sailors onto its sheltered waters all year. Courtesy, Tacoma Chamber of Commerce

Far right
Men still tread the waters of Tacoma Harbor on logs from Washington forests in this photo by Nan Koon. Courtesy, Port of Tacoma

Tacoma's domes in the main terminal complex were built in the 1960s to store alumina imported mainly from Australia. The larger dome holds 100,000 short tons and the small dome holds 50,000 short tons. Courtesy, Port of Tacoma

The primary colors and oblong shapes of these freight containers give the effect of a Mondrian painting. Photograph by Rod Koon, Port of Tacoma

The Pioneer Farm shows children how the area's inhabitants lived in the days before electricity and central heating. Courtesy, Tacoma Chamber of Commerce

Steilacoom, the oldest town in Pierce County, has many houses over a century old. This one, near the waterfront, has been converted into a restaurant. Courtesy, Tacoma Chamber of Commerce

The Western Washington Fair, held every September in Puyallup, is a Puget Sound tradition. Courtesy, Tacoma Chamber of Commerce

Owen's Beach, on the Five Mile Drive around Point Defiance, is Tacoma's favorite spot for a picnic by the bay. Courtesy, Tacoma Chamber of Commerce

During the restoration of the Pantages Theatre, the architects discovered much decorative detail work that had been boarded, plastered, or painted over. Courtesy, Tacoma Chamber of Commerce

Facing page bottom left
The granary at Fort Nisqually, the oldest structure in Washington, can be seen here through the gates of the renovated fort at Point Defiance. Courtesy, Tacoma Chamber of Commerce

The American Savings Bank and the relandscaped Fireman's Park have changed the face of downtown Tacoma as it appears from the bay. Courtesy, Tacoma Chamber of Commerce

Two orphaned walrus babies, rescued from Alaskan waters, are favorites of the visitors to the Point Defiance Zoo. Courtesy, Metropolitan Park District

143

X

PARTNERS IN PROGRESS

by Rita Happy

Similar to a kaleidoscope, where individual pieces fit together to create a complete pattern that varies with every turn, the businesses and industries of Tacoma are parts contributing to the whole.

The patterns shift to fit the community's needs—the beginning years, the burgeoning of a boisterous young city, the expanding and developing stages, the growing into national and international commerce.

Initiating the changing phases, adventurers come to build a new town. They need lumber for homes, and a forestry industry evolves. The railroad selects a terminus, and promoters spring into activity. Markets, goods, and services expand; merchants, machinists, transportation workers, bankers, loggers, fishermen, farmers, and medical experts all find an opportunity to serve.

Herbert Hunt's *History of Tacoma* records that in 1883 the young town included 19 doctors and 30 lawyers, as well as 11 dry-goods houses; 19 grocery stores; 4 each of drugstores, bakeries, furniture stores, boot and shoe stores, tailors, and blacksmiths; 2 livery stables; 5 barber shops; 11 hotels; 12 restaurants; 18 saloons; 3 wholesale liquor houses; 6 laundries; and an undertaker.

Its 4,000 citizens were just beginning to add certain refinements to their lives. Horses towed carriages over the muddy streets during rainy seasons, and there were plank-constructed walkways for pedestrians. Also, quoting a recent anniversary article in *The News Tribune,* "one of the important issues of the year was the installation of 16 oil streetlamps and the hiring of a lamplighter at $70 a month."

The foresight of R.F. Radebaugh, editor of the pioneer Tacoma *Daily Ledger* who wrote, ". . . there is good reason to believe that out-siders . . . may, with confidence, invest their money here," proved perspicacious. A railroad city that attracted the money of eastern investors, Tacoma was selected as the terminus; this opened the door for other industries that needed or wanted rail facilities. Promoters called it the "City of Destiny," and they believed their prophecy would come true.

Not everyone succeeded, of course. Recessions wiped out dozens of businesses. The survivors learned to adapt, to alter to meet the challenges of a changing society.

Tacoma's pattern was influenced by nature from the beginning. The fine harbor, great forests, fish and wildlife, mineral resources, and temperate climate provided a versatility and bounty unequaled in most parts of the country. The port shipped lumber, coal, and wheat—an impressive combination. Many local industries flourished because they provided the tools, materials, and labor to develop the area's resources.

Among the enterprises that opened to meet a regional need, a surprising number outgrew their local connections. The first surge took goods to the Orient, and many firms now supply worldwide markets.

The Tacoma business kaleidoscope reflects a healthy optimism—in spite of a long economic recession. There is an obvious determination to produce high-quality goods or offer first-class services, a counterpart of an intense commitment to the community and its people.

A variety of organizations proudly share their stories here—patterns in words and photographs that mesh and complement one another to form the vivid kaleidoscope of Tacoma's partners in progress.

Tacoma shines across the water on a summer evening in this photograph by Richard Frederick.

PUGET SOUND NATIONAL BANK

J.B. Sutton was one of the original founders and first president of Puget Sound Savings Bank, a pioneer institution that became an important Tacoma-area bank.

The year was 1890 and Tacoma was in the midst of a population boom. Washington had just achieved statehood; businessmen, builders, and buyers were flocking to Tacoma to take advantage of the newly completed east-west rail link to Puget Sound. From a population of 1,098 in 1880, Tacoma had grown to 36,000 by 1890.

A perfect time and place for opening a bank? A Michigan salesman named J.B. Sutton thought so. He was so sure, in fact, that he persuaded D.S. Garlick and George Tibbits to leave their business interests in Michigan to explore the banking possibilities in the vast, unknown Pacific Northwest.

The trio sought financial backing in Tacoma and finally obtained the support of General J.W. Sprague and H.F. Garretson, two prominent Tacoma businessmen of the time. On June 10, 1890, their dream was realized: Puget Sound Savings Bank was born.

The bank opened at 2422 Pacific Avenue with $50,000 in capital and the grand sum of $838.12 in deposits, the latter provided by five savers who were assured by *The Tacoma Daily Ledger* that the bank's 7,000-pound, chilled-steel vault would "resist the efforts of the enterprising safecracker and his diamond-pointed drill."

As it turned out, safecrackers would not be a problem for the fledgling bank — but a faltering economy would. A financial panic that began to sweep the country in 1891 closed 14 of 21 Tacoma banks within two years. Due to some savvy financial leadership, however, Puget Sound Savings did not become one of the victims. In fact, by 1907, three years after J.B. Sutton died and D.S. Garlick became president, the bank's deposits had swelled to a total of $210,000. Another financial panic tested the institution in the following years, but once again the bank survived beautifully: By 1915 deposits amounted to $838,000.

Through this rocky period the bank relocated three times, but in 1920 it began negotiating for purchase of the National Realty Building, a splendid structure completed in 1912 as the tallest office building west of the Missouri River. The 1119 Pacific Avenue address eventually became the Puget Sound Bank Building.

The bank also changed its name a few times during the early years of its existence, to Puget Sound State Bank and then to Puget Sound Bank and Trust Company. In 1923 the bank was nationalized as The Puget Sound National Bank of Tacoma — by this time an institution with deposits of three million dollars.

But hard times were again just around the corner. In 1933, after the bank-closure order issued by President Roosevelt, the bank's officers refused to lay off employees; instead, the entire staff took salary reductions and dug in, waiting for the end of the Depression. By the end of the decade the struggle paid off: The bank rallied into a spectacular era of growth. Deposits reached $10 million in 1941,

In 1933 bank officers signed clearinghouse certificates during President Roosevelt's "bank holiday" in case they needed to circulate the substitute currency. Banks reopened, and the certificates were not needed.

and a year later the bank was even able to remodel its headquarters.

The 1950s were a stable period for PSNB, and the bank began an expansion program. The K Street branch opened in 1951, and the Lincoln branch (acquired with the purchase of the Lincoln Bank in 1934) moved to new quarters at 37th and G streets. Five other branches opened during the busy 1950s: Lakewood Center, the 84th and Pacific Avenue branch, the Narrows branch, Midway on the Seattle-Tacoma Highway, and the Fife branch.

Besides being one of the first banks in the area to start full branch-banking services, PSNB has also been an innovator in other customer services. In 1942 the institution was the first commercial bank on the Pacific Coast to use machines for checking-account deposits. In 1963 modern magnetic-ink character machines were installed, and "Quickbank," a system of automated teller machines, was

Puget Sound Savings Bank opened on June 10, 1890, at 2422 Pacific Avenue.

introduced in the 1970s. In January 1981 Puget Sound completed a new operations center with sophisticated equipment to streamline operations. A new "on-line teller system" incorporates terminals located at all teller stations to post customer transactions and update balances instantly.

Creative advertising campaigns traditionally have accompanied the new services. The "hometown bank" campaign won national awards in the 1960s and was imitated by banks all over America. Tacomans will remember dashing "Ace Busby" presiding at bank openings, grinning from billboards, and lettering bank slogans in skywriting swoops over Puget Sound communities in the 1970s. The *Wizard of Oz* Tin Man came to town in the 1980s, searching for a bank "with a heart." He found it at the Puget Sound National Bank.

Today Puget Sound is the largest bank headquartered in Pierce County, the sixth largest in the state, and one of the 200 largest commercial banks in the United States. A subsidiary of Puget Sound

In 1920 bank officials negotiated to buy the splendid National Realty Building, completed in 1912 as the highest office building west of the Missouri.

Bancorp, the bank has assets of approximately one billion dollars. Over the years growth has come through mergers and an expanding branch system, which now totals more than 50 branches serving not only Pierce County but also four surrounding counties.

PSNB's presidents, from Sutton and Garlick through C.A. Brower, Homer N. Tinker, Forbes P. Haskell, Reno Odlin, A.E. Saunders, and W.W. Philip, have believed in strong commitment to and involvement in the city of Tacoma. Over its 90-year history, the bank has joined actively with the city to stimulate the entire area's economic vitality and cultural resources. Many years separate today's Puget Sound National Bank from the tiny, struggling Puget Sound Savings of the 1890s, but its continuing strong commitment to Tacoma provides a sturdy bridge to the bank's past—and its future.

NALLEY'S FINE FOODS

Thirteen-year-old Marko Narancic arrived in New York from Croatia in 1903. He had 15 cents in his pocket, and he couldn't speak a word of English.

First employed as a water boy in a West Virginia steel mill, where he learned a little English, the teenager changed his name to Marcus Nalley. When he had saved enough money, he traveled to Montana where his older brothers had settled.

A Jewish meatpacker in Butte gave the youngster his first exposure to the world of business and "the first real human kindness I had known since coming to America." But young Nalley, restless and ambitious, returned to the East to find work in Chicago's large Kaiserhof Hotel—where he progressed from kitchen flunky to pantry boy to fry cook. He liked to prepare food that pleased the public, and decided this was a good career opportunity.

The young cook did not mind the hard work—10 to 12 hours a day, seven days a week. But when the hotel owners toured the kitchen on Christmas morning without even greeting their employees, he quit—taking with him knowledge, ambition, and a resolve to treat his fellow men as equals.

Marcus Nalley, founder of Nalley's Fine Foods in Tacoma, courageously led the firm from a small kitchen facility to an international corporation.

In 1913 Nalley became chef on the first "Olympian" of the Milwaukee Railroad running between Chicago and Tacoma. He liked the Pacific Northwest and left the railroad to work in Tacoma. His last job as chef was at the Bonneville Hotel, where he became a specialist in preparing and serving a new potato delicacy, the "Saratoga chip."

Deciding to start his own business and produce potato chips, Nalley carefully sliced 50 pounds of potatoes in his small kitchen. He fried them in cooking oil, added salt, packed the slices in paper bags, and left his house to peddle the product from a 15-cent market basket.

Merchants were skeptical about the new product. Potato chips were served only by exclusive hotels, and many people didn't know what they were. Refusing to accept defeat, the young businessman countered, "I'll guarantee them. If they don't sell, I'll buy them back from you."

Soon the public began to buy his chips, and he rented a $5-a-month storeroom behind his apartment—equipping his operation with a stove, sink, and table. It was 1918.

Nalley added other products to expand his line, moved into a storefront, and soon expanded his business to all of the building's store space and to adjoining storage structures.

While the former chef knew how to prepare appetizing foods, packaging them for sale was a problem. He hired a chemist and improved production techniques; losses turned into profits.

In 1928 the business was incorporated and became known as Nalley's, Inc. Nalley helped design a new building on Puyallup Avenue, which was the "pride of Tacoma, the model of the industry," according to a local historian.

Although sales fell during the Depression, Nalley arranged with his creditors to continue business and by the end of the 1930s his debts were paid. " 'This is only the beginning' was his favorite comment during all this trying period," L. Evert Landon, a longtime employee and second president of the company, related. "What more inspiring motto could have been composed? He furnished leadership to his subordinates to seek new products, new methods of manufacture, and new ways of doing business so that his flourishing enterprise might keep up with, or step ahead of, competitors. Better still, he delegated the authority and provided the opportunity to try new things."

A tract of land that became known as "Nalley Valley" was purchased in 1940. A pickle plant and a meat products

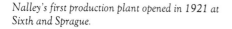

Nalley's first production plant opened in 1921 at Sixth and Sprague.

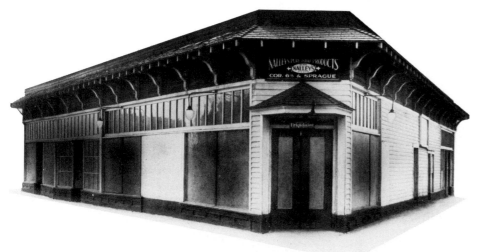

cannery were erected there first; after World War II structures were built for potato chip production and a sales warehouse.

In 1953 the Puyallup Avenue building was sold to the Salvation Army, and operations were consolidated with other company activities at Nalley Valley on South 35th Street. Two years later the founder completed full transfer of his ownership to members of the organization, a program he had initiated in 1930.

During the next decade the firm began to acquire small family-owned businesses within its market area. These included IXL of San Leandro, XLNT Food Company and Venus Foods of Los Angeles, Red Seal Potato Chip Company of Denver, and King's Potato Chip Company of Tulsa. All but IXL of San Leandro were later divested.

The corporation became a division of a multibillion-dollar international conglomerate, the New York-based W.R. Grace Company, in 1966. The following nine years brought substantial volume growth. Then in 1975 Nalley's became a division of Curtice-Burns, Inc., of Rochester, New York. A unique concept in the Curtice-Burns and Nalley's operation is that of having growers who produce the raw materials participate as

Nalley painted his motto, "If it's Nalley's, it's good," on his 1924 fleet of delivery trucks.

partners in ownership of the business.

Featuring a wide range of products, including a variety of chips, pickles, mayonnaise, syrup, salad dressings, chili, and soups, Nalley's has a food-service division that supplies restaurants, schools, hospitals, military bases, and caterers. The firm continues to incorporate effective advertising techniques, with both radio and television commercials advocating

Marcus Nalley's own slogan, "If it's Nalley's, it's good."

Modern employees have matched the spirit of sacrifice, cooperation, and hard work of the pioneer industry workers to bring Nalley's to new sales and profit records, culminating in 1982 with sales of $128.2 million.

Nalley Valley land was purchased in 1940, and the first structures housed a pickle plant and a potato chip operation. This photo shows Nalley's operations today.

GORDON, THOMAS, HONEYWELL, MALANCA, PETERSON & O'HERN

In the early days of Washington statehood, three young attorneys—Michigan native Elmer M. Hayden and Illinois natives Joseph H. Gordon and Scott Z. Henderson—opened law offices in the small mill- and port-town of Tacoma.

The men emerged as community

elected president of the Tacoma Bar Association. Henderson also served as president of the state bar association, and was recognized as a peerless trial lawyer.

Early associates of the group included J.T.S. Lyle from Wisconsin, who in 1917 was appointed special attorney to represent Pierce County in condemnation

federal district court judge, presided over some of the state's most controversial cases during his quarter-century on the bench. Floyd V. Hicks served as state supreme court justice as well as U.S. congressman. William N. Goodwin was named U.S. attorney for western Washington and then federal district court judge.

Scott Z. Henderson, who came to Tacoma from Illinois, gained a reputation as a peerless trial lawyer.

Joseph H. Gordon, who conducted a successful general practice, served on the first board of governors of the Washington State Bar Association.

Elmer M. Hayden, an expert in corporate law, came to Tacoma in 1894.

leaders and became involved in events that helped shape the future of Tacoma and the Puget Sound area. Their offices evolved through a series of mergers into a multi-service law firm known as Gordon, Thomas, Honeywell, Malanca, Peterson & O'Hern.

The careers of these pioneer lawyers kept pace with the growth of the young city. Hayden, well known for his expertise in corporate law, served as president of the Washington State Bar Association before his death in 1938. Gordon, who conducted a successful general practice, was a member of the first board of governors of the organization and was

proceedings for the 65,000 acres upon which Fort Lewis was established; Frederick G. Remann, who served as Pierce County prosecuting attorney and then as superior court judge for 23 years until his death; Rhodes scholar Frederic D. Metzger, a specialist in corporate law and a president of the state bar association; and Lindsey L. Thomson (whose father arrived in 1853 and served in the first territorial legislature), a state attorney general in the years following World War I.

Successors continued in the forefront of the legal profession. George H. Boldt,

The law firm—which ranks among the largest in the state—maintains offices in Tacoma on the top floors of First Interstate Plaza, and in Seattle at One Union Square. Its attorneys handle a broad range of matters in labor, land use, real estate, mortgage banking, securities, family, criminal, and immigration law. Trial work represents a significant portion of the service. Regular corporate work includes securities litigation, contract disputes, and other forms of business litigation.

Tools and methods have changed since Hayden, Gordon, and Henderson began practice, but the goal of the organization remains the same: to provide competent legal services to a diversified clientele.

BROWN & HALEY

Brown & Haley is the oldest, largest candy company in the Tacoma area and one of the oldest and largest in the United States. It hasn't always been.

In pioneer Tacoma sweets were made only in small "candy kitchen" retail shops. By 1895 Wiegel Candy Company emerged as the leading general-line manufacturing wholesaler of confections to nonproducing retailers. In 1905 Tacoma Biscuit and Candy Company began making a wide range of candy under the brand name "Everybody's."

Wiegel Candy Company and Tacoma Biscuit and Candy Company dominated confectionery wholesaling in Tacoma until the 1920s, when a host of competitors opened plants in the area. Newcomers included Brown & Haley, Hamilton, Johnson, Marcoe & Sons, Humphries, Mack's, and Dorette.

Most candymakers learned their craft in Wiegel's and Tacoma Biscuit's kitchens or in the kitchens of Tacoma's many retail confectionery and ice cream shops— places such as The Pheasant, Paradise Confectionery, The Cave, Johnson Confectionery, Josslyn's, The Chocolate

Harry L. Brown (left), general manager and head of manufacturing, and Jonathan Clifford Haley (right), president and chief salesman of Brown & Haley when it originated in 1914.

Fred T. Haley has been president and chairman of the board of Brown & Haley since 1954.

Shop, and the famous Muehlenbruch's. Muehlenbruch's, owned by a German family, was boycotted out of business in 1917-1918 after the United States entered World War I.

In 1902 Harry Brown began working at Josslyn's, where he stayed until he learned enough to open his own retail candy shop on Broadway in 1907. His friendship with Jonathan Clifford Haley turned into a business partnership when J.C. began selling Harry's "Oriole Chocolates." Haley was selling Schilling spices, but he offered the chocolates to his clients throughout the south Puget Sound area.

By 1914 the partnership became formal with the organization of Brown & Haley. Haley was president and chief salesman, and Brown was general manager, chief candy formulator, and head of manufacturing.

John D. Hamilton, Haley's brother-in-law, learned candymaking as plant superintendent at Brown & Haley. He started Hamilton Candy Company in 1923 and continued until 1970.

Humphries was a Tacoma candy bar house that flourished and faded in the 1920s. Wiegel Candy Company had a fire from which it never recovered, and closed its doors in 1936. In 1931 Nabisco bought out Tacoma Biscuit, and the firm still markets Tacoma Biscuit's "Honey Maid Grahams."

Brown & Haley owes its success to several factors—loyal and hard-working employees, a commitment to producing candy of the highest quality, and the remarkably happy circumstance that turned Brown's candymaking talents in 1923 to creating a unique "English toffee" later given the brand name ALMOND ROCA®.

The recipe for ALMOND ROCA® Buttercrunch calls for a great deal of fresh butter, and at first had a shelf life problem. ALMOND ROCA® Buttercrunch was turning rancid before people could buy and eat it. The firm discovered a solution in 1927, and the company believes that ALMOND ROCA® Buttercrunch was the first candy in the world to be put in vacuum-sealed tins.

This famous Tacoma product has developed into one of the largest selling gift confections in the United States. It is marketed in 30 countries on six continents.

MULTICARE MEDICAL CENTER

Bishop John A. Paddock founded the Fannie C. Paddock Memorial Hospital in 1882 to honor his wife, who died before she could see her dream fulfilled.

Mary Bridge Children's Hospital, 1955.

As the Tacoma community grows, three area hospitals are answering the need to provide the best health care in the most cost-effective manner by joining forces under a consolidated banner. Each hospital, in its uniqueness, is part of the whole program—with health services reaching out into the southwest Washington region.

TACOMA GENERAL HOSPITAL

In 1880 Tacoma had a population of 1,098 and little available medical help. Epidemics of smallpox, malaria, pneumonia, and typhoid fever wracked the railroad men, loggers, and mill workers who struggled to build the new city.

A clergyman in New York City, John Adams Paddock, was appointed the first Protestant Episcopal bishop of Washington Territory. When his wife Frances learned of the desperate need for a hospital in Tacoma, she went to work to raise the needed funds and gather equipment to carry to the West. However, falling ill during the last lap of the trip, Mrs. Paddock died on April 29, 1881.

Bishop Paddock continued his wife's dream, and in 1882 established the Fannie C. Paddock Memorial Hospital in a former

dance hall on Tacoma Avenue and Starr Street. A larger memorial hospital opened in 1889 in a four-story house on J Street. The new K Street hospital was built in 1915 and "Tacoma General Hospital" became part of the official name.

Tacoma General Hospital celebrated its centennial in 1982. An expansion that year provided a patient-care tower for medical, surgical, and trauma patients and a new adult 24-hour emergency department, increasing bed facilities to 412.

The Marian Cheney Olrogg Regional Center, providing comprehensive services for cancer patients and their families, uses the scanning capabilities of nuclear medicine and diagnostic radiology and radiation therapy services of the Tacoma Radiation Center. Maternal and child care facilities have extended into a new wing, including areas for neonatal intensive care for the critically ill newborn and perinatal care for the at-risk pregnant mother. Tacoma General goes into its second century of service with hope for the future.

MARY BRIDGE CHILDREN'S HEALTH CENTER

With the combined resources of the estate of Dr. A.W. Bridge, longtime area physician, and the Tacoma Orthopedic Association, Mary Bridge Hospital was opened on L Street in 1955. The program

at Mary Bridge focuses on four major areas: hospital services, rehabilitation, specialty support services, and community health care services. Now known as Mary Bridge Children's Health Center, it continues to provide the children of the region with complete health care in a loving and caring manner.

THE DOCTORS HOSPITAL OF TACOMA

Doctors Hospital, a facility operated by the Pierce County Medical Bureau, was opened in 1946. Eleven years later several Tacoma physicians purchased the hospital from the bureau and operated it as a private facility. With private donations and a private bank loan, a new hospital was built on South Fawcett Avenue and opened in 1967. It serves a growing aging population and large downtown business and residential community. The institution has assumed a leadership role in eye care, and has established a modern same-day surgery program as part of a non-profit consolidated health care system.

These three hospitals serve the ever-changing diversified health needs of the Tacoma community with the most sophisticated medical techniques, over 2,000 skilled staff members, and a forward-looking consolidated management team.

THE TACOMA NEWS TRIBUNE

"An Independent Journal Devoted to the Development of Washington Territory."

That is what R.F. Radebaugh and H.C. Patrick promised when they arrived from California by sailing vessel to publish the first edition of *The Tacoma Ledger,* dated April 21, 1880. They set all the type by hand, letter by letter, and printed the paper on a hand-operated press.

In 1885 The Tacoma News, *located at 12th and Pacific Avenue, chronicled the growth of a bustling new city.*

But the most important date to *The Tacoma News Tribune* is April 7, 1883, the day *The Tacoma Daily Ledger* began daily publication. The year 1883 has additional importance, for that September 25 *The Tacoma Daily News* made its entrance into the newspaper field.

The *News* was started by Patrick, who had sold his interest in the morning *Ledger* to start the afternoon *News.* The *Ledger* took the lead in circulation, advertising, and prestige. Patrick became discouraged and sold his paper in 1885. By 1890 Radebaugh found himself in financial straits because of real estate investments, and sold a half-interest in his paper to Nelson Bennett. In 1892 he sold the remaining half.

Although subsequent years brought the linotype mechanical typesetting machine to Tacoma and improvement of editorial content, financial difficulties persisted.

After a series of investments and sales, both papers became the property of Sidney A. (Sam) Perkins.

In 1908 the flood of optimism motivated Radebaugh, a healthy 62-year-old, to launch another Tacoma daily. Publication of the *Tacoma Daily Tribune* began June 12, 1908; but once again Radebaugh came to the end of his resources and he sold the paper to Richard Roediger—who had just returned from the Klondike and Alaska with $40,000. The *Tribune* moved into a new building on St. Helens Avenue, but new management could not get the paper into the black.

At that point John S. Baker, president of a trust company and one of the paper's principal creditors, traveled to Cleveland to urge his cousin, a publisher, to buy the Tacoma paper.

Elbert H. Baker published the Cleveland *Plain Dealer,* one of the foremost newspapers of the country. His son, Frank S.—also a publisher—came to Tacoma, decided the city offered fine opportunities, and convinced his father to assist in the purchase. The two acquired the paper and formed the Tribune Publishing Company, printing the first issue October 26, 1912. In only six years the *Tribune* became so dominant that it absorbed the *News* and the *Ledger* to become the major daily newspaper in the city.

Frank Baker completed more than 47 years as publisher before his death in 1960. The majority ownership in *The News Tribune* went to his three children, son Elbert H. Baker II and daughters Mrs. George F. (Mary) Russell and Mrs. Bruce (Betty) Kelly.

From 1960 until 1969 his son-in-law, George F. Russell, longtime general manager of *The News Tribune,* continued as president and general manager. Elbert Baker succeeded his father as publisher and, in 1973, led 500 employees in welcoming tour groups to a new multi-million-dollar offset printing plant at 1950 South State Street.

Elbert Baker II continues his father's criteria that *The News Tribune* be fair, that editors present conflicting views adequately, and that the paper be alert in defending the rights of the people. That is a publishing philosophy the pioneer newspapermen would approve.

In 1973 The News Tribune *moved into this multimillion-dollar offset printing plant, located at 1950 South State Street.*

NORTH STAR GLOVE CO.

Tacoma's North Star Glove Co.—one of the foremost glove manufacturers in the United States—was founded in 1910 by an enterprising Swedish immigrant named Albert Wekell.

When his family immigrated to the Pacific Northwest, the young man joined the Gold Rush to Alaska but failed to strike it rich. He returned to his new home and formed a partnership with his brother-in-law, T.O. Johnson, bought two sewing machines and the name "North Star," and began to manufacture various styles of canvas gloves. Tacoma was a workingman's town primarily comprised of loggers, mill workers, fishermen, and construction workers who needed sturdy gloves; the business grew steadily.

In the 1920s Albert's brother, Charles, replaced Johnson in the firm. The brothers moved their factory from Tacoma Avenue to larger quarters at South 24th and Pacific Avenue, employing 35 people to make both canvas and leather gloves.

During the Depression years of the 1930s, workers relied upon quality products. Consequently, North Star survived that lean period and Charles' sons, Shirley and Cliff, joined the family operation on a part-time basis while attending high school. Shirley, who sought ways to modernize production, quickly became a sparkplug for the company.

World War II brought an increased demand for gloves, prompting Shirley to move to Orting and to open another plant. Throughout the 1950s the firm continued to run both facilities at full production, with 80 workers turning out 250 styles of gloves.

Shirley bought his uncle Albert's share of the business in 1960, inheriting full control the following year when his father died at age 83. By then his sons, Tom and Rob, were associated with the organization.

In 1965 the Wekells purchased Oregon Glove Company of Salem, and obtained the Granet line of coated and dipped gloves. Later investments included Universal Rubber Company, manufacturer of waterproof gloves; Western Glove Company, added in Tacoma to handle hides, leather, and retail sales; and Brown Enterprises, producer of welder and lined gloves, which was incorporated into the main factory at 2916 South Steele when additional warehouse space was opened.

The corporation—now fabricating more than 350 styles and sizes to meet a wide range of industrial and personal needs—distributes to wholesalers and to industry. While its principal market is in the western states, highly specialized gloves are sold throughout the nation and overseas.

North Star specializes in heavy-weight gloves that "most of our competitors won't manufacture," says Rob Wekell, president and sales manager of the family firm that now employs fourth-generation family members.

Albert Wekell, left, began manufacturing gloves in 1910. His brother, Charles, joined the firm in the 1920s and together they supervised the operation for almost 50 years.

North Star employees display some of the 350 styles and sizes of gloves they manufacture in one of the nation's top 10 glove-making operations.

Albert Wekell (shown here) and his brother-in-law, T.O. Johnson, bought two sewing machines and the brand name "North Star" and began manufacturing gloves at 1349 Tacoma Avenue.

STANDARD PAPER COMPANY

Paper products were offered to pioneer Tacoma residents at Richmond and Stoppenbach's store on Dock Street. That small firm evolved into the H.N. Richmond Paper Company by 1896. Richmond sold his interest in the business in 1909, and the enterprise was reorganized as Standard Paper Company.

Officers of the new organization included Roy E. Davison, president and treasurer; Frank A. Wilhelmi, vice-president; and Adolph Schantz, secretary. Printing, wrapping, and building paper and a full line of stationery and other papers were offered for sale at the store at 1728 Pacific Avenue. Eight traveling salesmen represented the firm throughout Washington, east to the Columbia River, south "as far as freight rates will justify," and into the territory of Alaska.

Adolph Schantz had emigrated from Switzerland in 1904 and began working for the paper company the following year. In 1921 he bought an interest in the firm and became secretary. G.W. Paul, a longtime employee who had worked as manager of the printing paper department, became the company's fourth partner in 1928.

In the early 1930s Standard Paper Company's partners included (from left) Adolph Schantz, Roy E. Davison, Frank A. Wilhelmi, and G.W. Paul. The man second from left was a prominent customer.

In 1931 Standard Paper Company purchased a site at 1950 Pacific Avenue, the location of the old West Coast Wagon Works. The firm moved into the building in 1934 and remained there until relocating to 3701 East 20th Street, adjacent to Interstate 5, in 1969. The new site includes a 35,000-square-foot facility on 3.5 acres of land.

At the turn of the century the H.N. Richmond Paper Company, forerunner of the Standard Paper Company, was located at 1728 Pacific Avenue.

Schantz, the surviving partner of the company, retired in 1959 after serving in positions from errand boy to president in a span of 52 years. He died later that year. Howard C. Tatman, who had been associated with Standard Paper for 30 years, became president in 1959 and served the organization until his retirement in 1966.

Howard Schantz had started with the firm in 1952. In 1966 the business came under total Schantz ownership, and he became president. Mrs. Albert (Jean) Hallstrom sold her stocks to her brother Howard at that time. H. Douglas Schantz, Howard's son, helped in the company from high school days. In 1978, at age 23, he became vice-president. Also involved in the business has been W. Earl Anderson, vice-president and controller.

Standard Paper decided to enter the retail office supply business in 1973. It first acquired Tacoma Office Supply Company, formerly owned by the Osborne family. Acquisitions increased the firm's influence in the retail office supply business. Standard purchased Evergreen Stationers of Auburn in 1976 and Northwest Office Equipment Company of Seattle in 1977. In 1982 Standard Paper opened a new store in Seattle at Fifth and Union, and changed the names of all its retail outlets to Northwest Stationers and Interiors.

Mariann P. Schantz manages the retail operations as president of the corporation. Sue L. Schantz is assistant manager. The retail division employs approximately 45 persons, and annual sales exceed three million dollars. The wholesale products operation of Standard Paper distributes printing paper, industrial papers, restaurant supplies, and industrial chemicals. It is also a wholesaler of office products to retail outlets.

Standard Paper Company markets in the states of Washington, Oregon, and Alaska. One of the first paper houses in the state, it continues to make a significant contribution to the economy of the territory it covered before the turn of the century.

PENNWALT CORPORATION

In 1850 five Philadelphia Quakers organized the Pennsylvania Salt Manufacturing Company and constructed a plant to produce lye and other alkaline salts of soda from natural salt. The enterprise flourished, thus planting the roots from which Tacoma's multimillion-dollar Pennwalt Corporation plant has grown.

year as Tacoma ElectroChemical Company. Although it produced less than 15 tons of chlorine a day, it added a vital component to the growing pulp and paper industry.

The Great Depression brought "tough sledding" for the new operation, according to company officials. However, dedicated,

Tacoma ElectroChemical Company evolved into Pennsalt Chemicals Corporation when the parent firm decided to diversify its manufacturing and chemicals production. Then, in 1969, Wallace and Tiernan, Inc., merged with Pennsalt and the corporate name was changed to Pennwalt Corporation.

The eastern firm accepted an invitation in 1928 to build a caustic soda and liquid chlorine plant on 14 acres of filled ground adjacent to the Hylebos Waterway. It was not a crowded site — vast expanses of undeveloped land stretched between the new industry and the heart of the city. The plant began operations the following

Pennwalt barges, the new Totem *at left and* Tyee *at right, tied up at the Hylebos Waterway dock. Pennwalt and its neighbors form part of an expanding industrial area.*

hard-working employees at all levels were influential in its survival of the economic slump.

The local facility, which became part of the Inorganic Chemicals Division after the merger, uses enormous quantities of salt in its operation. Ships bring 175,000 tons of salt each year from Baja California, forming glistening mountains north of the plant that diminish as production demands erode the supply.

Pennwalt is a leader in the Northwest in the production of chlorine, caustic soda, muriatic acid, and sodium chlorate used in pulp and paper bleaching, water and sewage treatment, and the manufacture of such items as solvents and refrigerants (chlorinated organics), PVC (polyvinyl chloride), and inorganic chemicals. With

and sodium chlorate also are utilized in pulp production whereas muriatic acid from the Tacoma plant is applied in oil well drilling and in the metal-plating industry.

The corporation has worked with community agencies in developing a modern emergency-response system that

Pennwalt and other chlorine-related industries also carry radios with direct access to the fire department.

Pennwalt's 150 employees participate in the United Way, and the Pennwalt foundation has played a supporting role in such local projects as the Pantages Theater restoration, Mary Bridge Children's

modern production techniques more than 250 tons of chlorine are shipped out daily in tank cars, barges, and smaller-quantity cylinders. While the major customer of Pennwalt chlorine is the Northwest pulp and paper industry, a significant portion is used in water purification, bleach, and the manufacture of adhesives. Caustic soda

Pennwalt began as Tacoma ElectroChemical Company on the sparsely populated tideflats industrial area in 1929.

functions throughout the tideflats area. A hotline telephone system alerts fire department personnel of potential problems.

Health Center, Tacoma General Hospital building fund, Tacoma-Pierce County Family YMCA, Junior Achievement, funding for local boys' clubs, and others.

Pennwalt Corporation, with headquarters in Philadelphia, is a worldwide manufacturer of chemicals, health products, and precision equipment.

TUCCI & SONS, INC.

Michael J. Tucci founded Tucci & Sons, Inc., which has grown from a small construction company into a major paving, grading, and utility operation.

In 1950 Michael J. Tucci purchased part ownership of Burrows & Milone, a small utility construction company, and in 1958 he purchased the remainder of the business and changed the name to Tucci & Sons, Inc. Harrison Bros., a local earth-moving firm, was purchased in 1960. In 1975, two years after Michael J. Tucci's death, Asphalt Paving & Engineering Company was purchased and, in 1981, the asphalt division was expanded by acquiring the paving operation of the J.D. Shotwell Company.

Beginning in 1950, with 15 employees and an annual volume of $150,000, by 1981 Tucci & Sons, Inc., had grown to employ 200 workers and had an annual volume of $18 million.

Some of its major projects recently constructed are the first segment of the Lakewood/Parkland sewer project in the Custer area; the Flett Creek flood-control project, for which Tucci & Sons received the American Public Works Association State Contractor of the Year Award; and

the Tacoma Dome Sports and Convention Center, for which Tucci was one of the joint-venture partners and responsible for site construction and asphalt paving.

Tucci & Sons, Inc., operates three major divisions—paving, grading, and utilities. From its three asphalt plants located throughout Pierce County, it manufactures, hauls, and lays asphalt for such projects as freeways, roads, subdivisions, and commercial parking lots. The grading operation can involve moving up to two million or more cubic yards of earth and serves both public agencies and private customers. Tucci's utility division installs mainline sanitary sewers, storm

Years of experience, knowledgeable personnel, and modern equipment enable Tucci & Sons to undertake public and private contracts.

sewers, and water mains.

The founder of the firm, Michael J. Tucci, was born in Davenport, Iowa, and came to Tacoma as a child. He was a 1930 graduate of Bellarmine Preparatory School and a 1935 graduate of Gonzaga University, where he was an All-Coast Football selection. Tucci was one of the original participants in establishing the Action Committee for Minority Employment (ACME). Additionally, he served as a member of the board of regents of Gonzaga University and was inducted into the Tacoma/Pierce County Sports Hall of Fame.

The company officials are Michael A. Tucci, president; John V. Xitco, executive vice-president and secretary/treasurer; and James G. Tucci and Thomas D. Tucci, vice-presidents.

HUMANA HOSPITAL TACOMA

In 1928 a Canadian nurse opened a seven-bed hospital in the Washington Building on Pacific Avenue. It was called Washington Minor Hospital because it handled only minor surgical cases.

The nurse, Mabel Patterson, soon found herself in financial difficulties, and took time off to investigate the possibility of moving her hospital to Toronto where

1930 she opened a 14-bed hospital on the building's fifth floor. The 17-story facility was touted in the press as "the most modern building ever erected in the Far West for the medical-dental fraternity."

Humana Hospital Tacoma grew from the determined efforts of a young nurse to become an important local medical facility.

wing and nursing tower in 1975 to expand facilities to a total of 155 beds and six operating rooms. Mrs. Gaetz, the tenacious nurse, participated in the dedication of the new wing.

In 1978 Humana, Inc., acquired Allenmore Community Hospital. This acquisition was reflected with a name change to Humana Hospital Tacoma in

her brother was a physician. She asked a nurse friend, Henrietta Sowa, to run the hospital in her absence. After determining to move to Toronto, Nurse Patterson packed up everything—taking the dishes, surgical equipment, and bedding.

On September 1, 1929, the manager of the Washington Building asked Nurse Sowa to reopen the hospital. Wasting no time, she lined up medical suppliers, purchased all the equipment, and reopened the facility on September 4.

When developers planned the celebrated Medical Arts Building on St. Helens Avenue, the young nurse decided to move her fledgling hospital to the new structure. She worked with the architect to design the facility, and in December

The hospital included two surgeries, a four-bed men's ward, five private rooms, a three-bed children's ward, and a two-bed women's ward.

"We never turned anyone away," Mrs. Henrietta Sowa Gaetz said, "regardless of whether they could pay. Some patients paid bills with chickens, vegetables, and fruits."

In 1955 Washington Minor Hospital was enlarged and relocated on the sixth floor of the Medical Arts Building, and became Medical Arts Hospital, Inc. In 1964 a group of 20 local physicians asked the facility to move to Allenmore as part of a new medical complex. Opening on the 20-acre site as a 50-bed care unit, the renamed Allenmore Hospital added a new

May 1982. Up-to-date facilities and services include diabetic instruction, nutrition counseling, electrocardiogram, emergency, gastroenterology lab, hypertension clinic, intensive and coronary care, nuclear medicine, ophthalmology lab, physical therapy, respiratory-pulmonary studies, radiology and ultrasound, radiation oncology, short-day surgery, surgery, pharmacy, laboratory, and a social services department.

Young Henrietta's little hospital pioneered a concept of locating hospital facilities in a medical office building. Humana Hospital Tacoma proves the validity of her approach—a modern hospital conveniently located in a medical complex.

MODEL LUMBER & ACE HARDWARE COMPANY, INC.

Morris Kleiner (front) founded Model Lumber Company in 1929. Joining in the management of the firm are his son Herman and grandson Greg.

The year 1929 marked the start of Model Lumber Company at 2424 Bay Street.

Three generations of the Kleiner family have brought Model Lumber & Ace Hardware Company, Inc., through the Depression, World War II, a serious flood, and relocation.

Morris Kleiner, son of a Polish truck farmer, immigrated to Canada in 1907, celebrating his 18th birthday aboard ship. He first moved to Calgary, Alberta, where he worked in a relative's lumber mill, tallying lumber for one dollar a day and eventually managing the mill for a salary of two dollars a day. All this time he attended college and studied English.

In 1914 Kleiner came to Tacoma. He purchased the Liberty Lumber Yard at South 40th and M streets and hauled wood and lumber by horse and wagon.

Kleiner married Pauline Weinfield of Montreal in 1919 and brought her back to Tacoma. For two years they lived on the third floor of the lumberyard building. Horses were stabled on the ground floor, and offices occupied the second floor.

The year 1929 marked the start of Model Lumber Company at 2424 Bay Street. Kleiner bought the land and developed the lumberyard. He brought employee Art Gummere from Liberty. Gummere retired in 1953 after 33 years with the company. Other men who assisted in the early days at Model included Bert L. Vaughan, who began at Model in 1929 and worked with Morris for 18 years; Bill Grass, who is still with the firm after 23 years; and Charles P. Serritella, a friend and associate who could do virtually anything that needed doing.

A serious flood in 1934 could have destroyed the business. The Puyallup River rose over its banks, and water poured into the lumberyard. A crew went in on a Saturday night to lift goods out of the floodwater. When the water receded Kleiner held a sale, and nails and other flood-damaged items went at bargain rates.

Model expanded in the '30s and again in the '40s. Kleiner needed reinforcing steel for the floor of a new building, but couldn't obtain the material because of wartime shortages. Serritella solved the problem: He collected enough cast-off bed springs to reinforce the concrete so that construction could proceed.

Morris Kleiner has been respected as a creative merchandiser. In 1936 he attracted national attention by building a model home at the lumberyard. The bungalow, a 28-foot by 24-foot, two-bedroom home, sported a roof sign with its price—$1,600. Thousands of Tacoma residents toured the bungalow, and a photograph of the house was featured on the cover of a national trade publication.

Herman Kleiner, Morris' son, attended Stadium High School and the College of Puget Sound and served a tour in the Army Air Corps during World War II before joining the company on a full-time basis in 1946. Herman purchased the business from his father in 1959. Herman's son Greg joined the business in 1974 and his youthful energy has contributed greatly to the growth of the firm. Morris' wife Pauline, Herman's wife Barbara, and Greg's wife Jaque also have played important roles in the business.

A turning point for Model Lumber came in 1972, when the city needed the site for an improved road system. Herman decided to reopen the yard at a new site, 4105 Pacific Highway East in Fife. Model, which had spent 43 years at the old location, reopened in its new quarters in 1973.

The Kleiners have a strong commitment to Tacoma and have participated in many special projects and community organizations, including Kiwanis, Goodwill, NAACP, Urban League, Salvation Army, and Boys' Club. Morris Kleiner has spent more than 70 years as a Mason and is still working in the business at age 94.

KELLY TELEVISION CO.

The tallest tower, the largest coverage area, and the finest-quality picture are features of KCPQ—owned by Kelly Television Co. and broadcast on Puget Sound's Channel 13.

Erection of the tower, on the summit of Gold Mountain near Bremerton, began in September 1980 after the Federal Communications Commission approved transfer of the station from the Clover Park School District to the Kelly Television Co. When construction was completed a few weeks later, the structure became the first maximum-height and -power television service in the area. The tower and circularly polarized antenna reach 708 feet, while the site's elevation lifts the tower to 2,395 feet above sea level.

Kelly employees beamed a test pattern with the station's first promotional announcement and initiated programming on November 4, 1980. The station provides a strong, clear picture for many Puget Sound areas that previously received poor transmission.

Broadcasting on Channel 13 originated as KMO-TV (the area's first NBC affiliate) on August 2, 1953, by Carl E. Haymond. J. Elroy McCaw of Seattle purchased the station in 1954 for $300,000 and renamed it KTVW-TV. Several years later the operation was purchased by Blaidon Mutual Investment Corporation of Seattle; that venture ended in bankruptcy court in 1974. With public support, the Clover Park School District acquired the bankrupt station in 1975 for $378,000. The school district changed the call letters to KCPQ-TV, and received permission to operate the channel on a non-commercial basis while reserved by the FCC as a commercial channel. Then, on January 2, 1979, KCPQ was purchased by the Kelly Television Co. for $6,250,000.

Formed to operate KCPQ, Kelly Television Co. is part of a family group established by Ewing C. Kelly in 1945. Initially a radio broadcasting business, the organization expanded to FM and to TV in 1955. After the founder's death, sons

KCPQ's maximum-height tower and antenna on Gold Mountain allows Kelly Television Co. to broadcast a clear picture to Puget Sound residents.

Robert and Jon formed a partnership with their mother, Nina.

As the Sacramento television station grew, the Kellys gained experience in the television industry. By the summer of 1978 they sold the radio stations and concentrated on television and banking. The family had founded River City Bank in Sacramento in 1974.

"We were especially interested in independent stations instead of network affiliated stations," Robert Kelly says. "An independent station succeeds or fails on its own efforts."

KCPQ's acceptance by the public and support by advertisers has been good. The Kelly Televison Co. renovated its studio on Steilacoom Boulevard, in the Clover Park Vocational-Technical School complex, and now has a staff of over 90.

"Our goal is to bring to Tacoma and the Northwest a professional television broadcasting station that is fully competitive with others in the area," Robert Kelly relates. "To do so we intend to be innovative and to contribute to the region and the people who live there."

WOODWORTH & COMPANY, INC.

One of the earliest entries in the old corporate ledger of Albertson, Cornell Brothers and Walsh, Inc., notes that Harold S. Woodworth was authorized to be manager of the paving division. That entry in 1921 marked the beginning of a general contracting firm that calls itself "problem solvers for three generations."

Originated at 113½ A Street, the company, in 1929, bought property on City Waterway—where its main office and plant were built in 1936. Woodworth and his son, J. Alden, became stockholders on January 28, 1936; a few months later, on May 7, the firm became Woodworth & Cornell.

Woodworth was named president of the firm in 1940, which became Woodworth & Company, Inc., the following year. The firm's leadership has been handed from generation to generation; J. Alden succeeded his father as president in 1952, and his son, John A., assumed the post in 1973.

In its early years the corporation took crews all over the state on paving contracts. A major project during World War II was paving plane-shelter areas for

In 1948 Woodworth & Company, Inc., did part of the construction and the asphalt paving for the new Tacoma Narrows span.

the U.S. Army, and in 1942 the firm built wartime housing in Lincoln Heights.

Contracting to demolish the remains of the old Tacoma Narrows Bridge, which had collapsed, in 1948 Woodworth constructed the center and end piers and anchors and did the asphalt paving for the new Narrows span.

Crushed and screened rock are

provided at both Woodworth's Hylebos and Lakeview gravel pits and any variety of hot-mix asphalt is available from asphalt plants located at both sites.

The building construction division assists in engineering, designing, and erecting structures of all types— warehouses, office buildings, and industrial and commercial facilities. The road construction division has brought Woodworth recognition as a leader in highway construction, specializing in such complex endeavors as freeway overpasses and bridges, state and federal highways, county roads, city streets, and private roads.

The corporation has paved a variety of large and small projects, including subdivisions, parking lots, and playgrounds. It also custom designs and builds tennis and pickleball courts and other types of recreational areas.

Woodworth's ledgers and contract books contain a capsule history of important Tacoma-area development. The firm, which has provided three generations of community leaders, now looks to the future.

Harold S. Woodworth (right, front row) worked on early Tacoma streets and became head of the asphalt crew.

Harold S. Woodworth (at left, in suit) supervised this road crew at North 29th and Union streets in 1909.

SOUTH TACOMA MOTOR COMPANY

When Peter Wallerich acquired South Tacoma Motor Company in 1919, its top line was a four-cylinder open touring car that featured wooden wheels, weighed approximately 1,900 pounds, came with a spare rim (no tire), and cost $735.

The firm was originated in the late 1800s as Union Street Livery; but with the growing popularity of automobiles in the early 1900s, the owners combined the livery business with a service store and garage.

Wallerich, who also owned North Pacific Bank in South Tacoma, sold interests in the ventures to his son, Clarence, and later to his grandsons, Peter and John. Clarence brought South Tacoma Motor Company through the Depression-wracked 1930s and into the World War II years. The company served as a wartime subcontractor, receiving bits and pieces of Army trucks and jeeps to assemble and forward to the Mt. Rainier Ordnance Depot, while its mechanics did a brisk business servicing Fort Lewis vehicles and private cars.

At the war's end men returned to their regular jobs, resulting in a postwar boom that saw the firm selling 200 cars and

trucks a year. John had started working with his father, pushing cars into the showroom and lots at a time when Clarence complained, "There's not a car on the floor under $1,000."

Although John had been associated with North Pacific Bank across the street, and Peter had entered the automobile business, later, by mutual agreement the two switched roles; John became head of the motor company and Peter became president of the bank.

South Tacoma Motor Company is probably the oldest Chevrolet dealer in the United States owned by the same family. It became one of the area's first Honda dealers in the early 1970s, and remains one of the West Coast's largest Chevrolet and Honda dealers. In addition, the firm was recently appointed the Rolls-Royce dealer for the state of Washington.

John Wallerich describes the fascination of watching the evolution of the motor vehicle, noting that the

---

South Tacoma Motor Company does business at 5602 South Tacoma Way, site of the original livery stable and turn-of-the-century garage.

automobile industry today is experiencing its greatest technological changes since it started at the turn of the century. Cars are made of fiberglass, plastics, aluminum, and space-age metals, and depend upon microchips for computerized ignition and fuel systems. Robots form an integral part of the production line.

"I like Tacoma," Wallerich states. "The people of Tacoma have been good to me." And he has made an impact on the city: His purchase of Northern Pacific headquarters prevented destruction of the building and spurred a significant historic-preservation movement; he served as president of Tacoma-Pierce County Civic Arts Commission and has been involved with Tacoma Philharmonic, Tacoma Art Museum, Tacoma Actors Guild, and the Pantages Theater restoration. Additionally, the company leader has enhanced his father's antique car collection.

South Tacoma Motor Company was one of the first to hire saleswomen. The staff includes 100 employees, and the plant features computerized office and shop-testing equipment—real progress from the horse and buggy days.

SELDEN'S FURNITURE & CARPET

S.C. Selden graduated from Lincoln High School in 1923, and went to work as a stock boy at Schoenfeld's Furniture. Almost 10 years later the young man left as assistant manager of the carpet department to become manager of home furnishings at People's Store. He resigned there in 1940 to open his own store.

Operating with a borrowed $3,000, Selden opened a 30-foot by 90-foot shop at 1145 Broadway—featuring linoleum, window shades, and carpeting. His staff included a secretary, three salesmen, and a carpet layer.

With the eruption of World War II, shades and linoleum became priority items; correspondingly, carpet mills wove blankets and other war materials. The company had neither linoleum nor carpet to sell to the public for more than two years. However, one phase of the business garnered thousands of orders: Customers were frantic to buy blackout blinds. At one point in 1942 the firm had a backlog of 30,000 shades for wartime housing, operating its shade assembly 16 hours a day, six days a week, producing a shade every 45 seconds.

Selden's went into government work with projects at North Fort Lewis, McChord, Bremerton Navy Base, Coulee Dam, Richland, and Hanford, Washington; Tongus Point and Hermiston, Oregon; Farragut, Idaho; and

Fairbanks, Alaska. A highlight of wartime business was a contract with the Navy to apply battleship linoleum in 77 Liberty Ships. Installation had begun on the seventh ship when orders came to remove all the coverings—officials had discovered the material was combustive under bombing conditions. Left with more than 11,000 yards of linoleum it could not sell without authorization, the firm was finally paid for the product by the government, shipped it to a Seattle warehouse, and repurchased it after the war.

During 1944 Selden's delivered and installed 96 rail carloads of asphalt tile in government buildings to become the largest floor-covering outlet by volume on the West Coast; but when the war ended business volume dropped from $3 million annually to $1.25 million. A difficult adjustment period followed. However, the postwar building boom developed to provide continued growth.

In 1948 Selden's won the Sweepstake's Trophy for its entry in the annual Daffodil Parade. The float was designed and built by company staff, and used 60,000 daffodils. The photo was taken in front of Selden's old location—1141 Broadway—now the site of the new downtown financial center.

In 1957 Selden's became a complete home-furnishing center when it acquired Kegel's Furniture and moved to those larger quarters at 11th and A streets.

That building was torn down in 1974, and the subsequent move to the newly redeveloped Broadway Plaza proved untimely. The downtown store was then merged with its Lakewood Center branch in 1978.

In 1981 all operations were relocated in a fine, complete, and larger facility at 27th Street West and Bridgeport Way in University Place, and an additional expansion of the sales area was opened in spring 1983.

Today Selden's Furniture & Carpet, in University Place, is a complete home furnishing store featuring top brands of furniture such as Thomasville and Century, and fine carpets by Karastan and Lees. Selden's draperies, ceramic tile, and hardwood floors are being installed throughout the greater Tacoma area. Selden's interior designers and installation crews are working in many outstanding homes and commercial buildings in the Northwest.

Stanley Selden became president in 1973 and is the owner/manager today.

In 1981 Selden's Furniture & Carpet consolidated all retail and commercial sales in its new location at 27th Street West and Bridgeport Way.

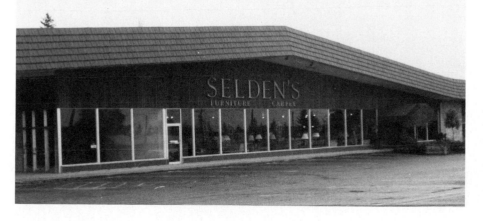

GEHRI SHEET METAL COMPANY, INC.

Stadium High School, the armory, St. Patrick Church, Lincoln High School, the impressive old courthouse—all of these display the craftsmanship of Adolf Gehri, a native of Switzerland who arrived in Tacoma, Washington Territory, in 1888.

The entrepreneur founded his business in Tacoma in 1892 at 11th and K streets. His signboard advertised "stoves set up and connected" and "jobbing promptly attended to." Script window-lettering promised "tin, sheet iron, and copper work" and "tin and granite ware." Early trade sent hot-air stoves to Alaska for the 1896-1899 Gold Rush.

In order to expand his operation, Gehri sent for two of his brothers, Emil and Alfred, who were plumbers. By 1904 the brothers had vacated a second shop on 11th Street between K and L, and had moved into the firm's permanent location at 1117 Tacoma Avenue South. The company letterhead announced Adolf Gehri and Company, "dealers in general and builders' hardware, sanitary plumbing, tinsheet iron, and copper work."

Prominent contracts of the pioneer firm included the finials on turreted Stadium High School, copper roofing for the original courthouse, and metalwork on schools, churches, and local businesses. During World War I the enterprise hired extra crews to turn out smokestacks for Camp Lewis.

When Adolf Gehri died in 1917 at 47 years of age, the authority was assumed by Ernest Feix. Under his leadership the organization installed the ventilating systems of two major hotels—the Winthrop in Tacoma and the Olympic in Seattle.

George Gehri, the founder's son, began as an estimator for the company and later became president. He developed Silent Air units (a tubular air conditioning system) for home use, and guided the firm in extensive work in the construction of Fort Lewis housing developments.

Gehri Sheet Metal Company, Inc., continues as a general jobbing and contracting shop with commissions in

In 1892 Adolf Gehri, a Swiss immigrant, opened his first shop at 11th and K streets.

heating and ventilating systems, general architectural sheet metal, school contracts, and commercial jobs. While most assignments are in Pierce County, there are others in Thurston and Kitsap counties. The corporation subcontracted as well for Alaska's Prudhoe Bay project, with work completed in Tacoma and shipped to Alaska.

By 1982 Margaret Gehri, daughter of the founder, had spent 64 years with the organization. After graduation from

Stadium High School, she came to work as bookkeeper for her father and now serves as treasurer. Joanne B. Gehri, who began working for the company in 1959, has been its president since 1965.

The roofline of Tacoma is a visible tribute to the industrious Swiss-born community leader who originated the family business known as Gehri Sheet Metal Company, Inc.

Margaret Gehri, a longtime employee and treasurer of the family firm, was born in the apartment above the company's second building on 11th Street.

ROMAN MEAL COMPANY

A German baker, an ailing physician and the legions of ancient Rome all played a role in the development of Tacoma's Roman Meal Company.

The baker, Henry Matthaei, learned his trade as a teenager in Germany. At 20 years of age, Henry immigrated to America. The year was 1878. Plying his trade, he eventually established a bakery in Kansas City, which would grow to be the city's second largest. Henry had a son, William, who worked in the bakery business with his father. Following the merger of Henry's bakery with four others, William decided to leave his father's company to become a technical salesman for Fleischmann's, which was introducing compressed yeast to the industry. He was assigned the Northwest region, and while in Tacoma discovered a bakery that was for sale. He bought the bakery and later built a new, modern one at the corner of South Seventh and Sprague.

The ailing physician was named Robert Jackson. Around 1910, unable to heal himself, he moved from Victoria to Tacoma to seek medical care. A historian, Dr. Jackson had read accounts of the legions of ancient Rome and the fact that their diet consisted of a daily ration of two pounds of wheat or rye. On this simple fare, they had the strength and stamina to conquer the then-known world. With his health failing, Dr. Jackson decided to make a final attempt at recovery by modifying his diet and conditioning his body. He developed what he called Dr. Jackson's Roman Health Meal, based on the diet of the Roman legionnaires. It was

a breakfast mush consisting of a mixture of whole grain wheat, whole grain rye, bran, and flaxseed.

By consuming the cereal regularly, he corrected what was a vitamin and mineral deficiency and his health improved. Dr. Jackson prescribed the mixture to many of his patients and the demand for the product became so great that he established a small factory in Tacoma to produce it.

In 1927 William Matthaei bought Dr. Jackson's Roman Meal Company; he developed a bread which he called Roman Meal and distributed it in the Tacoma area.

Two years later the Continental Baking Company purchased Matthaei's baking interests. However, Matthaei retained control of the Roman Meal Company and spent his time concentrating on the sale of Roman Meal Cereal. His business survived the Depression, and many a hungry stomach was filled with his nutritious cereal.

Since he no longer owned a bakery, Matthaei turned his energies to licensing bakeries throughout the country to produce Roman Meal Bread. Two divisions were created, the grocery products division to sell the original Roman Meal Cereal, and a bakery division to sell Roman Meal Baker's Mix to those bakers throughout the nation licensed to produce Roman Meal Bread.

Consumer demand for Roman Meal

Located at 2101 South Tacoma Way, the Roman Meal Company headquarters features a modern test kitchen and a quality-assurance laboratory.

After more than five decades of expansion, Roman Meal Company produces the number one non-white bread in the country.

A Victoria doctor combined grains to create the nutritious cereal first introduced to American consumers.

Bread and cereal grew to the point that the company decided to build its own mill. Fargo, North Dakota, was selected as the site. There, wheat and rye are still milled and blended with bran and defatted flaxseed to produce Roman Meal Cereal and Baker's Mixture. Cereal is boxed for home use and Baker's Mixture is packed in 50-pound bags or loaded into bulk carriers for bakers' use.

Roman Meal became, and still is, the largest-selling non-white bread in the country. It is currently licensed to approximately 150 bakers throughout the United States as well as Canada, Bermuda, the Bahamas, and Japan.

Good nutrition is the reason Roman Meal was originally developed, and the nutrition program is a very important part of Roman Meal's marketing activities. The company funds a nutritional studies laboratory at the University of Miami School of Medicine in Florida.

William Matthaei's son, Charles W.H. Matthaei, is now president of the Roman Meal Company. Assisting their father in the firm are Bill Matthaei, senior vice-president and secretary/treasurer; Fred Matthaei, vice-president of marketing; and Dick Matthaei, assistant director of research and development.

CAMMARANO BROTHERS, INC.

With money borrowed from their sister Rose, Edward Cammarano (shown here) and his three brothers founded the Tacoma bottling firm in 1921.

Orange Julep Bottling Company: That's how the city's oldest beer-wholesaling operation under single management began during Prohibition.

Four brothers—one born in Italy and the rest in Pennsylvania—came with their family to the Wilkeson-Carbonado area and then to Tacoma. James (who worked for a bottling plant), Philip, William, and Edward were determined to start their own business. They borrowed money from their sister Rose, and formed the bottling company on May 31, 1921.

The entrepreneurs mixed soft-drink concentrates according to the franchiser's directions, put beverages into bottles, and went out to sell. When they marketed their own product under the "Paradise Club" label, they bottled the beverages at night and made deliveries during the day.

Although the firm name initially changed to reflect the product it peddled, eventually it seemed simpler to use "Cammarano Brothers." The enterprise supplied stores and restaurants with soft

drinks until the repeal of Prohibition in 1933.

Company plants operated on Jefferson Avenue, on A Street near Puyallup Avenue in 1933, and in a block built by Cammarano Brothers at 2307 A Street in 1937. In the late 1930s the firm maintained five satellite warehouses at Seattle, Auburn, Olympia, Bremerton, and Centralia; all had beer and soft drinks. The headquarters is now at 2324 Center Street.

During the gasoline rationing days of World War II, Cammarano Brothers resorted to horse-drawn wagons for deliveries.

Cammarano Brothers actually bottled beer at the 23rd and A Street plant, becoming the only non-brewer bottling beer in the country. Schlitz shipped full barrels of beer from Milwaukee. Tacoma workers tapped the kegs, put the beer into quart containers, pasteurized it, and sold it at low cost under the Schlitz label. Efforts to draft legislation to halt the procedure failed; however, World War II rail needs prevented Midwest brewers from shipping their barrels to the West.

Cammarano stopped distributing soft drinks in 1970, and began selling beer and wine exclusively. Rainier is the primary beer brand, but the company also supplies other beers as well as California, local, and imported wines. More than two million cases are dispersed annually in Pierce, south King, Mason, and Thurston counties.

Distribution areas differ from the early days when a soft-drink area was determined by how far a driver could travel in a day in a Model A. Most early distributions were to taverns, but with the change of state liquor laws, marketing and packaging techniques, and refrigeration, approximately 60 percent of the beer now goes to groceries and convenience stores.

The original Cammarano brothers entered semiretirement in 1965. William and Edward were still living in 1983. Current management includes William Cammarano, Jr., president; James Cammarano, Jr., vice-president; David Cammarano, vice-president; and Robert Cammarano, secretary.

NATIONAL BLOWER AND SHEET METAL COMPANY

From a blacksmith shop in Old Tacoma to an important role in the energy and nuclear age—that is the history of National Blower and Sheet Metal Company.

Founded in 1890 by Frank Rikard, the blacksmith shop was later sold to Otto Resic and C.W. Williams. In 1912 Peter F. Finnigan bought the establishment, and a year later moved the operation to property on St. Paul Avenue.

The firm was incorporated in 1942 with Finnigan as president. His son, Dayton, succeeded him in 1953, with Maurice Finnigan becoming vice-president. In 1982 Robert Kirrage assumed the presidency, and Pad Finnigan, third generation in the company, was named vice-president.

Initially specializing in blow pipes for sawmills and planing mills, in 1916 National began work on ventilating systems and other industrial sheet-metal work. In 1938 the business expanded to include general building sheet-metal work.

World War II forced National into around-the-clock shifts, manufacturing sheet-metal products for the construction of military bases that formed part of the coastal defense system. The organization added a roofing division in 1946 and expanded operations to Alaska, doing extensive work on postwar defense systems there until 1952.

When the nation burst into the nuclear age, the Tacoma firm went to work at Hanford, constructing ventilation systems and creating stainless-steel liners for 200-foot concrete stacks. It also assisted in the construction of a key air-defense post at McChord Air Force Base. National fabricated and installed many structural frames and command platforms on military bases around the country that enclosed transparent data panels used by Air Force personnel to plot aircraft movements.

Pete Finnigan began a tradition of pioneering industrial and commercial systems. He developed a forced-air furnace before the idea was generally accepted. In addition, National fabricated

equipment made of aluminum instead of steel—because of aluminum's non-sparking qualities—for Du Pont's explosives-manufacturing operation.

The corporation's executives have always believed in serving their community. For many years Pete Finnigan was on the industrial committee of the Tacoma Chamber of Commerce. Dayton served as president of the Tacoma Rotary Club, on school bond committees, and as president of the Tacoma Country and Golf Club. He also was a member of the national board of directors for the American Institute of Steel Construction for seven years. Maurice served on the city council for nine years, and Kirrage works with Elks committees on local projects.

Top
Peter Finnigan (second from right) acquired this sheet metal shop in 1912.

Above
A worker welds sections of ductwork for an air pollution control device for the ASARCO plant.

National Blower and Sheet Metal Company has expanded to provide custom products and services in four departments: sheet metal, structural steel, roofing, and steel cleaning and painting. While engaged in extensive work in the Alaska oil industry, the company fills more than 4,000 orders a year—and has earned a reputation for experience and leadership in the innovative design and use of metals.

RASMUSSENHOBBS

Peter Rasmussen

Del Hobbs

RasmussenHobbs is a multi-discipline design firm located in one of Tacoma's most interesting historic residences.

Peter Rasmussen and Del Hobbs are architects who offer a complete spectrum of planning and design services to their clients. This architectural firm has a professional staff active in facility programming and design, space planning, and graphic design.

With their own design and financial resources, they have acquired and renovated the historic Henry Drum House at Number 9 Saint Helens Avenue. The architects were honored by the American Institute of Architects with a Special Citation Award for their restoration and adaptive reuse of this building. The Henry Drum House has been listed on the National Register of Historic Places since 1977.

Both firm principals have participated in historic-preservation programs. Del

Hobbs has served on the Tacoma Landmarks Preservation Commission, and Peter Rasmussen was a founding member of the Pierce County Landmarks Preservation Committee.

Both Rasmussen and Hobbs hold Bachelor of Architecture degrees from Washington State University, and were classmates from 1963 to 1968. Hobbs served as a Navy civil engineer with the Seabees in Vietnam in 1969 and then returned stateside to work with a Tacoma architectural firm. Peter Rasmussen was born in Esbjerg, Denmark, as his mother hid under her featherbed with a midwife while Allied Forces bombed that port city during World War II. His family later sailed to Tacoma in 1958 when Peter was 14.

The two men decided to form their own business in 1974, a difficult choice in the midst of a recession. Their first office, barely large enough for the two of them, was located in University Place.

In 1977 the firm purchased the Drum House. The partners made a commitment to retain the historical nature of the 1888 structure and make it work for their current and future needs. They moved into the only habitable floor, and the maid's room became a darkroom. Architectural design facilities were moved to the renovated attic with its view of Commencement Bay. Restoration of the building continues today, with attention to the final details. The architects have enjoyed studying the history of Henry Drum, who designed the home for his family. Drum, the fifth mayor of Tacoma, was instrumental in achieving Washington's statehood. He later served in the historic first legislature of the State of Washington.

Major projects designed by RasmussenHobbs include the Pierce County Detention and Correctional Center, a $19.2-million facility. The firm has also continued to work with the Tacoma Public Schools on remodeling and restoration of school facilities throughout the district.

Other notable projects include the

renovation of the Old Town Gold Coast Building into contemporary offices, and the renovation of the old Steilacoom Fire Station into town administrative offices. The firm's regional design practice has included projects for the federal government at Whidbey Island Naval Air Station and Puget Sound Naval Shipyard. RasmussenHobbs has been commissioned to design offices throughout the state for the Department of Natural Resources, as well as multiple-family dwelling complexes and private residences around the Puget Sound area.

Del Hobbs is a past president of the Southwest Washington Chapter of the American Institute of Architects, secretary/treasurer of the Washington Council AIA, past vice-president of the Tacoma Chamber of Commerce, a member of the Tacoma Dome Design Jury, and an officer in Downtown Rotary. Peter Rasmussen is past chairman of the Tacoma Planning Commission and was twice elected to the Tacoma City Council. He also served on the Civic Arts Commission, the executive boards of the Economic Development Corporation and the Comprehensive Mental Health Center of Pierce County, and is past president of the Danish Brotherhood.

Peter Rasmussen and Del Hobbs are two men with a strong community commitment and an investment in Tacoma's future.

The Henry Drum House, listed on the National Register of Historic Places, is used by RasmussenHobbs for its architectural design facilities while the restoration of the 1888 building continues.

BODDIE'S BUILDING CONSTRUCTION, INC.

Algernon "Al" Owens Boddie spent eight years in the U.S. Air Force, completing his service career as a captain at McChord Air Force Base near Tacoma. He liked the community and the people. He also "believed that the opportunity here was excellent, that this was an area experiencing a boom."

Obtaining a contractor's license in March 1963, Boddie opened shop at 2321 South 12th Street—specializing in remodeling, building houses, and constructing kitchen cabinets, vanities, and furniture. The cabinet shop outgrew its space, and in 1965 was moved to 2356 Tacoma Avenue South. The following year the firm purchased a building at 2102 South 12th Street, its present address, and expanded operations to include commercial construction while increasing emphasis on custom homes.

Among the few minority contractors to initiate work under the Small Business Administration's 8 (a) program established in the late 1960s, Boddie's company erected the Number 2 fire station for Trident—the first operational building completed at the site. A major endeavor was the construction of Totem Marina on City Waterway, for which the contractor was project manager. The firm, incorporated on October 7, 1970, now specializes in commercial and industrial work.

Boddie's Building Construction, Inc., has been an integral part of several training programs to assist minority workers. One plan, in cooperation with the Conifer Company, involved teaching carpenter apprentices through an outreach office. Boddie served as catalyst for the program in two ways: He helped the Tacoma Urban League form a union-apprentice operation, and he assisted with the state's training program in which the workers were registered.

Another project entailed working with high school students in the cabinet shop—through a cooperative effort with the Tacoma Public Schools' Vocational Rehabilitation prevocational program. Boddie also supported a minority training

The firm's main office, at 2102 South 12th Street.

program sponsored by the National Alliance of Businessmen.

The contractor serves effectively in several civic positions, including the board of trustees of the Tacoma Public Library since 1975 and the Tacoma Dome Jury. Twice elected president (in 1971 and 1981) of the Minority Contractors' Association of Pierce County, he is an executive board member of the Tacoma Chapter, Associated General Contractors of America. He is a Mason (Prince Hall) and a member of Omega Psi Phi fraternity.

A native of Montgomery, Alabama, Boddie was graduated from Tuskegee Institute in Alabama in 1954 with a degree in industrial education. His wife Velma also attended Tuskegee Institute. Secretary/treasurer of the construction firm, as well as office manager, Mrs. Boddie belongs to the Tacoma Chapter, Associated General Contractors of America; the People's Community Center

Algernon "Al" Owens Boddie, founder of Boddie's Building Construction, Inc.

advisory board; and the National Association for the Advancement of Colored People.

PACIFIC STORAGE, INC.

As early as 1889 one Hotspur O. Piercy operated Pacific Transfer Company wagons from stables at 1531 D Street, which later became Market. His teams hauled goods from the docks, where sailing vessels discharged their wares.

Almost a century later Pacific Storage, Inc.—a successor to the pioneer firm—still works off the waterfront, but it stores commodities in two giant warehouses and maintains a fleet of 100 trucks.

Pacific Storage and Warehouse Company also was organized by 1889. Conducting business from "Adams opposite 24th," the enterprise apparently

moved to 1721 Jefferson, a brick building modern Tacoma diners will associate with the Old Spaghetti Factory. That structure, originally planned as a hotel, served as home of the company until 1970.

In 1907 the storage firm was purchased by Edward J. Lanning; at the close of World War I, when Piercy retired, he also bought the Pacific Transfer Company. The organization became Pacific Storage and Transfer Company.

Upon Lanning's death in 1924, the

John Dyer (right), chairman of the board, and son William Dyer, president of Pacific Storage, Inc.

went through several changes of ownership and then combined with another warehouse to form Pacific Security Storage and Warehouse Company. In 1904 or 1905 the business

corporate stock was transferred to his daughter, Sally Newell. Her husband, Matt Newell, became president at that time.

Terminal Warehouses, Inc., bought

Pacific Storage and Distributing in 1946 from the Newells, and the name was changed to Pacific Storage, Inc., in October 1956.

John Dyer, who has spent his entire life on Puget Sound, became chairman of the board in 1965. His son, William, became president at that time. Donald Dargan, who was vice-president, retired from the firm.

When the company moved in 1970 to a modern office and warehouse facility at 440 East 19th Street, a retired employee telephoned Dyer to ask if he had removed the contents from the old building's "secret room." Dressed in his business suit, he located the site, and pushed his way through decades of cobwebs and grime. Stored in the long-forgotten place were horse trappings, three barrels filled with small cream containers, a wooden milk separator, and two dental chairs marked for delivery to a Tacoma office before the turn of the century. A selection of the artifacts was donated to a local museum.

Pacific Storage, Inc., grew from its pioneer heritage to become the largest repository for copper in the United States. Its negotiable warehouse receipts have been bartered on the commodities exchange.

Included in storage facilities on 19th Street and on Port of Tacoma Road are petroleum products, paper products, chemicals for manufactured goods, and telephone-switching equipment. The corporation distributes imported Izusu diesels nationwide.

A household-goods division represents Allied Van Lines in movement of goods. Two major moves handled by the firm transferred The Weyerhaeuser Company to its new headquarters, and local government departments into the City-County Building.

The freight-trucking division is primarily oriented to handling import/export container-cargo unloaded at the Port of Tacoma—a modern interpretation of Hotspur Piercy's wagon-transport business.

B&I SHOPPING CENTER

Earl Irwin, a World War II veteran, and Leo Bradshaw erected a 30-foot by 70-foot concrete block building at 8012 South Tacoma Way in 1946, offered a collection of war-surplus goods and hardware, and dubbed the business "the biggest little store in the world."

The owners chose a combination of their initials to name the store "B&I," then the Irwins bought out Bradshaw's shares and went on to increase the shopping complex to a total of 285,000 square feet by 1982. The Irwin family owns and operates sporting goods, drug and housewares, and stereo departments. Other tenants offer goods and services in leased space.

Irwin, a flamboyant advertiser, in 1948 brought in animals, set up a full-size carousel indoors, and featured clowns, balloons, and animal rides. Consequently, the concept of the "circus store" was born. He acquired more property, added buildings and tenants, and used his promotional skills to bring children and their parents to the shops.

The most prominent publicity gimmicks featured the 1953 visit of the Cisco Kid, the famous television cowboy; Miss B&I, a hydroplane supported partially by the store; the appearance of Bert Thomas, the first man to swim the Strait of Juan de Fuca; and the contest in 1957 when Irwin ordered a quarter of a million pounds of ice delivered to the parking lot. A Fort Lewis soldier won 500 silver

Earl Irwin's flamboyant advertising stunts brought the Cisco Kid to Tacoma in 1953. The Irwin family members, Constance and Earl (in back) and Mary Lou and Ron, pose with the television cowboy.

dollars for guessing the time—within five minutes—of the day, hour, and minute the last bit of ice would melt.

But Irwin's circus promotion was the most successful of all. When he hired the

Ringling Brothers Circus to play in the parking lot, people flocked to the store. Exotic animals remain a major attraction. Ivan, a silverback gorilla, is the best known of the Irwin animals. Purchased for the B&I after his birth in 1964 in the Belgian Congo, in 1966 he appeared as a guest on the popular television series "Daktari." At age 18 the 500-pound Ivan eats and acts something like a human teenager, entertaining shoppers with his antics. He lives in a three-room compound, which includes a spacious play area and waterfall.

Earl Irwin died in 1973 at age 64, and his wife Constance succeeded him as president. Ron Irwin, their son, is vice-president; daughter Mary Lou Borgert is secretary/treasurer. Five grandchildren form the third generation of the B&I family.

In 1982 a $720,000 project expanded and upgraded the shopping center and in 1983 an indoor water slide was added—progressing, Mrs. Irwin said, "the way Earl would have done."

The B&I shopping center in 1983.

PUGET CORPORATION

Aluminum castings and injection plastic moldings for computers, winches, valves, telephones, and knives are representative of the many custom parts produced by Puget Corporation.

The business was organized as Puget Die Casting Company in 1946 by George A. Lund, Marco Heidner, and T.H. Monroe, with Otto A. Sturdy as plant manager. The firm began operations in the former boiler room sawdust bin of the Clear Fir Lumber Company on Day Island Waterway.

The first die-casting machine produced zinc license plate frames, cabinet hardware, and coin changers. Within the first year the fledgling enterprise had to decide whether or not to buy an aluminum die-casting machine.

When a local businessman, Dick Camp, pioneered the process for the chrome plating of aluminum and sought a Tacoma plant to produce bathroom hardware, Puget Die Casting became the first firm in the Northwest to install production aluminum die-casting equipment. Another boost came from Washington Steel Products in Tacoma, headed by C. Morrison Johnson, which manufactured builders' hardware for the national market. Titan Chain Saws of Seattle, the pioneer manufacturer of chain saws in the United States, was an early customer for magnesium castings. In the early 1960s

Puget innovated with the production of brass die castings for use in water meter housings and lawn sprinklers.

In 1959 the company moved to a new plant at 2101 Mildred Street West, which has been expanded from an initial 10,000 square feet to 60,000 square feet. The operation has remained essentially the same, concentrating on the manufacture of die castings. While the early market was local, business branched to the Portland area and kept spreading; Puget currently makes castings for virtually every West Coast industry and other businesses in all parts of the United States and Canada.

Specializing in close-tolerance, precision castings, Puget is heavily involved in the production of parts for the computer industry, serving such firms as Western Electric, General Telephone, IBM, and Hewlett-Packard. To provide a complete service, Puget designs the tools, produces the die-casting molds, does the casting, completes the secondary machining, and provides completely finished, plated, and painted parts.

In a 1979 expansion phase, the firm built one of the most modern casting facilities in the United States. Metals are

Puget Corporation has pioneered casting procedures and is recognized in the United States and other countries as a manufacturer of precision products.

In 1946 George Lund opened Puget Die Casting Company in the former boiler room sawdust bin of the Clear Fir Lumber Company.

melted in electric furnaces that provide absolute quality control. Robots are used to pour the molten metal and to extract castings from the molds. This turn to automation created more technical jobs for employees and offers more exact control over the casting process.

A Portland, Oregon, die-casting plant was established in 1967. In 1973 this plant was converted to the production of plastic parts and is currently a leader in the injection-molding industry in the Northwest. Also in 1973, the company was renamed Puget Corporation and is headed by Patrick J. Lyon, president in Washington, and Geoffrey L. Levear, president in Oregon.

SCHWARZ, SHERA & ASSOCIATES, INC.

While stationed in Tacoma during World War II, North Dakota native V.A. Schwarz determined to return to the city and turn his attention to finding a peacetime career.

Urged by his father to get more life insurance coverage prior to his marriage, Schwarz visited an insurance agent— which led to an aptitude test and a decision to enter the business, initially by selling insurance door to door. In 1953 he founded V.A. Schwarz and Associates. In 1964 E.C. Shera and Dorothy Connor, both natives of Tacoma, joined him to form Schwarz, Shera & Associates, Inc.

Shera, a Yale University graduate who worked for a large insurance company, accepted Schwarz's offer to join in forming a new corporate firm. Ms. Connor had been a member of Schwarz and Associates since 1957, and she came into the firm as a principal at incorporation.

The enterprise opened in the Security Building in Tacoma with six personnel; it is now the largest independently owned brokerage-consulting operation in the Northwest specializing in employee benefits, and the staff includes

Schwarz, Shera & Associates, Inc., began in 1964 with six on the staff and grew to become the Northwest's largest independently owned brokerage-consulting firm specializing in employee benefits.

35 associates. A Seattle office was added in 1967, and Tacoma offices now occupy the 15th and 16th floors of the Puget Sound Bank Building.

Schwarz, Shera is an organization of actuaries, consultants, and licensed and bonded insurance brokers. Actuaries and consultants work as agents of the client in the employee-benefit and insurance industry, under obligation to no insurance company; this autonomy allows them complete objectivity in selecting the plans and insurer that best suit the needs of the client.

Continuing professional education has been a tradition at Schwarz, Shera. A majority of the staff holds the Chartered Life Underwriter (CLU) designation, one of the highest professional achievements available in the field. Several associates are professional actuaries and others are Certified Employee Benefit Specialists (CEBS) or Chartered Financial

Consultants (ChFC), difficult and prestigious professional designations.

Professional skills provide well-balanced programs at the lowest possible cost for the thousands of clients served by the firm. First using computer support in 1967, Schwarz, Shera today utilizes its own computer systems to combine many small buyers to form large groups, which qualify for insurance coverage at volume discounts.

The company also sells individual life-insurance policies, serving as a consultant working for the client. Coverage in employee benefits is provided to such clients as financial institutions, labor-management trusts, manufacturers, the wood-products industry, governmental units, and retail and wholesale establishments.

Schwarz, Shera is licensed in a majority of states, although the majority of its clients reside in the Northwest, and it has built a national reputation in a steady pattern of growth and expansion. Its members have served as officers and board members in civic, social, fraternal, professional, and educational groups.

PYRODYNE CORPORATION

Just before the close of World War II, a 14-year-old boy turned a small investment in fireworks into a sizable profit. His business venture evolved into a multimillion-dollar retail fireworks enterprise—Tacoma's Pyrodyne Corporation and Pyrotronic Corporation of California.

W.P. (Pat) Moriarty bought a quantity of fireworks that had been confiscated from Japanese-Americans who were moved from coastal areas to inland relocation centers. The fireworks were on sale for $60; Pat dickered until he paid only $15. He sold the fireworks to V-J Day celebrators for approximately $100.

The earnings motivated the entire family, and the following year, 1946, Mrs. Elizabeth Moriarty and her two sons, Pat and Jim, sold fireworks they had assembled and stored in their home.

Mrs. Moriarty traded the residence for property on the King County line in 1947. The family added a Quonset hut to the property for storage, rented a small office building at 2521 Pacific Highway East, and originated Zebra Fireworks Company. For 15 years the enterprise operated stands at Milton on Highway 99, offering a wide variety of fireworks that retailed about $50,000 a year.

During its first year Zebra added a display fireworks division and presented an aerial show at the Western Washington Fair in Puyallup. The display has been an event in the annual festival since then.

In 1959 the Moriartys and four other investors purchased Red Devil Fireworks Company in California and later, in 1962, the Atlas Display, Black Panther, and United Fireworks Company of Dayton, Ohio, Zebra Fireworks became Red Devil Fireworks of Washington, expanded its facilities at a new site on Highway 99, and began to wholesale fireworks to local charitable, civic, and religious organizations that operate stands as fund-raising projects as Red Devil had done in California.

The company name was changed in 1973, to Pyrodyne Corporation, an additional 40,000-square-foot complex

Elizabeth Moriarty, a founder of Pyrodyne's parent firm, Zebra Fireworks Company, also served as state Democratic chairwoman.

was added for rental income, and Toys Galore—a four-store retail chain—became part of the organization. Five more toy stores were added in 1976, 1979, 1982, and 1983 for a total of eight retail outlets. In 1978 the firm bought four more acres of land and constructed an additional 40,000-square-foot office/warehouse.

Pyrodyne Corporation consists of five divisions: Red Devil Fireworks; Red Devil Display, which presents an average of 160 aerial display shows a year; Toys Galore; Toyco, a wholesale toy outlet; and Pyrodyne, which owns rental lands and manages property in Tacoma and Spokane.

Pat Moriarty is chairman of the board. Darrell L. Byington, associated with the family as investment counselor since 1951, is president; Bernard Crowell, who sold fireworks as a youngster, is vice-president; and Jerry Elrod, who started as a summer employee, is vice-president and manager of Red Devil Fireworks.

For 15 years Zebra Fireworks sold a variety of holiday fireworks from a 72-foot-long stand on Highway 99, Milton. Annual sales at that time reached $50,000. Total combined sales now exceed $6 million a year.

FICK FOUNDRY COMPANY

Three devastating fires have not stopped the progress of Fick Foundry Company, a father-and-son operation that grew to become one of the nation's leading ferrous-jobbing foundries.

Samuel Fick came to Tacoma from Burnett to work as a cupola tender at the shipyards during World War I, and the experience he gained motivated him to go into business for himself when the war ended. Renting a double garage in the 600 block of East 11th Street in the spring of 1922, Fick hired his two teenage sons, Theodore and Joseph, for six dollars a week and organized Fick Foundry Company—primarily producing iron manhole rings and covers and window sash weights. Daughter Mary was bookkeeper.

One morning in 1928 the Ficks arrived at work to find their foundry destroyed by fire; undaunted, they moved their operations to a small location on East D Street, hired two molders, set up a cupola for melting scrap iron, and went to work again.

By 1937 the growing firm needed more space and purchased adjoining property from Nelson Boiler Works, which more than doubled the work area. Three years later the sixth employee, Richard Zydek, was hired for 50 cents an hour; he remained with the organization to become plant superintendent and corporate officer.

While the foundry continued producing cast-iron castings as the main line, brass and aluminum parts were added. Additionally, for a short time during World War II, Fick produced hand grenades—a top-priority government item. Unfortunately the facility was again razed by fire, and could not be rebuilt in time to continue war-effort work.

The tenacious family not only reconstructed its foundry, but expanded production and began manufacturing many new items. In 1946 an electric melting furnace was installed that allowed the foundry to produce steel castings— some of which were parts for cranes used to raise sunken ships at Pearl Harbor. A

An electric melting furnace installed in 1946 enabled Fick Foundry to begin the production of steel castings.

metal-testing laboratory was added in 1953.

The death of Samuel Fick, Sr., in 1940 at age 56 was followed by those of Theodore in 1944 at age 36, and Samuel Jr. in a 1951 automobile accident. At the time of incorporation in 1956, Joseph Fick was named president; Kay Fick, vice-president; and Richard Zydek, secretary/treasurer. Two years later Theodore Fick, Jr., began to learn the business.

Following a destructive fire in June 1959, the firm purchased waterfront property at 820 East D Street. In 1964 it acquired Star Iron and Steel Company property at 435 East 11th Street and installed the X-ray department, which increased the kinds of castings and added customers.

The corporation was purchased in June 1969 by Mitre Industries, Inc., a small conglomerate with headquarters in Dallas, Texas, that reduced its holdings until only Fick Foundry Company remained. David G. Ritter, a major stockholder, acquired 100 percent of the stock, and in 1975 formed the present parent company, Fick of Texas, Inc. Under his leadership as

chief executive officer, and Ted Fick as president and general manager, the organization has progressed from pedestrian to high-integrity castings to meet the component demands of modern technology.

Production workers pour molten metal for one of Fick Foundry's high-integrity castings.

PEDERSON FRYER FARMS, INC.

At the outbreak of World War II, Jody and Dorothy Pederson were operating gas transports between Kansas City and northern Minnesota; but when subsequent war needs prevented them from obtaining tires and fuel, they had to find another use for their large building. "For some reason Jody took a liking to chickens," Dorothy Pederson recalls. He installed more than 1,200 layers in the building, then left to find work in Washington while she tended the hens.

Reunited a year later the family continued to raise chickens in Enumclaw until 1947 when they bought a poultry farm at 72nd Street and Waller Road in Tacoma. While Pederson worked, his wife dressed and sold chickens off the back porch—75 cents a pound dressed and cut up. Chickens were scarce, and the price was high. One rural grocer stopped by each Friday to buy six chickens to sell over the weekend.

The enterprise thrived and began marketing chickens commercially to owners of small restaurants, as well as a market at Fife. While normal production varied from 50 to 200 birds a day, which were hand-killed and dressed by 10 employees, in the early 1950s the firm broke all its records by preparing 4,000 chickens for the 4th of July. Several factors led to the success of the business. Clean, cold water came directly from the pipeline running beside the farm. County residents accepted the local product, and neighborhood women provided a loyal, competent work force.

One of the first operators in the area to prepackage cut-up chicken with cellophane wrap, Jody Pederson was selected in 1964 to serve on the National Broiler Council—the only person so named west of the Mississippi. By this time sons Jack, Harold, and Larry had joined the growing family venture.

Pederson first delivered its chickens in two Studebaker pick-up trucks to nearby stores; today a fleet of refrigerated trucks takes packages to major distributors in western Washington—including Safeway, Albertsons, Piggly Wiggly, Thriftway,

Jody Pederson, who "developed a liking for chickens," founded the well-known Pederson Fryer Farms and was named to the National Broiler Council.

Dorothy Pederson assisted her husband in the development of the fryer farm and contributed much to its production and marketing successes.

Associated Grocers, and West Coast Grocers. The poultry also is marketed from centers in Yakima, Spokane, and Vancouver to markets in eastern Washington, Montana, Idaho, and northern Oregon. Safeway distributes Pederson fryers in Alaska.

As a result of nutrition concerns and an economy that has prompted an 84-percent increase in the consumption of chicken,

From a production of 50 chickens a day in 1948, Pederson's expanded facilities now produce up to 40,000 chickens a day.

Pederson has increased production to 4,200 chickens an hour—packaging between 32,000 to 40,000 a day for a total of nine million chickens a year. Company representatives are exploring an international market, and experimenting with chicken sausage, smoked chicken, and other products.

The corporation, headed by Jack Pederson as president, sponsors several youth baseball and soccer teams and supports local food banks, an employee bowling league, the Pantages Theater restoration, and the Tacoma Dome project.

NORTH PACIFIC BANK

Around the turn of the century, the area now known as South Tacoma was a separate town called Edison. The community had grown up around the Northern Pacific Railroad shops, at the time the most imposing industrial enterprise in the Northwest. The town had board sidewalks, numerous saloons, a hotel, mercantile establishments, and a few houses of ill repute.

However, Edison lacked one important facility: a financial institution. So in 1906 a group of local businessmen established the North Pacific Bank in a small, red brick building on Union Avenue, "to promote the general trade and commerce of the area."

The first years were difficult for the little bank, and several times it nearly foundered. Ironically, however, as contrasted to its once-mighty industrial namesake, the bank is the survivor. The railroad is now long gone, its huge shops dismantled, the bricks having been salvaged and sold to builders enchanted with their decorative value.

The bank was acquired by Peter Wallerich, a German immigrant, in 1910. Arriving in America in 1885 with just five dollars, the enterprising young

Early North Pacific employees received deposits from railroad employees and encouraged the dreams of local business people.

man first worked as a farm laborer in Iowa—and owned the farm by 1909. He taught himself English, one letter at a time, using a Morse-code correspondence course, and then moved west as a railroad telegrapher. Ending up in Almira, Washington, he took a second job as cashier, bookkeeper, and janitor for the local bank. He taught himself banking by correspondence, and by 1910 owned the Almira bank, which he sold to purchase the North Pacific later that year.

Peter's son Clarence was raised by other family members in Iowa after his mother died. He was sent to military school, but ran away to seek his fortune in San Francisco at age 14. By age 19 he had become a vice-president of Crane Importers, and was sent to Japan as their representative in the Orient. He managed trading activities for them and speculated in foreign currency for his own account, a venture that proved disastrous when the Russian Revolution invalidated his holdings in Czarist rubles. Virtually broke, he shoveled coal on a steamer to return to San Francisco to start all over again.

Some years later, when his then-ailing father asked him to return to Tacoma, he did so, and by 1951 Clarence had acquired control of the bank.

Clarence's two sons eventually became involved in the bank. John P. was active in bank management until he went into business for himself as a Chevrolet dealer. At that time, his brother Peter K. bought sufficient shares from him and others to gain control of the bank, following his earlier experience with the U.S. Army and the General Motors Graduate School-Chevrolet Motor Division. Peter assumed management of the bank determined to preserve the unique mission and commitment to the independent business community foreseen by the founders in their charter of 1906.

In 1906 North Pacific Bank opened in Edison (later to become South Tacoma) on Union Avenue, now South Tacoma Way.

DAVIES PEARSON ANDERSON, P.S.

During the time Claude M. Pearson and Alvin A. Anderson were college friends at the University of Michigan Law School, a survey cited western Washington as one of the best areas in the United States in which to start a law practice.

The two were convinced. After graduation they traveled west and established a partnership that opened on September 11, 1949, in the Central Bank Building at 605 South Pine, Tacoma.

Two important developments occurred in 1951: Vernon R. Pearson, Claude's brother and also a Michigan Law School graduate, joined the original colleagues; and the men established close working ties with Wayne J. Davies, a Seattle trial lawyer, in a relationship that proved to be a key to the law firm's early success.

In 1959 Davies Pearson Anderson, P.S., relocated to what was then the Rust Building (now American Federal Building) in downtown Tacoma. As recognition and the reputation of the organization grew, so did its staff and areas of expertise.

Vincent L. Gadbow (a college associate of Pearson and Anderson) joined the group in 1962, followed by Bertil F. Johnson in 1967. Ray Hayes became affiliated in 1969, when Vernon Pearson was appointed a judge on the Washington State Court of Appeals.

In July 1975 the firm moved into larger facilities, its own building at 945 South Fawcett. One year later it merged with Seinfeld and Seinfeld, P.S., gaining Lester and Dennis Seinfeld as additional members.

Several factors combined to result in further demand for the lawyers at Davies Pearson Anderson: The new office building was accessible to the public, services were recognized for their high quality, and the organization had experienced growth in areas of specialization. Its lawyers carved an important place for themselves in Tacoma as members of one of the city's leading law firms.

In January 1981 the group moved to its present location at 920 South Fawcett

The prominent Tacoma law firm of Davies Pearson Anderson, P.S., now occupies its own three-story building at 920 Fawcett Street.

(one block from the courthouse), continuing the pattern of excellence and carefully planned expansion begun in 1949. Dedicated to providing the best possible advice and representation on a wide range of business and personal legal matters, the professional staff devotes optimum individual attention to every client. Each attorney is encouraged to develop expertise in specific areas of practice, and the firm has had substantial

Davies Pearson Anderson, P.S., began in 1949 with two law school friends as original partners and has grown to include more than 20 successful lawyers.

success in cases involving personal injury, product liability, business, tax, estate planning, real estate, family law, bankruptcy, and trials in all areas.

Total commitment to service is not a promotional slogan at Davies Pearson Anderson, P.S. — it is a working attitude. The reputation of the organization is based on a tradition of successful results, as well as excellent personal relationships with clients.

MINTERBROOK OYSTER COMPANY

Harold Wiksten was a scrub boy at a Purdy oyster plant in 1943. "Someday I'm going to buy you out," he joked with his employers. Eleven years later he did just that.

Wiksten credits Hubert and Mary Secor for planting the first oysters in the area. From 1932 to 1938 they raised oysters in beds and sold them by the sack to a processor. In 1938 the company started to open oysters. It moved a float house into the harbor by the oyster beds and processed its own oysters from that time.

Wiksten graduated from high school in 1947 and worked as a biological aide for the state Fisheries Department at a Purdy laboratory during vacations while he attended college. When he graduated, Wiksten wanted to conduct shellfish research, but there were no jobs available. He started looking for an oyster plant on the Sound.

In 1954 Wiksten and a partner, John Barr, purchased the Minterbrook Oyster Company from Wiksten's employers. The two started with a $250 trade acceptance check. Equipment included a landing craft, an old tug, an old panel truck, and an old tractor. They bought a used dump truck.

Wiksten was married that same year to Beverly Mielke of Seattle. He left the business the following spring to enter the armed services. He returned in 1956 and bought out his partner in 1966. By that time Wiksten had acquired good equipment to farm the property at Carr Inlet. He purchased additional lands at Case Inlet. Land bought for oyster farming is regulated by an 1889 state act which limits certain areas along Puget Sound for shellfish farming and growing. The firm owns close to 400 acres now, with approximately two-thirds of it suitable for oyster farming.

At first oysters were sold only to wholesale houses. Then large chain companies began to do their own buying. Today Wiksten markets to chains and wholesalers in the Seattle-Tacoma area,

Minterbrook Oyster Company processed oysters at this plant in 1943. Oysters have been farmed in the inlet since 1932.

and to brokers in Idaho, Oregon, Utah, Illinois, Nebraska, Alaska, and Hawaii. Minterbrook oysters also go to Canada.

In the late 1920s Japanese oysters were introduced into Puget Sound to spawn in areas where the water warms during late summer. The mature oysters were gathered with rakes at low tide, put into large baskets, loaded onto a barge, and transported to the processing plant. Today the same methods are used in some areas. Other areas are harvested by using dredges.

Unfortunately, the early plantings were infested with "drills," a type of predator. During World War II no seed from Japan was available, and growers survived using local oyster strains. After the war the state and the Japanese government cooperated in an inspection program that prevented importation of seed infected with drills.

The oyster seed was healthy, but it became increasingly expensive. Large oyster companies decided to raise their own seed at hatcheries under controlled temperatures. The industry developed research programs and hatcheries, and Minterbrook currently uses no Japanese seed.

Wiksten looks forward to increased benefits from U.S. research. Growers anticipate farming new genetic strains bred for size, survival, and disease resistance.

Minterbrook freezes some oysters for sale, but most are marketed fresh. Wiksten expects the U.S. industry to develop improved packaging for frozen oysters with meat prepared so that cooks don't handle the raw product.

Minterbrook Oyster Company employs 44 workers and maintains a fleet of refrigerated trucks. Land areas for farming oysters are shrinking because of pollution, but Wiksten expects that increased enforcement of pollution-control regulations will enhance the future of business and recreation on Puget Sound.

The Wikstens have two children, Erika and Aaron, who are very much involved in the family business. They work during their summer vacations at the plant and some day plan to manage the firm.

W.H. OPIE & COMPANY

Tacoma boomed with excitement and enthusiasm. Money from the East poured in to found businesses and industries; and although 50 percent of the men were carpenters, houses couldn't be built quickly enough to shelter the newcomers who flocked to Tacoma in the 1880s.

William Opie was already one of Tacoma's leading citizens. Born in Michigan to English immigrants, in 1880 the young man arrived in New Tacoma where he was employed in the Bank of New Tacoma which had been founded by his father-in-law, A.J. Baker, a notable financier.

Opie observed that the real estate business flourished. Convinced the city had a promising future, he and a friend, fellow-banker George Orchard, organized the firm of Orchard and Opie.

Their advertisement of the mid-1880s proclaimed that the company "operates as a real estate and loan broker, writes insurance, makes investments for non-residents, pays taxes and makes collections, has houses and stores for rent, money to loan on real estate securities, and has

In 1927 Orville W. Hunter joined W.H. Opie & Company as a bookkeeper. He went on to become owner, president, and chairman of the board.

Founder William H. Opie served as the real estate firm's president for 25 years.

choice lots for sale at $200 each." The men bought and developed land, as well as serving as marketing agents for many others.

By 1888 Tacoma was a bustling port and rail city. In that atmosphere of growth Orchard left to tend other interests, while Opie remained to prosper as president of the real estate firm.

William Opie retired at age 65 in 1913—after 25 years as the organization's founder and president. His son, Clarence C. Opie, became president; another son, Harry B. Opie, served as trustee and treasurer. Corporate offices were moved to the Fidelity Building at 11th and Commerce.

In 1942 Orville W. Hunter and Warren S. Lagerquist became directors, ushering in a new era of expansion. Health problems forced Clarence Opie to retire in 1948—succeeded by Hunter—and after his death in 1950, Hunter and Lagerquist became owners of the firm.

The company expanded into a series of offices—from the Fidelity Building to a location at 113 South 10th, and then to spacious quarters at 1001 Pacific Avenue, where it remained for 27 years.

During 1950 Hunter and Lagerquist

William Opie and George Orchard, Tacoma bankers, organized W.H. Opie & Company and opened for business on the second floor of Merchant's National Bank at 11th and Pacific.

organized Westgate Inc., which accumulated hundreds of acres of unimproved north-end land, and developed the Westgate shopping district, as well as miles of streets and hundreds of homesites.

Hunter became sole owner after the sudden death of Lagerquist in 1958. The organization continued as an influence on real estate development with the assistance of a management team consisting of Sherman L. Jonas, Reidar A. Hansen, Wayne H. Fuller, and William T. Good.

Orville Hunter, who joined the W.H. Opie & Company as bookkeeper in 1927, is chairman of the board. His son, Donald C. Hunter, is president. The corporate headquarters is in Westgate Shopping Center at 5738 North 26th Street.

MURRAY PACIFIC CORPORATION

A typical logging setup at L.T. Murray's West Fork Timber Company during the '20s and '30s included a yarder (center), which brought logs into the working area, and a loading donkey (right), which placed logs on trains.

Today's modern logging methods have long since replaced the steam donkey and wooden spar tree with a portable steel spar yarder and grapple loader.

When Lowell Thomas (L.T.) Murray arrived on Puget Sound in 1907—after studying a year at the University of Michigan—sawmills were operating around the clock to supply lumber to fill the holds of tall-masted sailing vessels, and the Ohio native had no trouble finding work.

The ambitious young man soon invested in the O.K. Logging Company where he made a little profit, then formed the Murray-Ripley Company with William Ripley. However, the logging industry suffered a financial crisis; consequently the company failed, forcing Murray to work as a logger for the next four years. His prospects looked bleak until one day Lady Luck went on a hunting trip in rough terrain with him: He traveled through some good timber on the west fork of the Tilton River.

Murray went to Tacoma and outlined his plan to Chester Thorne at the National Bank of Tacoma, securing his first bank loan—$500. By the fall of 1911, at age 26, he had put together his West Fork Logging operations and delivered his first logs to market.

In 1913 Murray organized West Fork Timber Company as a holding company for timberlands, then acquired additional land and equipment, built logging camps, laid out railroads, and bought rolling stock and logging equipment. He also purchased High Valley Ranch in Ellensburg in the early 1940s to become Washington's largest individual landowner. In the 1980s the firm owns some 75,000 acres on the west slope of the Cascade Mountains, land in central and north-central Washington, and cutting rights on 20,000 acres in central Washington.

Murray's son, Lowell Thomas (Tom) Jr., began learning the woods firsthand with his father when he was five years old. As a young man he served in the U.S. Navy during World War II, attended college, then worked in a logging camp for 18 months before returning to college to earn a master's degree in forestry. He joined West Fork Timber Company as a forester in 1949.

L.T. Sr. had sold his logging company—machinery, locomotives and railroad, hotel, and shop facilities—in 1943, but young Tom acquired his own small venture in 1951. In a few years West Fork bought out and expanded Tom's logging company, and Tom ran the firm's logging operations from 1955 to 1961. He again ran his own logging company until 1970, when he became president of West Fork Timber.

From the beginning the organization was a leader in the logging industry, one of the few privately owned companies that retained ownership of the land after harvesting timber. By 1938 the founder's "selective logging" methods had brought visitors from all over the country to his headquarters in Mineral and prompted an interview with President Franklin D. Roosevelt. L.T. Murray was the youngest man to serve as president of the Pacific Logging Congress until 1957 when his own son, Tom, was elected at age 31.

In late 1971 West Fork purchased Pan Pacific Trading Company, adding an exporting capability to the firm. In 1974 the organization was renamed Murray Pacific Corporation to reflect its diversification, worldwide expansion, and more complex financial and trading commitments.

After L.T. Murray, Sr., died in 1971, the family continued as directors. Tom Jr. is president and chairman of the board. The headquarters is in First Interstate Plaza.

TACOMA ICE & COLD STORAGE COMPANY

Tacoma Ice & Cold Storage Company was founded in the horse-and-buggy days of 1887 as the Tacoma Ice Company. The 400-pound blocks of ice were scored into 25-, 50-, and 100-pound blocks. Deliveries were made to residences and businesses on a regular schedule.

The building of the Northern Pacific-Point Defiance main line to Portland in 1908 necessitated the firm's relocation from Dock Street to Holgate Street, where a plant was erected. In 1923 a new five-story brick cold-storage building was added, the nucleus of the present-day facility.

Delivery trucks replaced the horse-drawn wagons, but the ice business eventually faced a crisis: the advent of electric refrigerators. With the decline in orders, elderly stockholders of Tacoma Ice Company, feeling more aggressive management was needed, decided to sell.

John and Pat Reisinger, who owned the Pacific Brewing and Malting Company buildings on Holgate Street, bought the firm in 1962 and renamed it Tacoma Ice & Cold Storage Company. The couple entered the ice business at a turning point in the industry. Packaged party ice was a new product that grew in popularity, with approximately 80 percent of sales going to young people.

Manufacturing and marketing techniques changed. Packaged block ice is still sold for use in boats and recreational vehicles. A newer product, packaged compressed 10-pound blocks, are made from party ice and snow and formed in a block press. Crushed ice is packaged in large and small bags. Dry ice is retailed for a variety of uses. All processes are automated and the product is never touched by human hands.

The company's Turbo ice-making machine, the largest in existence, produces up to 72 tons of ice a day. Two other machines bring the plant capacity to 132 tons a day.

In 1977 the Reisingers formed a new corporation, Silver Star Ice and Fuel, separating the cold-storage operation from the ice and fuel business. In 1980 they entered the fuel oil coal business,

distributing oil, bulk, and packaged Utah coal, pressed logs, and kindling, as well as stove and fireplace accessories.

In the early morning of March 5, 1979, a flywheel broke, rupturing an ammonia line. The resulting fire destroyed the original portion of the plant with its engine room and compressors. The ice-making facility was rebuilt in a separate, modern manufacturing structure.

Extensive storage facilities at the plant provide five stories and a basement to hold 440,000 cubic feet of commodities.

Included are foods for school lunches; ingredients for food-processing companies; tree seedlings for wood-products firms; and berries, poultry, other local produce, and numerous other items.

The Reisingers' eight children worked at the plant during high school and college vacations. One of the sons, David, is a supervisor in the cold-storage facility. The parents, John and Pat, are officers of Tacoma Ice & Cold Storage Company; Pat and another son, Richard, are officers of Silver Star Ice and Fuel.

Tacoma Ice Company moved to a large plant on Holgate Street and replaced the horses with a fleet of delivery trucks.

In 1887 Tacoma Ice Company delivered blocks of ice in horse-drawn wagons to homes and businesses.

GLOBE MACHINE MANUFACTURING COMPANY

In 1881, while still in his early twenties, Jesse Bamford arrived in the United States from England. He brought with him his skills as a journeyman machinist, and came with courage and determination. He worked for seven years in New York and Iron Mountain, Michigan. Always one to test new frontiers, he and his bride Lavina, in 1888, decided to move to the Pacific Northwest.

Jesse Bamford and James C. Ollard founded the Ollard Iron Works, located in Tacoma, in 1889. During the Gold Rush, he worked in the Yukon as a marine engine expert.

Jesse returned to Tacoma in 1902. During the next several years he founded the Olympia Iron Works and, with George Dupea, the Atlas Foundry. He also purchased the Tacoma Brass and Machine Works, which was later reorganized to become what is now known as Globe Machine Manufacturing Company. Jesse opened in the Triangle Building at 17th and A streets and manufactured specialties and brass goods. He later bought out the Young Ice Machine Company and before 1917, the firm's primary business was commercial refrigeration.

The year 1917 was a turning point for Globe Machine. At that time, Jesse passed the reins to his son, Calvin. Born in 1896, Calvin Sr. had served his machinist apprenticeship for his father in the early days. He considered the needs of local industry and set out to improve the design and manufacture of machinery used in the developing forest-products industry. They moved to 301 East 11th Street, which is still a part of today's plant.

Calvin Sr.'s decision to serve the forest-products industry proved to be an auspicious one. One major contribution was his design of a ball-bearing cut-off saw which increased production by reducing equipment friction. The firm went on to design and manufacture hundreds of other products for high-efficiency veneer, plywood, and board production. Globe Machine still continues to produce a refined version of that original ball-bearing saw.

Early company records show that employees worked six days a week and earned five cents an hour. Calvin framed two of his early paychecks which show that he earned a total of $4.93 for two weeks of labor. During the Depression, the partners' salaries plummeted like the stock market but Jesse and Calvin were sustained by a belief in their business and in the future of the forest-products industry.

In 1966 Calvin Bamford, Jr., grandson of Jesse and son of Calvin Sr., joined the company full time. He graduated from the Wharton School of the University of Pennsylvania, but began his initial career at Globe Machine as a young boy sweeping the floors and painting the machines. When his father died in 1975, Calvin Jr. became the president.

No longer does Globe Machine make just one machine or one component to fill a need. The company is a "systems" house, designing and manufacturing groups of machines with electronic controls to perform a complete plant function. These integrated large-scale installations have become a trademark of the company with three generations of leadership backing its advances in engineering, design, and technical development.

Jesse Bamford on his 90th birthday with his grandson, Calvin Bamford, Jr. Photo taken in 1949.

The Globe Machine work force of the late 1930s. Calvin Bamford, Sr., is in the top row, second from right.

RALEIGH, MANN & POWELL, INC.

Wilbur C. Raleigh, a civil engineer and real estate expert, was a founder of the nationally recognized insurance brokerage.

George Guyles entered the insurance firm founded by his father and built it into a successful enterprise which became the parent company of Raleigh, Mann & Powell, Inc.

The year 1889 saw the start of a unique Tacoma firm that has grown to nationwide stature as an insurance brokerage.

Raleigh, Mann & Powell, Inc., grew internally from its founding. Its growth was augmented by mergers and acquisitions in the early years. The firm traces its origins from Sampson & Guyles, 1889-1906; J.C. Guyles & Co., 1906-1935; Guyles & Mann, 1935-1948; Guyles & Co., 1948-1966; Havelock C. Boyle & Co., 1914-1929; Lyon, Davidson & Murphy, 1934-1958; Mitchell & Erdahl, 1947-1966; Raleigh-Hayward Co., 1929-1950; Raleigh-Mann Co., 1950-1957; to Raleigh, Mann & Powell, from 1957.

Early records are sketchy, but 1914 ledgers reveal the firm had a telephone and paid its president $3,000 a year. The insurance brokerage now has a team of 55.

Long ago the firm sold its real estate business and transferred its life, health, and employee benefits activities to its affiliate—Schwarz, Shera and Associates. This action permitted concentration on the protection of clients' assets. Officials

recognized that money used to pay insurance claims is clients' money, and in the 1960s they increased emphasis on reduction of losses.

Before "risk management" was a frequent item in business journals, Raleigh, Mann & Powell's brochure bore on its cover only the words "risk management." They knew a broker buying insurance for a firm with a strong loss-control program can drive a hard bargain. The company's safety specialist still assists in developing such programs. This approach was particularly effective in the woodworking industries of western Washington, many of which are clients of Raleigh, Mann & Powell.

Since the state first permitted self-insurance of workers' compensation in 1972, Raleigh, Mann & Powell has been among the leaders in assisting Washington firms to qualify for the program. Officials believe their assistance has brought substantial savings to those businesses and more prompt payments of benefits provided under the state's Industrial Insurance Act.

Another successful innovation was the development of unified coverage available to all local YMCAs in all 50 states. That program increased coverage at substantial savings. The firm also serves a number of

corporations with nationwide branches.

A division of Raleigh, Mann & Powell provides insurance on loans and leases by banks and loan and leasing companies. It operates the first and only Washington State-based and -controlled computer system for handling all insurance information on lenders' leases and loans.

Also unique is the company's team organization. Raleigh, Mann & Powell includes at least one expert in each area of operation, including eight in personal insurance. No one is paid on a commission basis. This approach provides free, effective access to expertise in every aspect of the clients' problems.

Members of the firm offer a proud record of community service. They have included the city engineer, when the 11th Street bridge was built; presidents of Rotary, United Way, Chamber of Commerce, and the Municipal League; treasurer of the National Board of YMCA; chairman of a hospital board; port commissioner; and a host of other service roles.

MILGARD MANUFACTURING, INC.

In 1958 Maurice Milgard, Jr., and his son Gary opened Milgard Glass Company in a small shop on South Tacoma Way. They diversified their business by selling a line of aluminum windows. As the venture grew they were able to start Milgard Manufacturing in 1962 in a rented building on Tacoma Avenue, enabling them to make their own line of single-glazed aluminum windows. The business was successful; consequently, two years later they built an 11,000-square-foot

plant on Port of Tacoma Road, adding to it twice to increase it to 33,000 square feet.

Jim Milgard joined the glass company in 1961. In 1973 the father and two sons agreed to merge the enterprises, with Milgard Manufacturing acquiring Milgard Glass. The family firm eventually expanded to employ 350 persons, to capture the largest share of the local market, and to provide service to Washington, Oregon, Idaho, Montana, Nevada, Alaska, and California.

The objective from the beginning was to provide a reliable source of quality aluminum windows and doors, styled and crafted to meet the unique architectural requirements of the western United

States. The original objectives of "outstanding quality, good service, and design consistency" have not changed.

Although the new manufacturing company initially made only window units, by 1968 the plant was producing its own doors. Two years later aluminum frames were redesigned to fit both single-pane and insulating glass. Realizing the future of insulated-glass windows and doors, the Milgards developed a type of aluminum frame to market in cold-weather areas—where formerly only wooden frames were acceptable.

In 1978 the company bought property at 1010 54th Avenue East for a modern manufacturing-office complex. An addition was built in 1980, which included an ultramodern glass-tempering facility that gives Milgard the opportunity to sell tempered glass in the residential and commercial markets. Nonetheless, the major emphasis remains on residential windows and doors. Plant employees build approximately 2,000 units of insulated glass daily, as well as large quantities of tempered glass used in the 1,000 windows and doors manufactured each day.

As specialty-glass products are gaining popularity, the organization offers garden windows, bay and bow windows, skywalls, skylights, and stained and etched glass along with its regular line of products. Windows can be tinted, and frames can be stock aluminum mill or anodized bronze finish.

Gary and Jim Milgard are partners in the business that started "on a shoestring" and has become the largest manufacturer of aluminum windows and doors in the Northwest.

In addition to its major plant in Tacoma and a manufacturing plant in Marysville, Milgard Manufacturing has warehouses and sales offices in Pasco and Spokane; Boise, Idaho; Portland, Oregon; and Sacramento, California.

Maurice Milgard, Jr., and his son Gary opened this small glass shop on South Tacoma Way in 1958.

Milgard's new manufacturing plant, at 1010 54th Avenue East, includes 150,000 square feet of office, production, and warehouse space.

JOHNNY'S ENTERPRISES

John Meaker and his father went into the Depression in Seattle as owners of a meat market. The young man saved his money; and when a local woman's restaurant went broke, John bought the business for $750 and $50 a month rental for the building and equipment.

Meaker made money on the restaurant, sold it, and leased a hotel near the construction site of the Grand Coulee Dam. His partner, Clyde Crawford, ran the hotel, and Meaker took meat and produce to eastern Washington every weekend for the hotel's restaurant.

When the lease expired in 1939, Meaker leased the property and constructed the building now known as Ivar's Captain's Table.

When his partner died, the Crawford family purchased Meaker's share of the business in Seattle. Meaker married Bea Wingard, a lovely Tacoma girl, and sold his meat market and other Seattle interests to establish a home in Tacoma in 1944.

Meaker purchased the Nelson Bennett home at 505 Broadway in Tacoma. This site was cleared for the new Crawford's Seagrill in 1946. He closed the restaurant in 1952 and leased the building to Pacific Northwest Bell.

Meaker decided Tacoma offered a "golden opportunity" for someone in the restaurant business. Few first-class restaurants existed at that time. Tacoma residents usually went out to dinner only on special occasions. Meaker opened Johnny's Dock at Port of Tacoma in 1953 and set out to educate people about the pleasure of dining out regularly.

Meaker knew about meat, and he built his reputation on the quality of meat he served. Diners from the 1950s also remember the elaborate strawberry desserts and the enormous baked potatoes. Farmers in eastern Washington saved Meaker their 16- to 18-ounce potatoes, and Meaker had them delivered by the truckload.

On Christmas night of 1961 a pot warmer burned through the floor and ignited the building. Johnny's Dock burned to the ground. Undaunted,

Meaker rebuilt the business and reopened the following August.

In 1978 he moved Johnny's Dock to a convenient location on City Waterway. The new building seats 350 patrons and features banquet rooms, a wine cellar, and a large dining room.

Meaker's restaurants now include

The original Johnny's Dock, built in 1953, attracted townspeople and celebrities to its Port of Tacoma site.

Johnny's Dock; Johnny's on the Mall; Johnny's at Fife; Johnny's Shrimp House, a fast-food outlet at Tacoma Mall; and Johnny's Shrimp House at Lakewood Villa Plaza. Meaker's grandson, John Crabill, a university graduate in restaurant management, assists with the business.

Meaker continues to buy the meat and fish for his restaurants. Approximately 90 percent of the produce, vegetables, flour, eggs, and other commodities are purchased from local sources. Salmon and steaks are still customer favorites, and diners still enjoy sundaes, shortcake, soups, sauces, gravies, and baked goods made "from scratch."

Many celebrities have dined at Johnny's Dock over the years. The guest list includes Marion Anderson, Lucille Ball, President Richard Nixon, and scores of others. Bing Crosby came in every Sunday during one three-month stay in the area.

The unique flavor of Meaker's food led to a second business venture. Bea Meaker operated a jewelry counter in the lobby of Johnny's Dock. Customers often talked with her after their meals, commenting on the food's flavor. "We have our own seasoning," she told them. They frequently asked how to obtain some, and Mrs. Meaker decided to bottle a seasoning blend.

The first 12 cases—filled by hand—sold in three days. Mrs. Meaker ordered 50 more cases. The seasoning was bottled in the restaurant kitchen, and labels were hand-typed. Those sold rapidly, and the seasoning business was born.

Johnny's Enterprises developed a variety of seasonings to enhance food flavors. A new product offers small quantities of spices in foil-sealed packs. Seasonings are now marketed all over the United States and requests come from many foreign countries.

TACOMA MALL CORPORATION

"It all started with a very big dream . . . What does it take to translate a big dream into reality? An army of artists and artisans—wizards in stone, finance, and merchandise? Planes, ships, rail cars bringing a steady flow of merchandise from around the world? These, yes. But more: an unshakable faith in a community's great future. . . ."

That was how the local newspaper described the opening of the first stage of Tacoma Mall, a complex touted as the "most modern shopping center in the nation." Bon Marche opened its doors on August 3, 1964, and a crowd of 150,000 persons thronged to the site, creating a massive traffic jam. A year later the mall—the first completely enclosed air-conditioned shopping center in the Pacific Northwest and the second on the West Coast—opened with 55 stores, fore-runners of a parade of participants that reached 72 by the end of the first year.

The dream began in 1961, when a group of investors purchased approximately 40 acres of land and proposed a retail development known as Freeway Mart; the reality began when the investors asked Bon Marche to become part of the complex, and the store's parent firm, Allied Stores, decided the freeway

The Bon Marche opened first on the Tacoma Mall site, signaling to the community that the regional center would become a reality.

location offered an opportunity to participate in a "first-class" project. With Connecticut General Life Insurance Company as the underlying investor, Allied acquired the proposed Freeway Mart site, sold the land to the insurance company, and leased it with the right to purchase at a later date.

Freeway Mart investors retained the right to reacquire up to seven acres of mall property for a future office building. They sold those rights to other investors, who built the Tacoma Mall Office Building—which is not owned by Tacoma Mall Corporation.

The complex, initially a $40-million investment, was designed by John Graham

and Company, designer of Portland's Lloyd Center and the Space Needle. Its original size was equal to nine football fields—containing 900,000 square feet of selling space, with more than 80,000 square feet of enclosed mall. Milo H. (Pat) Segner directed the team that spearheaded the mall's development. Marvin E. Boys supervised construction and planning. Richard S. Eichler served as director of leasing; while Lloyd Beaulaurier and James Johnson were hired as center manager and promotion director, respectively. Tacoma Mall Corporation, a subsidiary of Allied Stores, acquired title to the shopping center in 1979.

An extension on the west side increased the size in 1973, and the Sears, Roebuck addition opened in 1981 to bring the total to 135 stores. Completion of a Nordstrom expansion in 1983 brought the structural area to 1,400,000 square feet—thereby making the mall the largest on the West Coast north of San Francisco.

The center offers security and convenience, with no barriers for the handicapped, and provides a site for home shows, art shows, automobile displays, dances, craft shows, and other community events. An adjacent 13-acre site, owned by the Tacoma Mall Corporation, will be developed to provide compatible retail and business services, including a variety of restaurants. Officials point out that the mall will grow and change to meet the needs of the community.

A 1981 aerial view shows the continued growth of Tacoma Mall and the surrounding neighborhoods, which offer support to the regional shopping complex.

KNIGHT, VALE & GREGORY

Robert T. Knight, one of the original partners in the firm of Racine & Knight, the forerunner of Knight, Vale & Gregory.

A single light illumined the rutted wooden floors and calcimined walls of each small office. The two rooms, furnished with tables instead of desks, became schoolrooms for evening classes. Thus was Knight, Vale & Gregory originated in Tacoma.

Robert T. Knight joined the Seattle accounting firm of Samuel F. Racine and Company in 1921. Assigned to Tacoma in 1924 to manage the office and accounting school Racine opened after World War I, Knight said he probably was sent to "give the office an easy death." Instead, he searched for new business outside Tacoma. By gathering clients from Olympia, Grays Harbor, Bremerton, and the Puyallup Valley—and by teaching classes five nights a week—he kept the operation alive during the Depression.

The determined accountant continued as manager of the Tacoma office until October 31, 1934, when he was made a partner in the organization of Racine & Knight. After Racine became ill in 1950, Knight continued business under his own name for several years.

Peter V. Vale (who grew up in Gig Harbor) joined the firm as junior

accountant in 1943, serving as Knight's assistant on audits and assignments in Eastern Washington, Bellingham, and Oregon.

William R. Gregory (a Stadium High School graduate) applied for a position just before completing his degree at the University of Washington in December 1948, and began his association on December 27.

On January 1, 1955, the partnership of

Peter V. Vale joined the firm as a junior accountant in 1943 and became a partner in 1955.

Knight, Vale & Gregory was formed. This marked the beginning of an era of growth during which other partners joined the firm, bringing their individual skills and experience. The company eventually organized an executive committee, with Gregory appointed managing partner. That position is now held by Cecil W. Royer.

Dramatic changes in the organization began during World War II. Men and women found employment without special training, and declining enrollment caused Knight to close his accounting school in 1942. However, the war economy created increased demands for professional accountants, and the firm's

growing staff worked long hours. Before the use of modern computing equipment, income-tax time was an annual nightmare. Preceding the April 15 deadline, employees worked from 8 a.m. to 5 p.m. and 6:30 p.m. to 9 p.m. weekdays, an eight-hour shift on Saturdays, and six hours on Sundays.

Knight's first offices were in the old Tacoma Building. Relocating to space on the third floor of the Washington Building in 1935, up to the 12th floor in 1942, and back to an expanded office area on the third floor in 1963, in 1971 the organization moved to quarters on the 15th floor of the new Washington Plaza (First Interstate) Building. A Seattle branch opened in 1965, and an Olympia office was created in 1980.

Knight, Vale & Gregory—which continues to serve several clients from the 1920s, 1930s, and the busy war years—

William R. Gregory, the third partner in Knight, Vale & Gregory, joined the accounting firm in 1948.

today provides a wide range of comprehensive services. Its nearly 100 professional and support staff members also participate in important professional and community activities.

FIRST INTERSTATE BANK OF WASHINGTON, N.A.

On a dark March evening in Tacoma in 1885, 32-year-old Charles Masterson arrived by train from upstate New York to explore the possibility of founding a bank in the fastest-growing town in the Pacific Northwest.

An 1886 bank card names the officers and directors of Pacific National Bank. The firm was founded by Charles Masterson, a banker-lawyer from upstate New York.

The next day the banker-lawyer visited General J.W. Sprague, president of Tacoma National Bank as well as head of the Chamber of Commerce, who promptly introduced the newcomer to Thomas Wallace, a successful young realtor. Describing the need for both a Chamber headquarters building and banking facilities for Masterson, Sprague suggested the young men work together to build a structure to serve both needs. Intrigued by the idea, Masterson began conducting his banking business in Wallace's office, while Wallace secured two lots at 12th and Pacific. Masterson arranged for a real estate loan of $10,000 from eastern investors, and the two accumulated an additional $7,000 locally in cash, materials, and services.

The U.S. comptroller of the currency granted charter 3417 to Pacific National Bank of Tacoma, and an organizational meeting was held at the Tacoma Hotel on October 7, 1885. Officers selected were Masterson, president; Lucius R. Manning, another upstate New York banker, vice-president; and Wallace, cashier. They also served as directors in addition to James P. Stewart, Puyallup merchant and hop grower; and William D. Tyler, manager of the Tacoma Hotel.

Pacific National opened its doors on January 2, 1886, to a slow beginning; however, 1887 was an auspicious year.

The bank's officers were responsible for the construction of Tacoma's first wheat warehouse, which was finished in time to receive the year's crop from eastern Washington that arrived on the newly opened Northern Pacific line across the Cascade Mountains.

The institution in 1888 constructed a building on the southwest corner of 13th and Pacific, which was sold a year later at a profit of $50,000 to George W. Vanderbilt of New York. It was a fortunate sale: By 1890 some 18 banks had been established in Tacoma, but by 1895 panics and depressions claimed all but five; liquidity resulting from the building sale helped Pacific National survive. A period of steady growth led to the acquisition of Citizens National Bank and a relocation to the southwest corner of 11th and Pacific in 1895, then a merger with Lumberman's National Bank in 1905.

In 1913 National Bank of Commerce of Tacoma joined with Pacific National to create the National Bank of Tacoma, with

Masterson's new bank and the Chamber of Commerce shared a building, completed in December 1885, on the southeast corner of 12th and Pacific.

headquarters on the northeast corner of 13th and Pacific. The former's president, Chester Thorne—a business and financial leader—became chairman of the board and served until his death in 1927. The new organization enjoyed rapid growth, building its resources to more than $19 million by 1919, when additional space became mandatory. An imposing new structure in Italian-Renaissance style was erected at the northeast corner of 12th and Pacific, the building that now houses the Tacoma Art Museum.

Transamerica Corporation acquired controlling interest in the bank by 1937. In 1938 the bank changed its name to National Bank of Washington. During the

Before the 1970 merger the National Bank of Washington constructed financial headquarters, Tacoma's most prestigious downtown building, on the site of its original bank. It is now known as First Interstate Plaza.

Women first joined the bank's teller line during World War II in the new headquarters on the northeast corner of 12th and Pacific; this building now houses the Tacoma Art Museum.

next decade the bank met critical war-effort challenges, financing shipyards and other war industries while answering the banking needs of its many thousands of customers.

The Pacific National Bank of Seattle, like the National Bank of Washington (with which it merged in 1970), provided for the needs of Seattle's businesses and industries from the Depression through the postwar boom.

Pacific National was founded in 1928 by a group of Seattle businessmen including William E. Boeing, chairman of Boeing Airplane Company, and William Calvert, president of San Juan Fishing and Packing Company.

When these successful institutions consolidated in 1970, forming Pacific National Bank of Washington, the bank became the state's third-largest commercial bank. It expanded as a full-service organization for both domestic and international customers, participating in additional mergers while developing sophisticated banking systems.

In the 1960s Transamerica Corporation separated its banking interests, which resulted in the creation of an 11-state bank holding company, Firstamerica Corporation, the predecessor of Western Bancorporation.

On June 1, 1981, Western Bancorporation became First Interstate Bancorp. At the same time, Pacific National was renamed First Interstate Bank of Washington, N.A. The names were changed to give all First Interstate Banks a common identity, reflecting the trend to offer services that transcend state boundaries.

An interstate service, TIPS (Teller Item Processing System), links tellers throughout the First Interstate system's multi-state territory so that customers can complete transactions quickly. Day and Night Teller services meet customers' needs at home and abroad. A new network of member banks (CIRRUS) will enable customers to withdraw cash from their accounts to automatic cash machines nationwide.

First Interstate Bank of Washington, N.A., has pioneered banking services since the days of Masterson, Manning, and Wallace. These were men of vision, but the services offered by this modern institution today must indeed surpass their most vivid dream.

BURLINGTON NORTHERN RAILROAD

In 1888 the new Northern Pacific headquarters building was completed at the north end of Pacific Avenue.

"No event in the early history of Tacoma was more important than the selection of Tacoma as the terminus of the Northern Pacific Railroad. . . ."

That is how historian W.P. Bonney described the impact of the first northern transcontinental railroad, which operated as Northern Pacific until a 1970 merger made it part of Burlington Northern Railroad. The account of site selection and line construction is a colorful tale of adventure, achievement, and finance.

A government charter authorized construction of the Northern Pacific line on July 2, 1864, stipulating that the western terminus was to be located on a site ". . . on a line north of the 45th degree of latitude to some point on Puget Sound." Every settlement along the Sound began competing for the pot of gold at the end of the rainbow. Editorial writers, land speculators, and citizens appealed to the decision makers, offering the "best" water access to the Pacific basin and a variety of other promises.

Northern Pacific had to build westward over the Cascade Mountains and north between Portland and Puget Sound. By mid-1873 the line from Kalama had reached to within 22 miles of Tacoma.

Financial conditions were desperate, and the line had to be completed to the Sound—somewhere—before the charter expired in December.

Someone had to decide quickly on a terminus. Mukilteo, Seattle, and Tacoma remained in the running, with Steilacoom a close fourth. A committee of the railroad's board of directors finally wired its report to the president. It described the advantages of its selection and related, ". . . shall unhesitatingly decide in favor of Tacoma."

Northern Pacific and its subsidiary, Tacoma Land Company, set out to build a city amid the stumps and muddy streets. Charles Wright, Henry Villard, and other railroad officials contributed to the growth of Tacoma. Northern Pacific built the Tacoma Hotel, an oasis of elegance and charm. The hotel, located on a bluff overlooking the Sound and Mt. Rainier, burned on October 17, 1935.

In 1888 Northern Pacific completed a general office building at the north end of Pacific Avenue. In 1891 the railroad opened car shops in South Tacoma, where hundreds found employment.

Construction began in 1909 on a splendid copper-domed passenger station, which was completed in 1911. The fine brick structure features terrazzo, Italian marble, and mosaic, with walls and partitions of antique oak and opaque glass. Both the headquarters building and Union Depot are listed on the National Register of Historic Places.

The financial crisis of 1893 forced several rail lines into receivership, including Northern Pacific. In 1896 the railroad was sold to a new corporation, Northern Pacific Railway Company, which reorganized on a sound financial basis. Purchases, mergers, and construction followed. Highway freight and passenger service was added to supplement rail service.

During World War II and subsequent years the company carried out a major rehabilitation program on its lines, eliminating main line curves and replacing bridges and tunnels. NP introduced a series of technological innovations and replaced its steam fleet with diesel-electric locomotives between 1938 and 1958. Computer installation in 1957 heralded a new era of efficiency.

In 1970 Northern Pacific became part of Burlington Northern Railroad, created by the merger of the NP, Great Northern, Chicago, Burlington & Quincy, and Spokane, Portland and Seattle railways.

A modern Burlington Northern train passes under the Narrows Bridge along the Tacoma waterfront.

HISTORIC TACOMA, INC.

Historic Tacoma, Inc. was founded in 1978 to fill a need for a city-wide organization dedicated to preserving and protecting the heritage of Tacoma. While there already existed neighborhood improvement groups, landmark preservation boards, and other special interest organizations, none had the sufficiently broad constituency, interests, and goals to be an effective instrument and advocate of historic preservation throughout the city. A group of Tacoma citizens was thus encouraged to form such a broad-based organization.

Fortunately Tacoma, unlike many cities which have "discovered" historic preservation too late, still had in 1978 many residential and commercial structures (as well as entire neighborhoods) of historic and architectural significance, well worth rehabilitation and preservation. Moreover, many business and civic leaders were already beginning to see the economic as well as social value in carrying out such projects.

It was apparent from the beginning that an effective historical preservation organization must combine the education of the public with community leadership in the public's behalf, and further combine the research and study of the past with its practical application to present-day community life. In keeping with this view, Historic Tacoma has sought to further historic preservation through such diverse activities as, for example, holding lectures on Tacoma history, sponsoring seminars on private restoration of older buildings, and advocating a "preservationist" position on public land-use and planning issues as they affect historically significant structures or areas of the city.

For Tacoma's 1984 Centennial

This pleasant Queen Anne-style home was built in 1898 for H.F. Alexander, a local steamship owner. The house has been included in the Stadium-Seminary Historic District, which was created in 1977. Courtesy, Tacoma News Tribune, photograph by Jerry Buck

celebration, we as members of Historic Tacoma wanted to sponsor a project which would both express our pride in the traditions and heritage of our city, and at the same time "spread the word" to those who might have forgotten (or never have known) just how rich that heritage has been. We are, therefore, extremely pleased to have had the opportunity to sponsor *South on the Sound*, a most fitting way for us to celebrate the Centennial of our city.

Mark Reutlinger
Vice President
Historic Tacoma, Inc.

PATRONS FOR *SOUTH ON THE SOUND*

The following individuals, companies, and organizations have made a valuable commitment to the quality of this publication. Windsor Publications and Historic Tacoma, Inc., gratefully acknowledge their participation in *South on the Sound: An Illustrated History of Tacoma and Pierce County.*

B&I Shopping Center*
Boddie's Building Construction, Inc.*
Brown & Haley*
Burlington Northern Railroad*
Cammarano Brothers, Inc.*
Davies Pearson Anderson, P.S.*
Dwyer, Pemberton and Coulson
Gail and Neal Elliott
Ken Ellison's Jardeen Elec. Inc.
Fick Foundry Company*
First Interstate Bank of Washington,
   N.A.*
Gehri Sheet Metal Company, Inc.*
Globe Machine Manufacturing Company*
Gordon, Thomas, Honeywell, Malanca,
   Peterson & O'Hern*
Greer-Patterson and Associates, Inc.
Humana Hospital Tacoma*
Tak Ikeda
Johnny's Enterprises*
Jones Washington Stevedoring Company

Kelly Television Co.*
Knight, Vale & Gregory*
Milgard Manufacturing, Inc.*
Minterbrook Oyster Company*
Model Lumber & Ace Hardware
   Company, Inc.*
Multicare Medical Center*
Murray Pacific Corporation*
Nalley's Fine Foods*
National Blower and Sheet Metal
   Company*
North Pacific Bank*
North Star Glove Co.*
W.H. Opie & Company*
Pacific Storage, Inc.*
Pederson Fryer Farms, Inc.*
Pennwalt Corporation*
The PQ Corporation
Puget Corporation*
Puget Paving and Construction, Inc.
Puget Sound National Bank*
Pyrodyne Corporation*
Raleigh, Mann & Powell, Inc.*
Harry R. Rasmussen
RasmussenHobbs*
Ronald, Karen, Suzanne, and Kriste
   Robbel
Roman Meal Company*
Schwarz, Shera & Associates, Inc.*
Sea-Tac Trophy and Engraving

Selden's Furniture & Carpet*
Sharp, Taylor, Hughes and Woodring
SME Corporation
South Tacoma Motor Company*
Standard Paper Company*
Mayor Doug Sutherland and The Tacoma
   City Council
Tacoma Ice & Cold Storage Company*
Tacoma Mall Corporation*
The Tacoma News Tribune*
Titus-Will Ford/Toyota
Robert L. Topel
Tucci and Sons, Inc.*
Bob and Bev Tweddle
Peter V. Vale
Wik Wiklund
Woodworth & Company, Inc.*

*Partners in Progress of *South on the Sound: An Illustrated History of Tacoma and Pierce County.* The histories of these companies and organizations appear in Chapter 10, beginning on page 144.

Marvin D. Boland recorded this quiet day at American Lake during the summer of 1924. Courtesy, Marvin D. Boland Collection, TPL

SELECTED BIBLIOGRAPHY

General

Bancroft, Hubert Howe. *History of Washington, Idaho and Montana*. San Francisco: The History Company, 1890.

Bonney, William Pierce. *History of Pierce County, Washington*. 3 vols. Chicago: Pioneer Historical Publishing Co., 1927.

Clark, Norman. *Washington: A Bicentennial History*. New York: W.W. North & Co., 1976.

Hunt, Herbert. *Tacoma: Its History and Its Builders*. 3 vols. Chicago: S.J. Clarke, 1916.

Morgan, Murray. *Puget's Sound: A Narrative of Early Tacoma and the Southern Sound*. Seattle: University of Washington Press, 1979.

Prosch, Thomas. *McCarver and Tacoma*. Seattle: Privately printed, 1906.

Quiett, Glenn Chesney. *They Built the West: An Epic of Rails and Cities*. New York: Appleton Century, 1934. Reprinted, Cooper Square, 1965.

Snowden, Clinton A. *History of Washington: The Rise and Progress of an American State*. 6 vols. New York: Century History Co., 1909.

Chapter I — The Indian Land

Gunther, Erna. "Vancouver and the Indians of Puget Sound," *Pacific Northwest Quarterly*, 51 (January 1960).

Hacking, Norman R., and W. Kaye Lamb. *The Princess Story: A Century and a Half of West Coast Shipping*. Vancouver: Mitchell Press, 1974.

Haeberlin, Hermann, and Erna Gunther. *The Indians of Puget Sound*. University of Washington Publications in Anthropology, vol. 4. Seattle: University of Washington Press, 1930.

McKee, Bates. *Cascadia: The Geologic Evolution of the Pacific Northwest*. New York: McGraw-Hill, 1972.

Meany, Edmond S. *Vancouver's Discovery of Puget Sound*. New York: MacMillan Co., 1907.

Menzies, Archibald. *Journal of Vancouver's Voyages, April to October, 1792*, edited by C.F. Newcombe, British Columbia Archives Memoir no. 5. Victoria: W.H. Cullin, 1923.

Smith, Marian W. *The Puyallup-Nisqually*. Columbia University Contributions to Anthropology, vol. 43. New York: Columbia University Press, 1940.

Wing, Robert C., with Gordon Newell. *Peter Puget*. Seattle: Gray Beard Publishing, 1979.

Work, John. "John Work's Journal," *American Indian Ethnohistory*, vol. 3. 1974.

Chapter II — Colonial Competition

Clark Jr., Malcolm. *Eden Seekers: The Settlement of Oregon 1818-1862*, Boston: Houghton Mifflin Co., 1981.

Heath, Joseph Thomas. *"Writ with a Quill Pen" — The Journal of Joseph Thomas Heath*. Edited by Gary Fuller Reese. Typescript. Tacoma Public Library.

Loewenberg, Robert J. *Equality on the Oregon Frontier: Jason Lee and the Methodist Mission 1834-43*. Seattle: University of Washington Press, 1976.

Stanton, William. *The Great United States Exploring Expedition*. Berkeley: University of California Press, 1975.

Tolmie, William Fraser. *Physician and Fur Trader*, edited by R.G. Large. Vancouver: Mitchell Press, 1963.

Wilkes, Charles. *Narrative of the United States Exploring Expedition*. Philadelphia: 1845.

Chapter III — Outlets to the World

Bergman, Hans. *History of Scandinavians in Tacoma and Pierce County*. Tacoma: Privately printed, 1926.

Carpenter, Cecelia Svinth. "Leschi: Last Chief of the Nisquallies," *Pacific Northwest Forum*, 1, no. 1 (January 1976).

Gates, Charles M. *Messages of the Governors of the Territory of Washington to the Legislative Assembly, 1854-1889*. Seattle: University of Washington Press, 1940.

Gimpl, Sister M. Caroline Ann. *Immaculate Conception Mission, Steilacoom Washington*. Master's thesis, Seattle University: 1951.

Huggins, Edward. *Reminiscences of Puget Sound*. (Newspaper articles gathered and edited by Gary Reese), Tacoma Public Library.

Meeker, Ezra. *Pioneer Reminiscences of Puget Sound: The Tragedy of Leschi*. Seattle: Privately published, 1905.

Reese, Gary Fuller. *A Documentary History of Fort Steilacoom*, typescript. Tacoma Public Library.

Rossi, Louis. *Six Years on the West Coast of America, 1856-1862*. Edited and translated by W. Victor Wortley. Fairfield, Washington: Ye Galleon Press, 1983.

Stevens, Hazard. *Life of General Isaac I. Stevens*. 2 vols. Boston: Houghton, Mifflin and Co., 1901.

Chapter IV — The Power of Steam

Cox, Thomas R. *Mills and Markets: A History of the Pacific Coast Lumber Industry to 1900*. Seattle: University of Washington Press, 1974.

Hedges, James Blaine. *Henry Villard and the Railways of the Northwest*. New Haven: Yale University Press, 1930.

Johnston, Norman J. "The Frederick Law Olmsted Plan for Tacoma," *Pacific Northwest Quarterly*, 66 (July 1975.)

Lavender, David. *Land of Giants: The Drive to the Pacific Northwest, 1750-1950*. Garden City, N.Y.: Doubleday, 1958.

Prosch, Charles. *Reminiscences of Washington Territory*. Fairfield, Washington: Ye Galleon Press, 1969.

Smalley, Eugene V. *History of the Northern Pacific Railroad*. New York: Putnam, 1883.

Wilkeson, Samuel. *Notes on Puget Sound*. Privately published, 1870.

Chapter V — A Delirious Decade

Harney, Thomas Porter. *Charles Barstow Wright, 1822-1898, a Builder of the Northern Pacific and the City of Tacoma*. Privately printed, 1926.

Hildebrand, Lorraine Barker. *Straw Hats, Sandals and Steel: The Chinese in Washington State*. Tacoma: The Washington State American Revolution Bicentennial Commission, 1977.

Morgan, Murray. *The Mill on the Boot*. Seattle: University of Washington Press, 1983.

Ripley, Thomas Emerson. *Green Timber: On the Flood Tide to Fortune in the Great Northwest*. Palo Alto: American West Publishing Company, 1968.

Schnackenberg, Walter C. *The Lamp and the Cross: Sagas of Pacific Lutheran University from 1890 to 1965*. Parkland: Pacific Lutheran University Press, 1965.

Spike, W.D.C. *Spike's Illustrated Description of the City of Tacoma*. Tacoma: Privately published, 1891.

Traver, George W. *Tacoma and Vicinity*. Tacoma: Privately published, 1889.

Woodbridge, Sally B., and Roger Montgomery. *A Guide to Architecture in Washington State*. Seattle: University of Washington Press, 1980.

Chapter VI — Hard Times

Hidy, Ralph W., Frank Ernest Hill, and Allen Nevins. *Timber and Men: The Weyerhaeuser Story*. New York: Macmillan Co., 1963.

LeWarne, Charles Pierce. *Utopias on Puget Sound 1885-1915*. Seattle: University of Washington Press, 1975.

Magden, Ronald, and A.D. Martinson. *The Working Waterfront: The Story Of Tacoma's Ships and Men*. Tacoma: Port of Tacoma and I.L.W.U. Local 23, 1982.

Schwantes, Carlos A. *Radical Heritage: Labor, Socialism and Reform in Washington and British Columbia, 1885-1917*. Seattle: University of Washington Press, 1979.

Chapter VII — The Challenge of Adversity

Browne, Belmore. *Camp Lewis*. Tacoma: Washington State Historical Society, 1918.

Chasan, Daniel Jack. *The Water Link*. Seattle: Washington Sea Grant Program, 1983.

Haines, Aubrey L. *Mountain Fever: Historical Conquests of Rainier*. Portland: Oregon Historical Society, 1962.

Mitchell, C. Bradford. *Every Kind of Shipwork: A History of Todd Shipyards Corporation 1916-1981*. New York: Todd Shipyard Corp., 1981.

Tacoma: Twenty Years of Progress, 1883-1903. Tacoma: Vaughan & Morrill Printing Company, 1903.

Walk, George W. "Fighting Fawcett: A Political Biography." Master's thesis, Western Washington University, 1976.

Chapter VIII — The Bitter Years

Ficken, Robert E. *Lumber and Politics: The Career of Mark E. Reed*. Seattle: University of Washington Press, 1979.

Gunns, Albert F. "The First Tacoma Narrows Bridge: A Brief History of Galloping Gertie." *Pacific Northwest Quarterly*. Vol. 72, No. 4 (October 1981).

Lucia, Ellis. *Head Rig: The Story of the West Coast Lumber Industry*. Portland: Overland West Press, 1965.

INDEX

Italicized numbers indicate illustrations.